The New Science of Intimate Relationships

The New Science of Intimate Relationships

Garth Fletcher

BLACKWELL
Publishers

First published 2002

2 4 6 8 10 9 7 5 3 1

Blackwell Publishers Inc.
350 Main Street
Malden, Massachusetts 02148
USA

Blackwell Publishers Ltd
108 Cowley Road
Oxford OX4 1JF
UK

Library of Congress Cataloging-in-Publication Data

Fletcher, Garth J. O.
    The new science of intimate relationships / Garth J. O. Fletcher.
        p.   cm.
    Includes bibliographical references
    ISBN 0–631–22077–1 (alk. paper) — ISBN 0–631–22078–X (alk. paper)
    1. Intimacy (Psychology)   2. Interpersonal relations.   I. Title.

    BF575.I5 .F54 2002
    158.2—dc21

                                                         2001003941

British Library Cataloguing in Publication Data

A CIP catalogue record for this book is available from the British Library.

Typeset in 10 on 12.5 pt Photina
by Ace Filmsetting Ltd, Frome, Somerset
Printed in Great Britain by T.J. International, Padstow, Cornwall

This book is printed on acid-free paper.

Contents

Preface

Beginning to write a book feels a bit like I imagine the experience of standing at the start of a trek across the Antarctic or a climb up Mount Everest. I do not know how other people manage this forbidding writing stage, but my strategy is to tell all and sundry that I intend to write such a book. After six months of such public declarations, I have worked myself into a psychological corner. If I do not start writing I stand to lose substantial face (or I am forced to tell lies). I started writing this book about three years ago. Book writing is never a full-time job for an academic. It has to be written in spasmodic bursts among a multitude of other activities including research, data analysis, other academic writing projects, grant-proposal writing, teaching, editing work, thesis supervision, and administrative work.

I have written this book mostly from the University of Canterbury in Christchurch, New Zealand, which usually strikes people as being located about as far away as it is possible to get from everywhere else. Fortunately, however, geographical distance does not matter much in today's world, with the existence of e-mail, powerful literature search engines, the Web, file attachments, and so forth. However, there is no replacement for personal contact and conversation with scientific colleagues when it comes to thrashing out ideas and keeping in touch with science at the coal face. I have been able to accomplish this through a research grant from the New Zealand Marsden Fund, along with generous financial aid from the University of Canterbury. These bodies have enabled me to travel every year to conferences and to universities in Europe, Australia, and the USA. I also thank the psychology departments at the University of Macquarie in Sydney, the University of A&M at Texas, and the University of California at Riverside, for giving me the space and resources to work there for periods of time over the last three years. Julie Fitness, Jeffry Simpson and David Funder respectively arranged and sponsored these stays, and provided stellar levels of companionship and intellectual intercourse to boot.

My aim in writing this book was to package and write about the innovative research and theorizing in scientific domains, concerned with intimate relationships, in such a fashion that it would be palatable and interesting to a lay audience, to psychology students, and to scientists and academics in fields other than psychology. Even my academic colleagues toiling in the same scientific vineyards as me may find what I have said to be of some value or interest. But, although I have struck a personal and conversational writing tone, I have striven to be true to the science, not to fudge important controversies, and to deal head on with complex and weighty material and arguments. One rule I have followed is to never rely on the interpretations or quotes from secondary sources, but to read the original material, whether it be research articles, ethnographies, theoretical pieces, or books. I have learnt a lot in researching for this book, and I have gained an even keener appreciation for the incredible quantity of thoughtful and intelligent research and theorizing being carried out in our universities and research institutions – I trust I have done it justice.

Science is a vast international club in which individuals meet at regular conventions and are involved in constant dialogue. It can be a harsh environment, because it involves the public scrutiny and criticism of ideas and research. However, a spirit of generosity and collegial support also prevails. I have asked many people to read specific chapters in this book in which they possess expertise. They have almost all responded willingly and have caught a good many mistakes and dubious interpretations, along with advancing many helpful suggestions. I could not have written this book without their help. They are Mark Baldwin, Russil Durrant, Bruce Ellis, Julie Fitness, Elaine Hatfield, Geoff Thomas, Anne Peplau, David Funder, Sandra Murray, John Holmes, Tom Bradbury, Geoffrey Miller, David Buss, Margo Wilson, Robert Brush, Mike Stoolmiller, Thomas Keenan, Beryl Fletcher, Ron Dahl, Simon Kemp, Bill Ickes, and Greg Newbold.

In addition, I heartily thank Jeffry Simpson, Roy Baumeister, and Anne Peplau, all of whom graciously offered to read the entire manuscript.

I also owe a debt of gratitude to the graduate students at the University of Canterbury who have worked with me as researchers and colleagues, and who have discussed many of the issues in this book with me personally or together as a group in our regular meetings. I especially thank Megan Stenswick, Jacqui Tither, Nickola Overall, and Claire O'Loughlin, who, above and beyond the course of duty, have willingly read, proofed, and commented in detail upon, the entire book.

I thank, above all, my good friend and colleague Jeffry Simpson. Jeff introduced me to evolutionary psychology, and has spent an inordinate amount of time discussing and debating issues in the science of intimate relationships with me over the years. Jeff's scholarship, intelligence, integrity, and generosity represent an ideal for others to aspire to.

I thank the team at Blackwell Publishers, especially Sarah Bird and Angela Cohen, for their enthusiasm, support, and advice, and extend my appreciation to Eldo Barkhuizen for his expert on-screen editing of the electronic manuscript.

Finally, and at the risk of making this preface sound like a speech after winning an Oscar, I thank Cynthia Upchurch for inspiring me to write such a book in the first place.

Any mistakes, errors, omissions, or flaws remaining in the book are, of course, mine alone.

Enjoy.

Chapter 1

The New Science of Intimate Relationships

*The emergence of a science of relationships represents a frontier –
perhaps the last major frontier – in the study of humankind.*
Berscheid & Peplau, 1983

The first known academic treatise on intimate relationships was Plato's
Symposium, written approximately 2,300 years ago. In this historic document Aristophanes tells a curious tale of a mythical being that was spheri-
cal in form with two complete sets of arms, legs, and genitalia. Because
of the strength and speed of these creatures (they cartwheeled around
on their four arms and four legs), they posed a threat to the gods.
Accordingly, Zeus split them in half and rearranged their genitals so
that they were forced to embrace front on in order to have sexual relations. Some of the original beings had two sets of male genitalia, some
had two sets of female genitalia, and some had one set of female and
one set of male genitalia. Thus, procreation of the species was only
possible by members of the original male-female creatures getting together. Possibly in deference to the sexual orientation of some of his
audience, or to the politically correct tenor of the time, Aristophanes
was quick to add that males who sought union with other males were
"bold and manly," whereas the individuals who originated from the
androgynous creatures were adulterers or promiscuous women.[1] Regardless of sexual orientation, the need for love is, thus, born of the
longing to reunite with one's long-lost other half and achieve an ancient unity destroyed by the gods.

   As this allegory suggests, individuals are alone and incomplete – an
isolation that can be banished, or at least ameliorated, when humans
pair off and experience the intimacy that can be gained in a close relationship. Such intimacy, the experience of reuniting with one's long-
lost other half, reaches its peak in parent–baby bonding, and in the

1

intimate high of romantic sexual relationships when looking into one's partner's eyes seems like staring into another's soul. But, intimacy is also experienced in powerful measures in platonic relationships, familial relationships, or in the long sunset of sexual relationships that have lost their passionate urgency and settled into a deep form of companionship.

Just like Plato's mythical beings, then, humans have a basic need to be accepted, appreciated, and cared for, and to reciprocate such attitudes and behaviors – in short, to love and to be loved.[2] And this is especially true in relation to finding a sexual partner, a quest that can range from a one-night stand to seeking out a mate for life. Indeed, for most people the goal of forming a permanent liaison with another human being is a pivotal aim in life, and one in which a massive effort and outlay of energy is invested. The importance of finding love, of forming relationships, is exemplified in Western societies in the ocean of information about love and intimate relationships pumped out in books, TV shows, plays, movies, newspapers, magazines, and so forth. Given the importance of forming satisfactory intimate relationships, it is only natural that individuals theorize about their own intimate relationships and what makes them tick. However, many individuals are inordinately curious about other people's relationships, even when they don't know the individuals involved, and the outcomes of the relationships could not possibly affect them. The love lives of fictional people on soap operas, as well as the rich and famous, audiences find endlessly fascinating.

One could claim that this attention to love, sex, and intimate relationships is a function of Western society, more specifically Western society as it has developed since the Industrial Revolution. I will argue throughout the book that this claim is wrong. As will be seen, romantic love has existed in all known human societies, and marriage, courtship, and sex, play pivotal roles in all cultures.

In writing this book I had several aims and audiences in mind. One aim I did not have was to write a self-help book. As the title indicates, this is not one of those books that gives six simple steps toward the perfect marriage or relationship, or gives recipes on how to meet or score with members of the opposite (or the same) sex. The bookstores are already full of such books, and I had no desire to contribute to the mountain of pap on the subject.

So, this is not a pop-psychology book, and it is not intended to save people's relationships or to render instant nirvana. Indeed, one goal of this book is to combat the avalanche of pop-psychology concerning relationships. It is not that I think all pop-psychology is rubbish, or that self-help books may not serve a function. However, the rule here is caveat emptor – let the buyer beware – because, frankly, there is a lot of snake-oil out there on talk shows, books, TV programs, the Internet, and so forth. Much pop-psychology, with its sloganeering and quick-fix solutions is simply false or misleading. Intimate relationships as they function in reality are fascinatingly complex – too complex to be captured in terms of achieving relationship utopia in five easy steps. Over the many years I have spent studying relationships in a scientific fashion, I have developed considerable respect for the way in which couples often heroically struggle to predict, control, and understand their own intimate relationships. All too often pop-psychology fails to connect to the real psychological world of intimate relationships and, thus, sells people well short.

This book, then, is an attempt to present an accessible account of the scientific work on intimate relationships. The audience I imagined peeking over my shoulder as I was laboring over my PC was a (curious and intelligent) lay audience. However, the book is not dumbed down, and it has, I hope, enough originality and scope to be of interest to my scientific colleagues, both in psychology and in other disciplines. One reason I have written this book is to combat some of the egregious stereotypes about work in this area. In the pecking order of disciplines in academe, psychology is regarded as a soft science, social psychology is one step down, and the study of intimate relationships evokes stereotypes like "unscientific," and "finds out what we already know." I come to bury such stereotypes, not to praise them. Given the profusion of pop-psychology and the lack of scientifically grounded books dealing with this topic, perhaps this ignorance is to be expected – indeed, this state of affairs is partly what prompted me to write this book.

My focus throughout will be on how the intimate relationship mind works. Thus, I will deal with phenomena like emotions, cognitions, expectations, desires, beliefs, and so forth. However, the relationship mind cannot be understood without also considering behavior, just as relationship behavior cannot be explained without taking the relationship mind into account. I will constantly explore the causal threads between mind and behavior (from communicating, to making love, to intimate violence).

I will confine my attention largely to intimate relationships that have a sexual or romantic connotation, rather than delve into platonic relationships. This is not to say that the study of intimate relationships does not include platonic relationships from familial to platonic friendships. This is not surprising, given that the different kinds of relationships are obviously related. Moreover, I will discuss particular categories of non-sexual relationships that are centrally related to adult intimate relationships, the most important being parent–child relationships. However, this book does not present a theory of interpersonal processes in general. The domain of sexual relationships possesses a natural coherence and a psychological significance that warrants study in its own right.

The New Science of Intimate Relationships

To understand why I have titled this book *The New Science of Intimate Relationships*, I need to explain a little of the history of scientific work in this area. Research relevant to human relationships has taken place for decades across several disciplines, including sociology, anthropology, biology, and, of course, the psychological subdisciplines including clinical psychology, developmental psychology, cognitive psychology, and social psychology. However, the study of human intimate relationships has been dominated by psychology, with social psychology playing a central role.[3] Within social psychology, up to the late 1970s, research into relationships concentrated on what factors lead people to be attracted to one another at the initial stages of relationship development. This research tended to be atheoretical and the results read like a shopping list of variables that influence attraction including similarity, proximity, physical attractiveness, and so forth.[4]

In the 1980s the psychological zeitgeist shifted toward the study of the greater complexity inherent in the development, maintenance, and dissolution phases of dyadic romantic relationships. This shift was prompted by several key developments in the 1970s. First, Harold Raush, John Gottman and others in the clinical area started carrying out research that, for the first time, actually observed and carefully measured the dyadic interchanges of married couples. The aim of such research was to find out what behavioral interaction patterns predicted marital satisfaction, a rather narrow endeavor compared to the more grandiose goals of social psychology.[5] However, this research gave other (social) psychologists some important methodological tools and, perhaps more

4

critically, firmly planted the idea that dyadic interaction can be profitably observed in relatively controlled settings. A second development was that Zick Rubin and others became interested in love, and devised reliable scales that could measure the concept.[6] This work on love has been maintained until the present day.[7] Finally, a group of social psychologists led by Harold Kelley produced a bell-wether book published in 1983 (*Close Relationships*),[8] which presented the first expansive and full-blooded treatment of intimate relationships from a social psychological perspective.

Social psychological research on relationships in the last decade has been marked by two major developments. First, there has been an explosion of work concerned with understanding the role that social cognition (beliefs, cognitive processes, etc.) and emotions play in intimate relationships. Second, there has been a burgeoning interest in how attachment and bonding processes contribute to adult romantic relationships. The social cognitive work on intimate relationships has borrowed theories and methodologies from both social and cognitive psychology. Attachment research in adults has appropriated the basic theories from the work in the 1960s and 1970s by John Bowlby and Mary Ainsworth concerning infant–caregiver attachment bonds. I will describe such work fully later in the book. But, what exactly is a social psychological approach to adult relationships, and how does it differ from other scientific approaches or disciplines that also study intimate relationships?

Scientific approaches to the study of intimate relationships can be differentiated according to their goals and to their level of focus. At a general level, all human sciences have the same aims – the explanation, prediction, and control of human behavior and cognition – although certain aims will be emphasized depending on the approach. For example, clinical psychology emphasizes the prediction and control of relationship phenomena (especially the prediction or control of relationship success or dissolution) whereas social psychology and evolutionary psychology focus more on explanation.

However, different approaches to the study of human relationships concentrate on different goals or questions, and thus vary in their domains of study. Developmental psychology, for example, is mainly interested in the development of bonding and attachment in childhood and in the development of intimate relationships across the life span. Evolutionary psychology is primarily concerned with understanding the evolutionary origins of human courting, mate-selection, sexual behavior, and so forth. Thus, evolutionary psychology is concerned with distal causes from the remote past for currently existent human behavioral (and cognitive) dispositions. Social psychology, in contrast, takes human dispositions (both behavioral and cognitive) as givens, and seeks to model the way in which such dispositions interact with external contingencies to produce interactive behavior, social judgments, and emotions. Thus, social psychology offers much more fine-grained predictions and explanations of specific behaviors and cognitions than does evolutionary psychology, and at a very proximal level. Sociological approaches, in contrast to both social psychology and evolutionary psychology, are concerned with the way in which the broader cultural and institutional contexts frame and guide the individual's or the couples' behavior. Social psychology focuses on the interaction between the individual and the dyadic relationship. Sociological (and anthropological) approaches tend to focus on the links between the couple (e.g., marriage, mate selection) and the wider culture.

Time to come clean. I am a social psychologist, and my research interests over the last two decades have concerned the role played by social cognitive processes and structures in intimate relationships. Accordingly, this book maintains an emphasis on a social psychological level of analysis. However, one reason I have written this book is to cast a wider theoretical net. My major thrust has been to combine a social psychological approach (and related research) with theories and research from evolutionary psychology. I have also liberally borrowed from developmental psychology and clinical psychology, along with dashes of anthropological work, and drizzled with contributions from cognitive science. In short, I have adopted an interdisciplinary path.

My ecumenical approach is based on my conviction that the most appropriate way to view the range of scientific approaches to relationships is in terms of a theory-knitting approach. Different theories often focus on different claims and deal with different parts of the complex causal nexus that drives human behavior. Accordingly, such theories are not necessarily in conflict but can be profitably treated as complementary – as dealing with different parts of the proverbial elephant.[9] For example, social psychological and evolutionary approaches are both compatible and complementary, given that they deal with different questions.

To take a concrete example, a social psychological approach to understanding how people select mates might be to build a psychological model in which the importance given to particular mate characteristics (which may vary across individuals) would be treated as mentally stored cognitive standards (such as the perceived importance of obtaining an attractive and healthy partner). Thus, individuals would then use such ideals as standards to compare with potential mates or to evaluate perceived satisfaction with an existing mate. Resultant levels of satisfaction and relationship commitment, in turn, might affect one's own behavior, which might influence one's partner's behavior, which might end up with the couple deciding to live together, or with one person breaking off the relationship. Thus, a social psychological model describes how cognitions, emotions, and behaviors interact, and how they causally interact with the behavior of each individual within the dyadic relationship. Such models can become quite complicated, describing, as they do, a complex reality. Nevertheless, they deal only with a certain slice of the causal field at work.

Evolutionary psychology asks questions that social psychologists typically do not ask, like why do people bother looking for mates who are attractive and healthy in the first place or what is the origin of characteristic gender differences in such ideals? (To avoid confusion, throughout the book I will use "gender" to refer to male versus female, and "sex" to refer to sexual intercourse or related behavior, appearance, and attitudes.) Answers for evolutionary psychologists lie in the evolutionary history of humans; specifically in the adaptive advantages that would have accrued to our ancestors in the ancestral environments in developing such mate preferences (which may be different across gender).

Evolutionary and social psychological enterprises are not, however, completely autonomous enterprises. Understanding the evolutionary origin of such ideals can help the social psychologist to identify and measure the appropriate categories of ideal standards, in addition to helping predict how people will feel, think, and behave with potential or existent mates in contemporary society. Understanding how the relationship mind works at the proximal level, in turn, will help the evolutionary psychologist to ask the right questions and gives important clues about what are mental adaptations (with an evolutionary history) and what are not. These points are not mere speculation, as I will show later in the book.

Now, this may seem a perfectly reasonable, even obvious, way of proceeding. Yet, it is often not the way that science, or scientists, actually do proceed. The history of the social sciences, including psychology, is depressingly often a history of internecine warfare and of takeover bids among theories and approaches that may be complementary (as it is of science generally). For example, a heated battle is taking place in psychology and relationship science concerning the merits of evolutionary psychology. The most fervent proselytizers of evolutionary psychology argue that it represents no less than a new paradigm, and that all psychologists should use it. Its fiercest detractors argue that it has little place in a "true" science of intimate relationships, and that it represents a largely unfalsifiable set of propositions based on the incorrect assumption that our genes are our destiny. Such critics are not creationist scientists nor do they want to argue with Darwinism. Their principal argument (which deserves attention) is that evolutionary processes have thrown up a marvelously malleable, all-purpose learning machine called a human being. Accordingly, our genetic inheritance does not build in any dispositions or predispositions to behave or think in any particular fashion. Humans, so the argument goes, have their desires, beliefs, personality traits, and so forth, almost wholly determined by the local and cultural environments in which they have developed. This view is termed by Leda Cosmides and John Tooby the standard social science model, and it is the approach that evolutionary psychologists wish to overthrow.[10]

To give another example, the sociological wing of relationship research and theory decries the overwhelming focus on the individual or dyad in the standard social psychological approach. They claim the bulk of the causal forces at work actually reside in the wider culture. Some proponents in this school of thought – the postmodernists – go further and argue that standard "scientific" approaches should be discarded, adhering, as they do, to outmoded, traditional models of science (termed *positivist* accounts). I will go into some detail here, because the arguments I consider throughout the book often come down to the kind of scientific model explicitly or implicitly adopted.

Positivist models of science were at their height in the middle of the twentieth century, but still maintain currency, at least in the received versions of science published in the media, or in the introductory sections of undergraduate academic textbooks.[11] In any case, such traditional scientific models adhere to the following four assumptions:

- A real world exists, independent of human existence, and the aims of the behavioral sciences are to explain, predict, and control human behavior.

8

- Scientific theories and hypotheses must be testable.
- Scientific theories and hypotheses are tested through replicable, empirical observations.
- Science is value free.

This list, to some extent, represents a cardboard stereotype. Nevertheless, it represents the traditional edifice of science that postmodernists yearn to jettison. First, postmodernism abandons the aims of science (explanation, prediction, and control) and replaces them with social and political aims such as enriching people's lives, or challenging the prevailing repressive male or white European ideologies. Second, scientific theories, lay theories, or the musings of astrologers or tea-leaf readers are viewed as simply different (and equally valid) accounts of an infinitely malleable reality that is actually a function of cultural forces. Third, the world exists as a function of how we perceive and interpret it. Thus, there is no world that exists independently of human culture and judgment. Fourth, science is not value free, but locked into the values of the wider society. Fifth, the notion that empirical findings give us gold standard tests for evaluating theories is regarded as a myth of positivist thought.

I won't launch into a full-scale analysis of postmodernism here.[12] But I don't need to in order to show why postmodernism is wrong. The Achilles' heel of postmodernism is its unremitting relativist approach to truth and reality, an epistemological stance that lies at its core. The notion that there is no reality outside human understanding is risible. However, it is not the absurdity of such a belief that is the nemesis of postmodernism, but the fact that such a thoroughgoing relativism is viciously self-contradictory. The argument that relativism is self-contradictory is not new – Socrates laid out the basic arguments against relativism convincingly more than 2,000 years ago. However, such arguments bear repetition.[13]

The way in which postmodernism kneecaps itself is revealed in a multitude of ways. Consider the following questions and their implications:

- Why do postmodernists bother trying to convince other academics to adopt a postmodernist approach? If postmodernism is somehow superior to other approaches, this means it is false because postmodernism is committed to the rejection of the idea that some theories or accounts are cognitively superior.

- How can the aims of postmodernist approaches be evaluated? If it is true that postmodernist theories enrich people's lives, or empower the masses, then postmodernism is false, because the theory is based on the postulate that such reality claims cannot be seriously advanced.

- What are we to make of the welter of empirical claims that are produced as part and parcel of postmodernist articles? If they are true, then postmodernism is false, because it is based on the view that empirical claims should not be interpreted as claims about reality.

In a nutshell, then, if postmodernism is true it is false, and if it is false it is false. Either way, it is false.

This argument may seem like a clever bit of sophistry, but it reveals a fundamental flaw that permeates postmodernism and produces astonishing displays of doublethink. Postmodernist arguments regularly make use of the same criteria of veracity, including empirical claims, which are simultaneously discarded as relics of a positivist tradition. In sawing off the branch that holds up the values of rationality, truth, and belief in a world that is (partly at least) independent of human cognition, relativists apparently fail to realize that they are perched on the same part of the branch they are busily attempting to sever. Postmodernism is self-refuting and is, thus, not tenable.

However, even postmodernism contains some germs of truth. In particular, few scientists today would maintain the fiction that science is value free, or somehow operates in isolation of the surrounding culture and its beliefs. Moreover, the positivist idea that science is marked out from pseudosciences, like astrology, by the commitment of science to leaving its theories open to falsification by empirical tests, has come under increasing attack by contemporary philosophers of science (who generally also hate postmodernism). In traditional models of science, scientists are supposed to ruthlessly evaluate their models and explanations by deducing empirical predictions from their theories and then subjecting the predictions to empirical tests. If the predictions pan out, fine: the theories can be allowed to stick around. If the predictions are proved wrong, then the theory is massively falsified, and should be unceremoniously dumped. This is the kind of scientific procedure many people learned in high school science, and it is associated with the work of Karl Popper in the mid-twentieth century.[14] The problem is that this is not what scientists actually do, nor is it even a credible normative model for what they should do.

What do scientists (including psychologists) actually do when faced with empirical evidence counting against a much-favored theory or hypothesis, and in favor of a new (maverick) theory? Well, they typically do one or more of the following: (1) point out that there are methodological problems with the evidence, including poor measurement procedures, inadequate sample size, inappropriate sample selection, poor general design, wrong statistical procedures, and so forth; or (2) argue that the data have been wrongly interpreted, and can be explained in terms of the supposedly wrong theory; or (3) argue that the maverick theory is implausible because it is illogical, or is not consistent with other well-accepted evidence, or is too simple and lacks the breadth of the supposedly wrong theory, or that it is bizarrely complex and nature is not like that, and the list could go on. This is what scientists tend to do in psychology, and what they do in every science.

This characteristic of science as it actually works does not ineluctably draw us back into the dreadful maw of a relativist postmodernism. To explain why, consider the model of the scientific process pictured in figure 1.1.[15] Such models are popular in philosophy of science circles, and have now penetrated psychology, as well as other scientific disciplines. Essentially it is a swept-up version of a positivist account, but one that drops positivism's most problematic features. As can be seen, scientific thought is composed of four major categories: criteria for theory evaluation, the aims of science, rules for good research, and the theories themselves. This model assumes that the theoretical structures or entities postulated in theories, which may be unobservable (such as electrons or cognitive processes), nevertheless refer to an independent reality. Accordingly, the principal aim of science is to develop theories and models of the causal processes and structures that accurately represent the real world. However, this aim is best represented as an ideal, which in practice may be impossible to reach (like democracy or justice). A fundamental part of a scientific approach is to admit that any part of the system (aims, theories, research rules, or criteria), may be mistaken. The whole scientific shooting match can be seen as a form of knowledge and theory-making that is constantly in flux and being improved upon as a function of experience.

A single research finding that counts against a well-accepted theory can be dealt with in two ways. First, the maverick evidence needs to be replicated in other labs or by other people to convince us that it is a real phenomenon (thus the need for replication, which is a common value

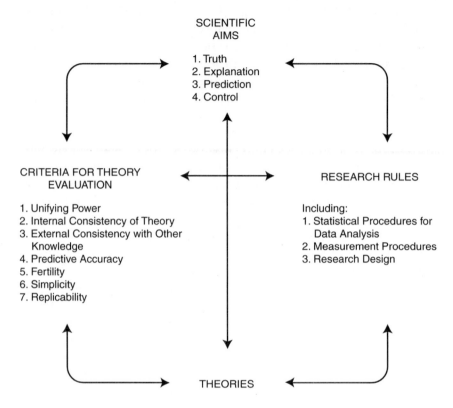

Figure 1.1 A model of the scientific process

in science). Second, empirical evidence that is convincing or compelling is likely to be generated by research programs rather than single experiments or observations. Research programs can examine and test phenomena in different ways, deal with alternative plausible explanations, provide evidence of replication, and so forth. But even this kind of empirical evidence will not save an overly positivist approach. The reason is that there are always other important criteria (some conceptual) that scientists consider when evaluating theories, including simplicity, coherence with other well-accepted knowledge, being logically consistent, having the capacity to unify phenomena that previously seemed to be quite independent, being a fertile source of other useful hypotheses, and so forth. The ability of the theory to make accurate predictions may be a central criterion in evaluating scientific theories. It

12

may even be the most important criterion. But is not the only criterion. This model shows that not only is science inherently conservative, but that this is a perfectly rational state of affairs.

When important episodes of scientific change are examined it is apparent that the slushy connection between theory and evidence is not idiosyncratic to psychology, but is common to all sciences. One of my favorite examples concern Lord Kelvin's arguments in the 1880s concerning the age of the earth (the connection with intimate relationships will become clear in due course). Kelvin's calculations were based on the laws of thermodynamics, and were derived from three arguments concerning the cooling of the earth, the age of the sun, and the action of the tides. His preliminary estimates for the age of the earth, published in 1862, provided a figure of somewhere between 20 and 400 million years. However, over the subsequent years, he promulgated figures that were supposedly more accurate, and were increasingly lower. By 1897 his best estimate of the earth's age was 24 million, with an upper limit of around 40 million years.

Kelvin's estimates, as we now know, were widely astray (the earth is currently reckoned to be around 4.5 billion years old). If ever there was empirical evidence that disposed of another theory this was it – if the earth were as old as Kelvin claimed, there was simply not enough time for evolution to have occurred along the lines suggested by Darwin's theory, which postulated natural selection working on random variation.

How did Charles Darwin and others respond to Kelvin's challenge?[16] Darwin was painfully aware that his version of evolution was ruled out by Kelvin's estimates. After much intellectual wrestling, Darwin recommended a wait-and-see attitude while continuing to push his own theory. Others, such as Thomas Huxley and Alfred Wallace (the co-discoverer of evolution), altered Darwin's theory to allow for natural catastrophes or rapid climatic changes to accelerate the pace of evolution that would be more usual in stable periods. However, as Kelvin's estimates of the earth's age became ever lower, geologists and others adopted a more confrontational perspective and began questioning Kelvin's original analyses. As was argued, if the evidence from physics and geology conflict, why should geology necessarily submit?

The decisive blow to Kelvin's estimates did not come until 1904, when Ernest Rutherford (the University of Canterbury's most famous student) realized that the discovery of radiation (an internal source of

13

heat) enormously increased the possible age of the earth and the solar system. When about to deliver the coup de grâce to Kelvin's arguments, while delivering a talk at the Royal Institution in England, Rutherford noticed Kelvin, old and frail by this time, sitting in the audience. Not wishing to unduly humiliate the great man, Rutherford phrased his talk in terms of substantiating Kelvin's original comment in his first paper on the age of the earth in which Kelvin expressed the qualification that his arguments held, unless some unknown source of heat inside the earth was discovered – *voilà*, Kelvin was right! Kelvin actually had never mentioned such a qualification again in his subsequent articles, which gradually became more trenchant, and he never publicly recanted his views, even after Rutherford's incisive realization. Individual scientists are not necessarily rational. It is the process of science over time with many scientists at work that provides the collective rational structure of science.

Note that this argument does not imply that scientists can rationally hold onto their extant theories come what may – that anything goes. Anything does not go. If it did, then scientists would hardly ever achieve consensus and we would be able to list dozens of scientific cases where one theory massively outpointed another on the criteria listed in figure 1.1, yet were unsuccessful. But there are no such cases in science (that I am aware of) – the reason being that when all criteria are decisively met, then the winning theory emerges triumphant. Remember that Darwinian evolutionary theory eventually overcame considerable resistance from the human egocentric view – that we are at the centre of the universe – to sweep all before it. On the other hand, cases where some criteria point one way and some another, or the evidence seems fairly evenly balanced, are a dime a dozen in every field of science. In such cases there is widespread argument and dissent. It bears repeating that science is inherently conservative when it comes to theory change, and for good reason.[17]

Let me deal with a few other claims, which are commonly expressed in relation to the scientific study of intimate relationships. Two hackneyed propositions often expressed are as follows:

(1) Studying relationships and love scientifically will destroy the magic of it all. (2) Studying intimate relationships scientifically only tell us what we already know from common sense – like "good communication produces successful relationships" or "arguing and getting angry are bad for relationships" or "men are more frequently aggressive in relationships than are women."

Loud boos to both claims! There is no evidence that studying any phenomenon makes it less puzzling or enthralling. Indeed, the very opposite is the case, especially in psychology, where what appear to be mundane and everyday behaviors (such as talking or explaining someone else's behavior) become mysterious – even magisterial – feats when seriously investigated. As to whether studying relationships will only tell us what we already know, well, the proof of the pudding is in the eating – once you have read the book you will be able to make an informed judgment. However, I have already laid a trap by citing in the above paragraph three commonly accepted notions that extensive research suggests are either questionable or flat-out wrong. It turns out that it is uncertain what the relation is between communication and relationship satisfaction, that arguing and getting angry are not necessarily bad for relationships, and that men are not more frequently physically aggressive than women in intimate relationships (I will document these claims later in the book). It does not pay to be overly confident about maxims learnt at one's caregiver's knee, or garnered from the latest column one has read about relationships in a magazine. Some popular stereotypes about relationships are true, others are false, and many are half-truths, as will be seen.

On the other hand, I do not wish to suggest that all lay beliefs or lay theories (whether shared, and hence commonsensical, or idiosyncratic) should be dispensed with as unscientific rubbish. After all, laypeople share the same set of aims as do scientists; namely, to explain, predict, and control their own relationships. Psychological folk theories and aphorisms concerned with love and relationships have developed over eons of time. Given that humans are still here and prospering, it is unlikely, to say the least, that such lay theories should turn out to be utterly false, and therefore useless as tools for people to use for predicting, explaining, and controlling their own relationships. However, this does not imply that lay conventional wisdom is necessarily correct or that it is adequate as a scientific theory. To adopt a scientific approach entails subjecting any theory or body of knowledge to the same critical scrutiny regardless of whether it comes from the Bible, from common sense, or from renowned authorities. Folk theories comprise a valuable resource that scientists can plunder, but it would be hardly surprising if it turns out that common sense offers a partial, limited, and partly false account of relationship phenomena.[18]

However, even if common-sense theories or maxims are false, this

15

does not mean that they are not worthy of scientific study. People's beliefs and theories influence their behavior, regardless of whether such mental states are true or false. A man may believe, quite irrationally, that his wife is being unfaithful, and accordingly has an extramarital affair of his own in retaliation. The man's belief, although false, partly explains his behavior. Accordingly, if psychologists wish to explain lay behavior or cognition they are forced to take the existence of commonsense beliefs and theories into account (unless the psychologists happen to be radical behaviorists and believe that mental states and processes do not cause behavior – rare animals these days). This is a commonly expressed point, and one that is apparently banal if not blindingly obvious. Yet it has a fundamentally important consequence for psychology or any social science that has at times been missed.

General models of scientific practice and thought share a common structure across the physical and the psychological sciences. However, the point just raised is one factor that demarcates the psychological sciences from the natural sciences. The psychological scientist is obliged to take into account the beliefs or lay theories of the individual, regardless of their truth value. In contrast, the paleontologist, or the astronomer, or the biologist is not obligated to take into account lay thinking or theories on related subject matter, because such lay theories and beliefs do not causally influence the phenomena being explained. The paleontologist does not need to consider folk theories of the origins of life, because human theories (scientific or lay) could not have possibly influenced the causal processes of evolution over the last billion years or so. Similarly, the astrophysicist may safely ignore origin myths or folk beliefs about the origin of the universe, since such theories could not possibly influence the phenomena being explained. All scientists, of course, may borrow ideas or concepts from common sense when building their theories. However, psychological scientists are obliged to do so, whereas natural scientists have no such obligation.[19]

Most scientists who study relationships examine how they *do* work, not how they *should* work. This may have been a superfluous point, if I was writing a book about anything other than relationships. However, the is/ought distinction is frequently confused when it comes to relationships. I suspect, once again, the dead hand of pop-psychology at work, which is typically expressed in terms of what people should do to have the perfect marriage, or to catch the ideal mate, or to have a wonderful sex life. I will never talk about what people should do, although

I will cover the research concerned with what predicts relationship happiness or longevity. To give an advance warning, accounts of how relationships actually work are not always a pretty sight. Many well-replicated findings concerning how relationships function seem almost designed to make a feminist shudder, or to reduce the politically correct to apoplexy.

I also reject the claims often made that science should not investigate or report findings that might maintain or justify behavior that is judged as bad or inappropriate (views that are kissing cousins to the sort of postmodernist approaches I have already repudiated). Such claims are a dagger aimed at the heart of science, which is not in the business of suppressing truth or conforming to current politically correct views. Science investigates and strives to attain the truth. Arguments that evolutionary theories, for example, are wrong or bad because they justify differences between men and women and legitimate discrimination or prejudice confuse the is/ought distinction. To be sure, scientific theories and findings can be used for invidious or evil purposes by unscrupulous or prejudiced individuals – evolutionary theories, for example, have a long history of such (mis)use. But the problem resides in the manner in which such theories are applied, not in the scientific merit of the theories themselves. If men and women are different as a matter of empirical fact, and we wish to prevent discrimination and encourage equality, then surely it is advisable to understand the causes of such differences – otherwise misdirected and expensive societal efforts are likely to eventuate. Science is not in the business of justifying, but of explaining. The two activities are related in human societies, but are *different* activities.

The final term I have not discussed in the title is the word "new" as in the "new science." Such usage might be thought odd, given that different scientific disciplines have been studying different aspects of intimate relationships for decades. If pressed, I might admit to a smidgen of fairground hucksterism in using such a word. However, my use is justified on the grounds of the extraordinary flowering of scientific research concerning intimate relationships over the last two decades. Much of this new research and theorizing has operated within scientific disciplines, but interdisciplinary work is also burgeoning. Recent interdisciplinary journals have been set up on relationships, new international societies dealing with relationships have been developed, the flow of academic books dealing with intimate relationships has increased, and

17

scientifically based courses on intimate relationships are becoming commonplace in universities. This activity has lead to a wealth of new knowledge and an expanded appreciation of the pivotal status that dyadic intimate relationships play in people's lives. Significant progress has been made toward an interdisciplinary, mature science of intimate relationships – enough progress to warrant the appellation "new."

In writing this book I have been inspired by the work of Ellen Berscheid, currently Regent Professor at the University of Minnesota, who has consistently championed the call for the development of an interdisciplinary scientific assault on intimate relationships (for the development of a science of intimate relationships) over the last two decades (and who has published some of the pivotal work in the field). It is richly ironic that Berscheid (and Elaine Hatfield) received the first so-called golden fleece award in 1975 from US Senator Proxmire, which he awarded for some years to recipients of research grants from government agencies for projects he judged as particularly foolish. The ex-senator's complaints were redolent of some of the misconceptions I have already challenged, to wit:

> I object to this not only because no one – not even the National Science Foundation – can argue that falling in love is a science; not only because I'm sure that even if they spend $84 million or $84 billion they wouldn't get an answer that anyone would believe. I'm also against it because I don't want the answer. I believe that 200 million other Americans want to leave some things in life a mystery, and right at the top of things we don't want to know is why a man falls in love with a woman and vice versa . . . So National Science Foundation – get out of the love racket. Leave that to Elizabeth Barrett Browning and Irving Berlin.

If you disagree with the good senator, then this book is for you. If you agree with his comments, then you really do need to read this book![20]

The contents page gives a flavor of the wide-ranging list of topics I have covered. In Part I, I discuss three key theoretical planks that undergird the science of intimate relationships – the roles of lay theories and cognition (chapter 2), the origins of the intimate relationship mind (chapter 3), and the nature of love and other emotions (chapter 4). The remaining chapters in the book examine how these three domains play out when investigating specific domains within intimate relationships. Part II covers topics that, in one way or another, are related to how intimate relationships unfold over time. How do people communicate and read each other's minds in relationships (chapter 5)? What factors predict relationship success and does communication matter (chapter 6)? Why does the capacity and need for psychological intimacy vary across people (chapter 7)? And, how do people choose their mates (chapter 8)? In Part III I deal with two themes that sell movies and books – sex (chapter 9) and (intimate) violence (chapter 10). In the concluding chapter I attempt to pull it all together, summarizing what we know (and do not know) about intimate relationships and offering an overarching theory about the origins and nature of the intimate relationship mind.

Because this book deals with the scientific study of relationships, I will offer few unadorned or iron-clad conclusions. Relationship science is a hotbed of argument and disagreement about issues big and small. Many intriguing questions will be raised, which are unanswered, and some issues will remain unresolved. Science is like that. On the other hand, I will generally strike an attitude, or present some integrated account that I believe is the best currently available. Science works like a courtroom, with the jury representing the wider scientific community, the judge representing the editors and editorial boards of scientific journals who set the rules about what is admissible evidence, and the lawyers, the warring factions presenting their own versions of the truth. When university students get past the inevitable bromides and false certainties of introductory textbooks and, usually at the graduate level, strike the arguments and uncertainties inherent in the primary scientific literature, it is tempting for them to throw their hands up in despair and revert to a postmodernist stance ("you can prove anything!") – and some do. I hope to show that such an attitude is unnecessary and wrong; that a balanced analysis of the scientific findings often lays bare the facts, and that an intelligent evaluation of the available theories that explain the facts provides signposts for the best paths to follow.

Conclusion

This book illustrates how the scientific work on relationships has a double-barreled role. It increases our understanding of intimate relationships, while simultaneously informing our scientific understanding of the basic building blocks of psychology: cognition, affect, and behavior. And this is simply because so much of human cognition, emotion, and behavior is interpersonal in nature.

Part I

Three Theoretical Planks

Chapter 2

The Intimate Relationship Mind: Theories about Theories about Theories

. . . there is nothing so practical as a good theory.
Lewin, 1951

Consider the following question. How do you know whether you are in a good relationship or a bad one? I have asked this question many times in university classroom settings. Initially, people normally give responses like "I just know," "Good relationships feel good," or "What an interesting question – I have never really thought about it." After an opportunity for more thought on the matter, my students typically come up with a set of criteria they believe establishes the nature of a "good" or "successful" relationship – good communication, similarity, good sex life, honesty, humor, support, and so forth.

One major goal of a cognitive approach to intimate relationships is to answer the same question, and explain how and why people make evaluations of the state of their relationships. However, the sweep of such approaches is exceptionally broad and deals with every imaginable kind of relationship judgment and decision, from those that occur at the very genesis of the relationship ("Gee, he looks interesting"), to the kind that occur at its end ("This relationship will never work!"), to the myriad of mundane judgments that accompany every relationship every day.

The model I propose operates at the general cognitive level, and is not intended as a description of the brain or even the microstructure of cognition. I disagree with an overzealous brand of reductionism in which

23

all phenomena are (on principal) reducible to one level of analysis. Thus, a "greedy reductionist" (to use a term coined by Daniel Dennett[1]) might insist on describing all phenomena (including biological and psychological material) in terms of the subatomic world of particles and forces. The implausibility of such a move becomes obvious when one imagines a full-blown description of some social activity (say going out on a date) by describing what is going on in terms of the atomic and subatomic physics involved. The resultant analysis in terms of swarms of particles and the fundamental forces involved may give an accurate account of the physical reality of the date. However, it would be unable to answer even simple questions, such as why the man paid for the meal or why the female pushed the man's hand away from her knee. The subatomic explanatory picture invoked is informative about reality at the level of fundamental particles, but cannot even begin to explain the way in which reality is structured and organized at the psychological or dyadic level.

I agree that there is only one reality to describe and explain. However, there exist multiple levels of description, interpretation, and explanation, which tap into different features of the causal structures and processes at work. These different levels of explanatory model building boil down to the physical level, the biological level, the cognitive level, and the interpersonal/social level. None of this implies that it is not a good idea, even a marvelous idea, to develop theories that both draw from and integrate such levels. Indeed, such grand theories include the most famous and impactful in all of science, of which Darwinian evolutionary theory is the pre-eminent example. Moreover, one major criterion for a good theory is that it is consistent with well-entrenched theories or knowledge from other domains. Cognitive theories ignore, at their peril, what we know about the neurophysiology of the brain, not to mention the laws of physics.

A longstanding, and apparently intractable, debate in philosophy and science has concerned the proper relation between minds and brains. The development of the computer changed this debate irrevocably, and created a powerful argument against a (greedy) reductionist approach in which cognitive descriptions of the brain (the mind) are simply reduced to descriptions of neurons and synapses. The same computer software or program can be used to access and manipulate the stored information in the memory store of two computers that differ in terms of their internal hardware. A precise description of the two computers in terms of electrical currents, stored electrical potentials, and hardware can be given. However, such descriptions fail to give an adequate description and explanation of what the computers actually do, which may be identical according to a higher-order description of how the information is processed (specified in terms of the programming).

The computer analogy with the human brain and mind is irresistible – the mind is akin to a higher-order description of the brain that details how information is stored, accessed, organized and the functions it is used for. The folk psychology of human behavior is pitched at exactly this level. When we say that Mary believes that Tom is unhappy and buys him a gift to cheer him up, we are explaining Mary's behavior in terms of information that is stored and acted upon, in the same way in which we explain how other intelligent systems work (such as in nonhuman animals and computers). If anyone believes that human behavior can be readily described and interpreted without the spectacles of folk psychological theory, then try imagining someone baking a cake without perceiving the actions as intentional, or inventing an informative explanation for why Fred drove his car to Mary's place without mentioning any of his goals, beliefs, wishes, wants, personality traits, abilities, attitudes, desires, intentions, or motives.

The theory I will present is general and complex, but I will anchor it to specific examples to render it digestible and plausible. Relationships are comprised of two people (as the bare minimum) but to simplify matters I will deal initially with just one individual in the dyad and his or her relationship mind. I start with a diagram showing the elements and basic causal links in (see figure 2.1). This is not a model I invented from scratch – it represents an amalgam of features that have currency in mainstream cognitive and social psychology.[2]

Here is an example to give an intuitive feel for the way the model works: Joan's partner unexpectedly pays her a compliment (Eliciting Event) which leads her to feel particularly happy (Eliciting Emotion) because she had begun to think her husband was taking her for granted (Local Relationship Theory). She recalls with pleasure the way her husband used to flood her with gifts and romantic notes when they first got together (Conscious Processing) and thinks what a sensitive, loving person he usually is (Cognitive Outcome). Joan decides to make his favorite meal (Behavioral Outcome). Her general belief that close relationships need a lot of work to stay successful (General Relationship Theory) and her positive evaluation of her relationship (Local Relationship Theory) are strengthened (feedback arrow from Outcomes).

25

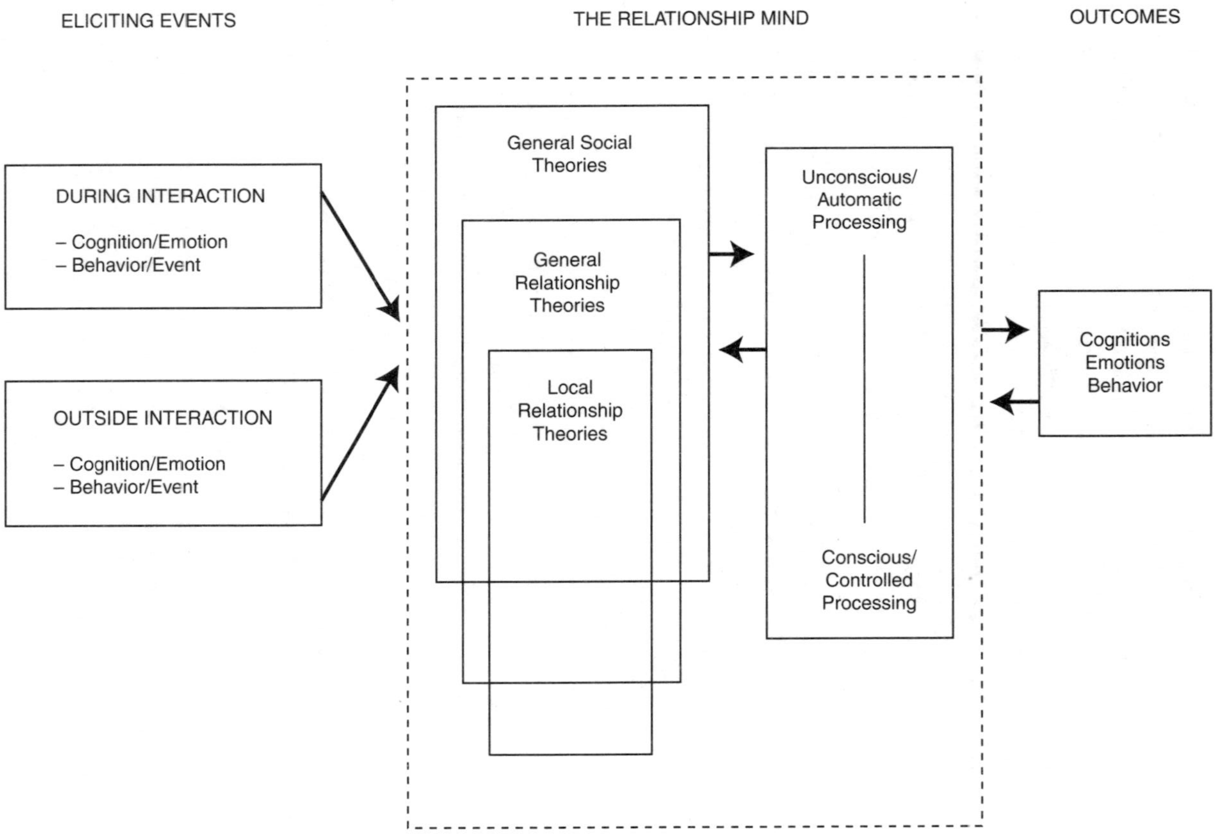

Figure 2.1 A model of the intimate relationship mind

The relationship mind is split into two basic components, which are crucially intertwined: stored relationship theories and online processing. This division is standard fare in traditional cognitive models, although the two components are often termed "long-term memory" versus "short-term or working memory." The notion that humans store every single event and behavior experienced as memory traces in long-term memory has long since been discarded as wildly implausible. Instead, according to stock cognitive theory, we encode, organize, store, and recall events and behaviors in terms of stored knowledge structures, in which the details are often lost or blurred. Of course, a small amount of information can be retained in working memory, but this memory store is severely limited both in terms of the amount of information it can retain (typically considered as close to seven items) and in the length of time it remains available. The reasons for my labeling these stored knowledge structures as "theories" (and my curious chapter title) will become clear in due course.

The Content and Structure of Relationship Theories

General social theories

The basic idea here is that people have a variety of rules, beliefs, and so forth that apply generally to interpersonal relations (from strangers to lovers). These include a general folk theory (often termed "theory of mind") that specifies when and how to attribute beliefs, attitudes, intentions, personality traits, and so forth. Hence, as can be seen in figure 2.1, they apply to intimate and nonintimate relationships alike. I will give an example using a much-researched model in social psychology, known as attribution theory, that deals with the way in which people explain (attribute causes) to their own and to other people's behavior.

Even a minimal level of anecdotal observation is sufficient to suggest that people try to understand and explain each other's behavior a lot, especially in relationship contexts. This impression is backed up by research. First, people talk a lot about relationships. When Robert Dunbar and colleagues eavesdropped in England on people's conversations in cafeterias, bars, and trains, he found that talk about personal relationships typically dominated the conversations.[3] Ethnographies of traditional cultures, including hunter-gatherer cultures, also often note that

27

sex and adult sexual relationships are a favorite topic of conversation.[4] Second, people often produce causal attributions spontaneously, both in the way they talk about relationships and in the way they think about relationships and relationship events.[5]

However, a central difficulty in developing a scientific theory about the underlying cognitive theories involved is that laypeople use an almost infinite variety of causes and reasons to explain behavior. The way that attribution theorists dealt with this problem was to hypothesize that it might not be the content of the cause that matters so much, as where the putative causes are located along a handful of dimensions including stability, specificity, and locus of attribution.

To understand how a standard attribution model works, and what these causal dimensions mean, consider the following example: Mary is unhappy with her marriage and is distrustful of her husband, Fred. Fred comes home and surprises her with a gift of flowers. Mary is likely to explain such an action with attributions such as "Fred is suffering from a rare excess of guilt because he has dented my car" or "Fred has had a rare win on the horses." In short, Mary writes Fred's positive behavior off using attributions that are unstable, specific, and external to Fred. The unstable nature of the cause means that the positive behavior will not continue, the specificity of the cause means that it will not leak through to lend a positive hue to Fred's personality or behavior, and the external nature of the cause means that Fred is not really responsible for the behavior of bringing home the flowers.

Contrast this response with the likely scenario if Fred were to come home and make a cutting remark, in response to a polite query about his day. In this case, Mary is likely to make an attribution to Fred's insensitivity, or to his lack of love for her, or to his general bad-tempered personality. Now the implications are reversed. The stable nature of the cause means that the negative behavior is likely to continue, the generality of the cause means that it will leak through to negatively infect the rest of Fred's personality or behavior, and the internal nature of the cause means that Fred is responsible for his insensitive behavior. This entire set of attributions, for both positive and negative behaviors, is clearly bad for the relationship.

Now, imagine that Mary is in a state of marital bliss. Fred comes home with the surprise gift of flowers. Mary now explains this behavior in a relationship-positive fashion according to Fred's sensitivity and caring nature (a stable, general, and internal cause). Conversely, a cutting remark by Fred will be attributionally written off with an unstable, specific, and external attribution (e.g., coming down with a cold, had a hard day at work, suffered from insomnia the night before). This set of attributions is clearly good for the relationship.

Not only is the standard attribution model a plausible account, but it also has the advantage of being true both within and across cultures.[6] A considerable body of research in Western cultures using a range of methods, examining relationships both cross-sectionally and longitudinally, and statistically controlling for a range of other variables (e.g., depression), has revealed strong evidence for this model. Strong connections have been typically found between the nature of the attributions and the level of relationship satisfaction.[7] In particular, large dollops of blame attributed to one's partner, for relationship problems or for negative features of the relationship, are corrosive.

One important feature of the standard attribution model is that attributions function to maintain existent levels of relationship satisfaction, regardless of the behavior of the partner. Fred is essentially powerless in terms of shifting his wife's evaluation of the relationship or himself. Regardless of whether he buys his wife flowers or barks at her, Mary will maintain her existing impression of Fred and her attitude toward the relationship. This feature is linked to a central tenet of attribution theories first enunciated by Fritz Heider in 1958;[8] namely, people have a basic need to sift out and maintain judgments of the dispositional and stable properties of the world, including the social world. Causal attributions are one powerful means by which the relative permanence of any pre-existent belief, attitude, or social knowledge structure can be maintained, including relationship and partner theories. Potent levels of love and positive personality impressions are money in the cognitive bank that allow people to ride out outbursts of bad behavior. On the other hand, the way in which relationship cognition works also explains why it is so difficult for relationships that have gone sour to be turned around, even when the couple are highly motivated to make their relationship work.

Such a cognitive strategy cannot hold out forever against behavior, otherwise relationships and relationship judgments would never change – which they obviously sometimes do. However, I am claiming that lay theories and beliefs are resistant to change, not incapable of change. Ordinary people, just like scientists, are conservative. They do not alter or jettison their relationship theories according to every behavioral nuance and day-to-day experience. To do so would be to live in a nightmarish and inexplicable social world, in which levels of love and commitment, and related mental models of relationships and partners (not to mention ourselves) would chaotically zoom around.

A Methodological Interlude: Correlations, Experiments, and Science

I previously referred to the existence of a strong relationship between how people explain relationship events and relationship satisfaction, and that such a connection holds up when controlling for other variables (such as depression). I want to explain further what this means. In the process I will describe the meaning of a key mathematical coefficient (the *correlation*) and also talk a little about the use of two basic research designs – *experimental* versus *observational* (or "correlational," as it is sometimes termed). I will be scattering around references to both correlations and to these two categories of research design throughout the rest of the book, so bear with me. My treatment will be as painless and as brief as possible for those who panic, or expire with boredom, at the suggestion of anything mathematical or methodological.

Correlations are mathematical indices that precisely measure the amount of similarity between two variables or factors (which need to be expressed in terms of numbers).[9] So, to use the above example, we would end up with two columns of numbers (the variables) with each row of numbers containing one pair of numbers coming from one person. The first number in each case would represent how positive the attributions were (derived, say, from a questionnaire) and the second number would consist of a score representing the levels of self-reported relationship satisfaction. A trick used by the correlational formula is to first convert each variable (each column) so that they are on the same scale – this is necessary in order for the scores to be properly mathematically compared. The end product of the formula is a number that varies from -1 to $+1$, where 1.0 represents a perfect relationship between the two variables. A correlation of zero means there is no relationship at all. A negative correlation would mean that as attributions became more positive, then relationship satisfaction would become more negative. A positive correlation, which is what we actually find in this research, means that as attributions became more positive, relationship satisfaction also becomes more positive.

Table 2.1 What a correlation of .50 between relationship happiness and relationship attributions means

	Negative attributions	Positive attributions
Happy	25%	75%
Unhappy	75%	25%

One good way of understanding what the size of a correlation means is a cute device, invented in 1982 by Robert Rosenthal and Donald Rubin, called the *Binomial Effect Size Display*.[10] Correlations between the positivity of attributions and relationship satisfaction typically range from .40 to .60. Let us assume a correlation of .50 and that we had used median splits to divide people up into either high or low groups in each variable. Table 2.1 shows what this correlation amounts to.[11] As can be seen, the result in this case translates into a 75 percent probability that people who have relationship-positive attributions will also be happy with their relationships, compared to a 25% probability of being happy if one has relationship-negative attributions. Clearly, it pays not to blame your partner for relationship problems if you can help it.

In the past psychologists have tended to dismiss correlations under .30 as being too insubstantial to bother about. But the binomial display suggests that such an attitude is ill-founded. For example, the average correlation found in four studies in which marital separation was predicted from relationship satisfaction for the husband only, was .29.[12] This figure translates in being able to predict divorce for more than 60% of couples – hardly an inconsequential predictive gain from such a brief and easily gathered self-report, and from one partner only.

At this point the skeptic might well (rightly) point out that we are dealing here with correlational data. The well-known problem with such analyses is that they do not necessarily reflect causal relations, or, even if they do, we do not know which way the causal connection runs: Do attributions cause relationship satisfaction or the other way around? This latter problem (which way does the causality flow?) can be dealt with in designs in which relationships are tracked over time, and multiple measures are taken. In such research, for example, both blame and relationship satisfaction can be measured at a given time, then both assessed again, say, a year later. One can then examine the size of the path from time one relationship satisfaction to time two blame, and from time one blame to time two relationship satisfaction. If we assume that causality cannot run backwards in time, then the possible direction of causality can, thus, be untangled. Research using this design has consistently found that increased blame leads to lower relationship satisfaction and more negative interactions, but not vice versa.[13] These findings give substance to the claim that the way people explain their partner's behavior causes relationship satisfaction to move around.

However, all correlational research designs (including longitudinal designs) suffer from the dreaded *third variable* or *missing variable* problem. That is, attributions and relationship satisfaction certainly move up and down together, but this connection may be purely incidental, with all the causal work being done by a third variable. For example, perhaps becoming more depressed causes people to become more unhappy with their relationships and independently produces less sunnier and optimistic attributions for almost everything. However, this specific causal possibility can be tested using a multivariate statistical technique termed "multiple regression."

The standard finding is that people who are more depressed are considerably less happy with their relationships, which is consistent with the hypothesis that depression is doing the causal work. However, using multiple regression, one recalculates the strength of the link between the positive attributions (the postulated cause) and relationship happiness (the postulated effect), while simultaneously statistically controlling for the effect that depression is having on both relationship happiness and attributions. The well-replicated results reveal that the link between relationship happiness and attributions remains solid and high. Thus, this analysis rules out the possibility of depression as a third or missing variable. [14]

Using the statistical wizardry of multiple regression does not unequivocally establish a causal link between attributions and relationship satisfaction – to accomplish such a task one would have to identify and measure *all* the potential third or missing variables. Apart from the practical problems involved (there may be hundreds of plausible missing variables) one can never be sure that an important third or missing variable is at work that remains unknown. Nevertheless, as researchers test and pile up evidence that the link between two constructs survives a lengthening list of plausible missing variables, confidence in the causal link between the two constructs in question is strengthened (as is true for the link between attributions and relationship satisfaction).

The most unequivocal way of establishing a causal link between the two variables would be to carry out an experiment, in which one would assign folk in relationships randomly to one of two groups. Then we would manipulate the positivity of the attributions for one group upwards, and for the other group downwards (using, say, a cleverly designed questionnaire encouraging or discouraging partner blame). Next, one would assess the subsequent levels of relationship satisfaction. Of course, such an experiment is not ethically feasible – psychologists cannot go around willy-nilly manipulating folks' relationship satisfaction. This is a general problem with scientific work in this arena, given the ethical dilemmas involved. Of course, as we will see throughout the book, experimental procedures are adopted in relationship research, where it is feasible to do so. Moreover, the attitude sometimes adopted by scientists – including psychologists – that experimental methods give us unalloyed tests concerning causal hypotheses cannot go unchallenged.

First, the act of manipulating a variable is not without problems. To take the above example, in the course of manipulating people's attributions for their relationships in a negative direction the experimenter may also unwittingly make this group of participants more depressed. The additional depression produced by the manipulation, and not the increased levels of partner blame, might well be doing the causal damage. Of course, we could measure depression and control for it in the same way as described previously (using multiple regression) but this lands us back into using the same statistical correlational techniques that experimental methods are supposed to obviate.

Second, and more seriously, experimental methodologies give us good grounds for claiming that x causes y, but do not necessarily tell us the correct causal story. Indeed, they can be downright misleading. Consider, for example, if I carried out an experiment to test the hypothesis that malaria was caused by the noxious gases emitted by swamps or stagnant water (which was, indeed, the commonly accepted theory in the Middle Ages). In this experiment towns with nearby swamps would be randomly split into two groups, the swamps for one group of towns would be filled in, and then the incidence of malaria over the next year or so assessed. The causal hypothesis that noxious gases cause malaria would, thus, have been confirmed. But, of course, this causal account is nonsense, because we would not have understood the correct causal story of how malaria is spread via mosquitoes that breed in swamps. Swamps indeed do have a part to play in the correct causal story, but we need to understand the mediating variables at work – that connect the presence of low-lying water to the subsequent illnesses – to come up with the correct causal account. So it is with all experiments. Experiments can tell us that x causes y, but do not necessarily reveal the intermediary causes that link the causal factor with the final effect. Thus, experiments have their own brand of missing variable problems, which is similar to the third variable problem in correlational research.

The way that phrases like "scientific method" or "scientific research" are often used in the media, and sometimes, alas, by scientists, suggest the existence of a single scientific method that authoritatively reveals the truth. However, there is no scientific magic bullet that authoritatively reveals the causal machinery at work. All research methods have their weaknesses and their strengths, and the process of discerning the causal connections, in psychology or any other scientific arena, is typically arduous, with multiple criteria being taken into account (see chapter 1).

Finally (honest), correlational and experimental procedures are not either-or techniques, and psychological research often combines both techniques in the same piece of research. Indeed, statistical algorithms nowadays do much more than simply assess whether correlations, or differences between groups, are "statistically" significant. On the back of the development of increasingly powerful digital computers, statistical techniques are now becoming widely used in psychology, and the other social sciences, that have only been developed in the last decade or two. Such techniques allow the researcher to test complex causal models and, thus, are admirably suited to the analysis of data from relationship couples.

Interlude over – back to the model.

General relationship theories

This category includes concepts (and related emotions) such as love, beliefs, expectations, and ideal standards that concern hypothetical relationships or beliefs about relationships in general (see figure 2.1). This category is distinct from the first category (general social theories) in two ways. First, it is more content-loaded. Second, it is specifically concerned with intimate relationships. Of course, a certain amount of idiosyncrasy exists with such beliefs. However, there is substantial evidence that people's general relationship theories are similar in some basic ways, both across cultures and within Western cultures. Research within Western cultures, for example, shows that both men and women share similar concepts and understandings concerning the meaning of love and commitment,[15] what emotions mean in relationship settings,[16] what factors cause relationships to fail or succeed,[17] and what criteria are used in searching for a mate.[18] Evidence for this generalization mounts steadily in the following chapters.

The critical feature of this category of lay theories is that they exist as mental baggage individuals bring with them into specific relationships. Consider the following short fictional story and note the multitude of ways in which items from John's general theory overlap with the information generated from a specific relationship.

John first met Mary at a party. She was poised and confident, which reminded him of his previous girlfriend. Almost unconsciously, he felt the old vague feelings of inadequacy surface. However, these feelings subsided when he got to talk to her over the onion dip, and he discovered they both liked *Seinfeld* (his old girlfriend hated *Seinfeld*). Mary laughed at a joke he made, her eyes seemed warm, and she had a quizzical look that intrigued him. She wasn't exactly good-looking, but John had never really gone after a conventionally pretty woman. He did not fit the tall, dark, and handsome stereotype, and beautiful women intimidated him. At one point in the conversation, Mary touched his arm, and he felt her rounded breast press briefly against him. He became vaguely aware of his sexual arousal, and he casually slid his hand into his pocket. Could she be interested in him? He wanted to put his arm around her, but held back. "If women think you after only one thing, that can put them off," John thought. The discussion became more personal, they asked about each other's jobs, what they wanted out of life, and their hobbies. John thought they were quite similar in many ways, and he warmed to her – she seemed interesting and intelligent. Mary's girlfriend (who he vaguely knew) came over and talked about leaving. John glanced at her hand – no wedding ring. Maybe this was the one? He took the plunge: "Does anyone feel like going for a coffee?" Mary smiles: "Why not – this party's dying."

John's evaluations, his emotions, his decisions, and his behavior only make sense when we understand that they have been generated as a function of what John's relationship mind brings to the interaction in relation to his perceptions about Mary. Intimate relationship scientists have extensively studied almost every aspect illustrated in the above story including the role that previous relationship experiences have, the characteristics people look for in a mate, the role of similarity in mate selection, how self-perceptions influence mate selection, the role of physical attractiveness, the causes of interpersonal attraction, the longitudinal development of relationships, the predictors of relationship satisfaction or longevity, sex and passion, and gender differences. This book duly covers all this work, and more.

A major thesis of this chapter, and of this book, is that focussing on the overlap between general lay theories and local lay relationship theories is a powerful lever in explaining how the intimate relationship mind works.

Local relationship theories

What do lay local theories of intimate relationships look like? I will take as an example, the following representative short account of a participant in one of my studies, who was asked to briefly describe her current relationship (she had been dating for three months):

> I first met Dan at a party. We seemed to hit it off immediately – he is attractive and outgoing and also seemed to lead an interesting life. We have since developed a rather warm and sweet relationship. He is sensitive and kind, although we have both had our problems with past relationships, and he seems a bit insecure. We do a lot of things together, and we talk about our hopes and dreams. The one problem we do have is getting our schedules together – he likes to spend a lot of time with his friends, which I think is fine (I don't want to have a relationship with someone who is super-dependent on me). But, I think we need some time on our own. I am not sure where the relationship is going, and I am happy keeping it fairly light at the moment, which seems to suit us both.

This written account represents a truncated version of this person's mental model (sex, for example, is not mentioned at all, which is typical of such brief accounts). Moreover, there are substantial differences in the sophistication and complexity of such accounts. If we had asked a person who was married to talk about his or her relationship (and if they did so frankly and freely) the resultant transcription would be likely to run into pages (if not a book for some of my friends). Nevertheless, this short and superficial description exemplifies some key points about the nature of local relationship accounts that researchers repeatedly find. First, the account has a story form, with the individual starting from the time they had met. Second, both the partner and the relationship are described in dispositional or trait terms that are really quite abstract (sensitive, kind, warm) – there is little in the way of specific episodes or activities mentioned. Third, there is a tendency to link the items mentioned in terms of causal connections (e.g., Dan is kind but insecure – perhaps because of past relationship problems).

From the time that a prospective partner is met, people begin to build a mental model of the partner and the relationship (self vis-à-vis the other). This model becomes more complex and integrated over time, with causal connections of various kinds drawn between the elements. Many kinds of judgments will be involved, including personality judgments of the other, relationship-level judgments, and interactions between the relationship and outside situations and other relationships. Within the context of the local relationship model, people will also develop sometimes quite elaborate explanations of specific problems or issues that concern them (one can see an embryonic version of this step in the above short account).

As local relationship theories develop, they also steadily become entwined with self theories. Art and Elaine Aron have documented this point in an extensive program of research, showing how perceptions of the self and the partner influence one another over time.[19] Their research has suggested that as couples become more intimate, they build and cognitively access a relationship theory, which represents the overlap between the self and the partner. Observing at least some couples who have been married for 40 years or more being interviewed illustrates how far such a process can go. These couples will answer questions for one another and routinely complete each other's sentences. They seem close to comprising a single unit, both cognitively and behaviorally.

At the center of lay local relationship theories exist a set of relationship evaluative judgments that are continuously updated on the basis of relevant information. The most studied evaluative categories include overall satisfaction, passion, commitment, trust, closeness or intimacy, and love. Social psychologists and social scientists have carried out a mammoth amount of research on such constructs. The number of self-report scales designed to measure relationship quality judgments runs into the hundreds. Just one of the most popular scales developed in 1976 (the Dyadic Adjustment Scale[20]) has been used in over 1,000 studies. As will be seen throughout this book, there is overwhelming evidence that these kinds of judgments play a critical role in generating relationship behavior, cognition, and emotion.

A perennial debate in the scientific literature concerns the following issue. Do people simply perceive and judge their relationship along a simple good–bad dimension, which then drives every evaluatively loaded judgment? Or do people distinguish between and cognitively store separate judgments about relationship domains such as satisfaction, passion, commitment, trust, closeness or intimacy, and love? The former assumption has guided the development of several scales designed to assess overall levels of perceived relationship quality, and is reflected in John Gottman's claim that "in fact, if one selects a sample with sufficient range in marital happiness, it is difficult to measure anything other than marital satisfaction that involves the couple's perception of their relationship."[21] Supporters of this thesis can point to the fact that self-report measures of constructs like relationship satisfaction, commitment, trust, and so forth are normally very highly correlated (typically around .70). Such data suggest that people evaluate their relationships in a holistic fashion: "If my relationship is great, then everything about it is great"; "If my relationship is horrible then everything about it is horrible."

However, there is good reason to believe that people develop evaluative judgments of their relationships that do differ across domains to some extent. First, it is easy to envision plausible examples that support such a thesis: "Joe loves his wife and is highly committed to his relationship, but is vaguely dissatisfied because he does not entirely trust her," or "Mary trusts her husband completely, and feels very close to him, but she is disillusioned about the waning of the fires of passion." Second, various studies have shown that self-report measures of commitment predict relationship breakup, over and above reports of relationship satisfaction. Third, some recent research I have carried out with Jeff Simpson and Geoff Thomas[22] (using a fancy data-analytic technique known as Confirmatory Factor Analysis) has supported a model in which individuals do keep their evaluations reasonably consistent across domains, but which also allows systematic variability across domains.

To understand further how these three levels of relationship cognitive modules are psychologically linked (general social theories, general relationship theories, and local relationship theories) and why I think the term "theories" is a felicitous one, I turn to the functions of these lay theories.

The Functions of Lay Relationship Theories

Why do we develop relationship theories? What are they for? The standard social psychological explanation is in terms of their goals or functions. These goals tend to come down to three main types: explanation (or understanding), prediction, and control (or regulation). From the moment we meet a potential partner these three goals kick powerfully into action, and remain potent throughout the evolution of the relationship:

> I meet Mary at a party – what sort of a person is she? Does she come within a bull's roar of my ideal partner? Will she agree to come out on a date? Am I happy? Is Mary happy? How can I persuade Mary to have sex with me? Will the relationship go on to bigger and better things, or crash like my last one? How will Mary get on with my parents? How will my parents get on with Mary? Why doesn't my mother get on with Mary? Should we live together? How can I convince Mary to marry me? Why was she upset at our wedding? Why wouldn't she lend me her car when I asked her? What present should I get her for her birthday? Will I get jealous when I meet her ex-boyfriend? Why does she want to talk about the relationship all the time? Why is Mary depressed? How can I get her to pay more attention to me? Why is our sex life getting stale? How can I add spice to our sex life? Will she find out about my affair at the office? Why are we having so many problems? How do I persuade Mary to visit a marriage counselor? Why did our relationship break up? How can I meet a new partner?

The questions I have just invented represent a tiny percentage of the countless number of problems, questions, and associated goals that arise in the course of a relationship, ranging from the most mundane and everyday (how will Mary react when Fred tells her he will be late?) to the most momentous (should we get married? have a baby? get divorced?). But these questions illustrate the degree to which these three goals (explanation, prediction, and control) are intertwined. That is, the causal understanding or explanation for a relationship behavior is tied into attempts to both control and predict the course of that behavior. Take the mundane question asked above which posed a question about prediction – "How will Mary react when Fred tells her he will be home late for dinner?" Fred's answer will depend on his understanding of Mary, which in turn will influence how Fred might frame his message to avoid any negative ramifications. If Fred believes Mary is thin-skinned, and thinks the relationship is a little shaky, then he might bend over backwards to apologize and bring flowers home. On the other hand, if he thinks Mary is imperturbable and that the relationship is rock solid, he might adopt a more matter-of-fact approach and not work so hard to diplomatically wrap the message up.

Although the goals of explanation, prediction and control are intertwined in lay psychology, they may nevertheless function autonomously, depending on the circumstances. For example, we are often intrinsically interested in how other people's relationships work, even when there is no possible way in which the outcomes of such relationships can be controlled, and the relationships have no direct impact on our lives. Examples include fictional relationships in books and films and television, and the (often prurient) interest we have in the lives and loves of film stars or other famous people. My family and I, for example, assiduously follow the longest-running TV soap opera in the world – *Coronation Street* – a realistic gritty drama that is set in an English working-class neighborhood. We analyze and discuss these "virtual" relationships on the show as if they were real (when, oddly, we know they are fictitious).

Perhaps the most important and central route by which people explain, predict, and control their relationships is via the development and use of key relationship quality judgments. If you are satisfied with your relationship and trust your partner implicitly, for example, this will allow you to make rapid predictions about the likelihood of the relationship lasting in the medium term, and also to give an immediate (albeit superficial) explanation for, say, why you communicate so smoothly.

Recall that I began this chapter by asking the question "How do you know when you are in good or a bad relationship?" I am finally in a position to advance an answer. We do so by comparing what we perceive we have in the relationship with pre-existing expectations, ideals, standards, and beliefs concerning what constitutes a good or a bad relationship. In short, we integrate and compare our local relationship theories with our general relationship theories (as depicted in figure 2.1).

A plenitude of evidence for this general proposition will be offered throughout the book, especially chapter 8. I will present one illustrative example here. If Max enters a relationship with the belief and expectation that plenty of passion and hot sex are indispensable elements (generally speaking) in producing a successful long-term relationship, then his satisfaction with the relationship will be pinned to his perceptions of how the sex and passion is going. In contrast, if Bill enters a relationship with the belief that passion and sex are not really important elements in long-term relationships, then his general levels of satisfaction with the relationship will not be influenced much by his perceptions of his sex life. Leah Kininmonth and I found evidence for exactly this scenario.[23] For individuals who strongly believed that sex and passion were important in intimate relationships, their overall levels of relationship satisfaction were strongly connected to how passionate the relationship was ($r = .48$). In contrast, for individuals who did not believe that sex and passion mattered much, their relationship satisfaction was unrelated to the amount of passion and sex in the relationship ($r = .04$).

Online Cognitive Processing

When and how do people think about their relationships? First, if my general model is correct, then online cognitive processing should not normally occur without also, willy-nilly, calling up various stored dispositional constructs that are relevant to the relationship, and these may include aspects from all three knowledge categories (general social theories, general relationship theories, and local relationship theories). Relationship cognition can be elicited by almost anything. Such triggering events may occur either inside or outside relationship interaction (see figure 2.1). Indeed, simply being with one's partner (without any interaction) may evoke some relationship cognition or affect. However, watching a play, reading a book, or merely noticing a stranger who resembles one's partner may elicit some thought or feeling concerning one's partner. Feeling angry with one's boss, or admiring the handsomeness of a stranger, might also serve to remind one of an existing local relationship.

However relationship cognition is evoked, an important distinction (or dimension) is between unconscious/automatic processing and conscious/controlled processing. The existence of two basic forms of cognition has been widely postulated in cognitive psychology and cognitive science. There exists a remarkable profusion of labels for the two forms of cognition, including associative versus rule-based, heuristic versus analytic, tacit versus explicit, conscious versus unconscious, implicit versus explicit, interactional versus analytic, experiential versus rational, intuitive versus analytical, automatic versus controlled, procedural versus declarative, reflexive versus reflective, and the list – remarkably – could go on.

Although such distinctions do not carve up cognition in exactly the same way, it is possible to discern some basic commonalities. The unconscious/automatic processing end of things is typically seen not only as unconscious and automatic, but also as relatively fast and effortless, not readily verbalizable, and as relatively undemanding of cognitive capacity. The conscious/controlled end of the dimension can be described in exactly opposite terms; that is, conscious, controlled, relatively slow, more readily able to be verbalized, and quite demanding of cognitive capacity. In cognitive processing terms, many automatic/unconscious processes can occur simultaneously (or in parallel), whereas conscious/ controlled processing tends to occur most efficiently one process at a time (or serially). This kind of distinction is typically presented in terms of a dimension, rather than a hard and fast set of categories. The reason is to catch the point that many cognitive processes represent mixtures of the two processes, and also that cognitive processes that may start out with people sweating blood at the conscious/controlled end of the spectrum end up as automated and automatic (e.g., piano-playing techniques, rules for driving a car, learning how to titillate or please one's partner).

Consider a standard conversation in an intimate dyad, which only seems ordinary because we adults have mastered the complex psychological processes involved. Each person in the dyad needs to encode and interpret the barrage of verbal and nonverbal information emanating from his or her partner, while simultaneously controlling the expression of his or her own verbal and nonverbal behavior (including facial muscles, eye-contact, gestures, and body position), and blending a suite of cognitive, affective, perceptual, and behavioral processes into a performance that is smoothly co-ordinated in an interactive dance with the other. At the same time, each person will be making rapid judgments, guided and influenced by a set of stored relationship theories, and according to higher-order goals of the kind already described, which will vary from the mundane (e.g., "I want my partner to take the rubbish out") to the pivotal (e.g., "I am trying to avoid my partner becoming suspicious about the affair I am keeping secret"). The only way such regular interactions can be effectively accomplished is if a huge amount of cognitive and perceptual processing is routinely carried out automatically, unconsciously, and simultaneously (or in parallel, to use the standard cognitive parlance).

The amount and extent of conscious and in-depth analysis of a given relationship will vary tremendously depending on the stage of the relationship, individual personality differences, and the local environment. The needs of explanation, prediction, and control are always with us. However, in a relationship that has reached a stable plateau, and has a long history, complex interactional episodes will become overlearnt and stereotypical in nature, with very little conscious attention or thought required. Research has clearly shown that even in the most boring and well-regulated relationship, two kinds of events will snap people back into consciously regulated analysis: negative events, and unexpected events.[24] If your partner forgets your birthday or unexpectedly buys you a present out of the blue, then you will ask Why? However, your answer will be guided and conditioned by your background relationship theories in a largely unconscious fashion, in ways I have already given examples of.

There exists a massive amount of research evidence that generally supports the existence of the unconscious/automatic versus conscious/controlled processing dimension from cognitive and social psychology,[25] although there is relatively little research that has directly examined such processing in relationship contexts. Automatic processing comes in various forms. In one variety, outside events may be perceived and processed, but in an automatic and unconscious fashion. This kind of automatic processing implies that people can process (at some level) what their partner is saying, even when the TV is on, the baby is crying, and they are reading the newspaper. An experimental demonstration of this kind of unconscious and automatic processing was provided by Mark Baldwin and others in a piece of research intriguingly titled "Priming relationship schemas: My advisor and the Pope are watching me from the back of my mind."[26] Graduate students who were exposed to a briefly presented scowling picture of their departmental chair (outside of self-reported awareness) lowered subsequent ratings of some of their own research ideas, compared to a control group. In a replication of the effect, Roman Catholic women who had just read a sexually permissive passage, and were subliminally exposed to a picture of Pope John Paul II with a disapproving expression on his face, reported higher levels of anxiety and negative self-perceptions, than did control participants who were not shown the subliminal slide. In both cases, participants reported being unaware of perceiving the stimulus figure.

However, even when one is paying complete attention to one's partner, one's thinking will still be automatically and unconsciously influenced by stored knowledge structures. Thus, general relationship theories or knowledge structures (e.g., expectations, ideals, and beliefs) are silently and constantly at work, subtly influencing online judgments of local relationships and partners. A study I carried out with Janette Rosanowski and Julie Fitness used a technique, initially developed in cognitive psychology, to provide evidence for just this hypothesis.[27] In this technique (termed a "memory-loading paradigm") one group is asked to judge whether a set of items is either true or not true of themselves. Items are flashed onto a computer screen and participants press *yes* or *no* on designated keys on the computer keyboard. A second group then completes the same task, except this group is also asked to carry out a parallel task (such as remembering, and then regurgitating a string of digits). The computer program is set up to surreptitiously record the time taken (in milliseconds) to respond to the items that appear on the screen. The effect of this additional task is to normally (not surprisingly) slow people down when answering the questions. However, if the focal task can be done automatically, then the average time people take to answer the questions in the memory-loading condition should be about the same as in the nonmemory-loading condition in which individuals make the same judgments but without having to complete parallel cognitive tasks.

In the experiment we carried out, a group of participants who held strong beliefs in the importance of passion or intimacy in producing successful intimate relationships were compared with a group who held comparatively weak beliefs in the importance of passion or intimacy respectively. All participants then rated the extent to which a series of descriptive items (e.g., passionate, warm) applied to their own relationships – *yes* or *no*? As we predicted, the mean time that individuals took to answer these questions – for those who had strong prior beliefs – was the same regardless of whether or not they had their working memory loaded up by having to do two cognitive tasks at the same time (making yes/no judgments and remembering six digits). In contrast, those who had weak beliefs in the importance of passion or intimacy, revealed the standard effect of taking considerably longer to process the answers about their own relationships when they had to do two cognitive tasks at the same time. We interpreted these results as showing that people who had strong beliefs in their general relationship theories, about the roles of intimacy and passion, will commonly and regularly make related local relationship judgments (such as how warm or sexy are their own partners and relationships) – to the point that they become unconscious, fast, and automatic.

I have deliberately steered clear of the dogfight currently taking place in cognitive science and psychology concerning the relative merits of two kinds of general cognitive models – traditional information processing accounts, which have been around for decades, and a more recent competitor termed a "connectionist" model. Both models purport to describe the workings of the brain in cognitive terms rather than in strict biological terms (although the similarity between connectionist models and the structure of the human brain is often cited as a point in favor of a connectionist model). Information-processing accounts essentially attempt to trace the stages of processing that take place between a stimulus and a response, breaking the journey into various discrete stages. For example, an item might be first visually perceived, then transmitted to working memory where it is combined with some prior relevant knowledge structure, finally producing a decision to act, followed by a behavioral response (e.g., "I apologized to my wife after I saw her frown, and realized I had forgotten to buy the milk on the way home"). Connectionist models throw out the idea that cognitive processing occurs serially or in stages, and postulate the existence of massive networks of nodes and connections, in which all information is processed simultaneously.[28]

The sort of distinction I have described (unconscious/automatic versus conscious/controlled) is consistent with a hybrid model, which many cognitive psychologists have come to favor.[29] That is, one form of cognitive activity is slow and effortful, often linked to the use of language, and takes place serially and in consciousness. The other form of cognitive activity takes place in terms of parallel processes that occur simultaneously. Indeed, I doubt whether any cognitive psychologist these days doubts that large chunks of cognitive activity take place fast, unconsciously, and with many streams of cognitive activity occurring simultaneously.[30]

Theories about Theories about Theories

I have chosen to use the word "theory" as a general description of relationship knowledge structures. Use of this terminology invites comparisons between lay relationship theories and scientific (psychological) theories. Indeed, there are some intriguing points of similarity. First, like scientific theories, relationship theories are directed toward the goals of explanation, prediction, and control. Second, like scientific theories, relationship lay theories are directed toward discerning underlying and dispositional psychological structures that play a causal role in generating behavior. Third, like scientific theories, relationship lay theories are resistant and slow to change, especially when they are entrenched, although local theories (like scientific theories) may collapse when they become utterly untenable. Fourth, like scientific theories, lay relationship theories do not just consist of shopping lists of propositions or probabilistic beliefs, but represent attempts to model the structures that cause or generate individual and relationship-level behavior. Finally, relationship lay theories are constituted at both the general or hypothetical level and the local level, as are scientific theories, and people try to keep these two levels of knowledge structure roughly consistent with one another.

It has sometimes been claimed that laypeople are interested in specific relationships and concrete events, not in producing principles or explanations that apply generally. In contrast, science is supposedly centered on the generation of generalizations and explanatory models that apply to general phenomena. Such claims manage the feat of getting both lay psychology and science wrong. There is abundant evidence, a fraction of which is canvassed in this book, that laypeople attempt to keep their general theories consistent with their local theories, and constantly exchange information across levels. For example, if Fred learns that conflict and arguments are healthy from reading a pop-psychology book, he might well alter his evaluation of his local intimate relationship. Conversely, if Fred learns from experience that his local relationship works fine, even though he argues incessantly with his partner, then he will be likely to bring his general beliefs about relationship functioning into line.

Scientists, in an equivalent fashion, intensely study individual case studies of volcanoes, earthquakes, supernova, animals, wars, insects, cultures, humans, and so forth. Such case studies are informed and guided by prior general theories, but can also suggest problems or gaps in extant general theories. When Fred tries to explain why Mary has left him for someone else, and adapts his general theories about relationships on the basis of his experience – and associated explanation – exactly the same process is in train.

However, there are also some obvious ways in which scientific theories diverge from lay relationship theories.

First, laypeople use their theories not only to explain, control, and predict, but also to lay blame and responsibility, and to seek reparation or forgiveness. In folk psychology the moral order often becomes entangled with the scientific order – justifications and excuses become intertwined with explanations and causal attributions. This feature of folk psychology can be seen most generally in religious systems of thought, which notoriously mix up the two orders. But this characteristic of folk psychology can also be seen in individual terms every time an individual blames his or her partner for something. In contrast, modern-day science (at least the mainstream brand I favor) attempts to exclude the moral order from the development of scientific theories – the aim of the science of psychology is not to produce theories designed to appeal to our moral scruples or to adjudicate on how just or nice the world is. Of course, whether and how scientific theories can be applied to people's lives, appropriately brings the moral order back into the equation.

Second, a key characteristic of lay theories is that both online processing and parts of the lay theories themselves remain tacit or unconscious. Indeed, the accessible parts of folk theories – that we have good introspective access to – probably represent only the tip of the theoretical and cognitive processing iceberg. This is not surprising given the long genesis and overlearned nature of such folk theories, and the unconscious and inaccessible nature of much of the related cognitive processing when such theories swing into action. It is true that scientific reasoning and scientific theories probably contain more substantial components of tacit and unconscious material than scientists either realize or would like to admit to (scientists are, after all, human). Nevertheless, scientific theories are explicitly designed to be laid out in specific detail. Folk psychologists, in contrast, will often be forced to admit ignorance, or to do some theorizing on the spot when asked to say how and why they perform what are routine behaviors to them, but to the scientist are impresario performances of lay social cognition and behavior.

When it comes to intimate relationships, people often have a good deal to say about how their own relationships tick, why their relationships are in trouble, why President Clinton had an affair with a young intern, and how to attract members of the opposite (or same) sex. But the critical point is that what laypeople offer represents their own explicit, conscious, and verbalizable second-order theories – about their own first-order theories. Whether such lay theorizing is idiosyncratic or is simply a standard spiel lifted from the conventional wisdom, such second-order theories may either be sound or abysmally foolish (or something in between). Indeed, as I will argue later, it is sometimes those aspects of mental and behavioral life for which folk psychology is most confident and authoritative, such as how we attribute our own emotional states, that folk psychology proves to be the most fallible, biased, or just plain wrong. Just, of course, as scientific theories can be fallible, biased, or just plain wrong.

However, even if second-order lay theories are addled nonsense (about relationships or anything else), this does not mean that psychologists can ignore them. Why? Because, addled lay theories exert causal influences on the individual's behavior, affect, and cognition every bit as much as true theories. Hence, lay theories – regardless of their truth value – must be taken into account by the scientist who seeks to explain human cognition and behavior.

So, we finally come to the third "theory" in the title of the chapter – the third-order theory – by which I mean the theories of the scientist. Such scientific theories deal with both the second-order lay theorizing (explicit and verbalizable) as well as the first-order tacit or unconscious set of cognitive structures and cognitive processes. Scientific theories also deal with questions that are scarcely countenanced in folk psychology, including the evolutionary origins of relationship cognition, the microcognitive processes involved, the neurophysiology of the brain, and so forth. Nevertheless, it is possible (and sometimes revealing) to ask how reasonable or sound explicit folk lay theorizing is – and I do so at various points throughout the book.

Conclusion

Theories are at the core of both scientific and lay thinking, and are quintessentially human. Everyone has relationship theories, whether they know it or not, but their inner workings and nature are often hidden from a simple-minded introspective gaze. In the pages ahead I will expand on this model of the intimate relationship mind, especially with regard to emotions like love, ask questions about the origins and development of lay relationship theories, and document their nature in detail.

Chapter 3

The Origins of the Intimate Relationship Mind

In a single stroke, the idea of evolution by natural selection unifies the realm of life, meaning, and purpose with the realm of space and time, cause and effect, mechanism and physical law. But it is not just a wonderful scientific idea. It is a dangerous idea.
Dennett, 1995

One of the main reasons that Darwin delayed publication of his magnum opus on the theory of evolution for some 20 years or so was his prescient fear of the storm of controversy it would provoke, and the associated personal and scientific attacks he (and his family) would be forced to endure.[1] In spite of its overwhelming acceptance in the scientific community, and the pivotal role it continues to play in science, Darwinian evolutionary theory remains a towering lightening rod of dissension and bitter argument more than 140 years after Darwin dropped his bombshell.

From 1859 (the publication date of *On the Origin of the Species by Means of Natural Selection*) to the present day there has existed a pitched battle fought between those who espouse Darwinian evolutionary theory and those who adopt fundamentalist religious beliefs. But, even within scientific circles, a less publicly visible internecine warfare has been the rule rather than the exception. Moreover, the acrimony of the debate does not seem to have diminished over the last 140 years. Perhaps the most famous contemporary popularizer and defender of Darwinian evolutionary theory is Stephen Jay Gould, who has slipped into a public debate, with other leading evolutionary scientists, of abusive proportions.

In a 1997 exchange in the *New York Review of Books*, for example,

Gould characterizes the arguments, views, and claims of his evolutionary opponents (who are mostly leading scientists in the area) variously
as "foolish," "fatuous," "egregiously simplistic," "downright silly,"
"pathetic," "blustering," "miserly and blinkered," "gratuitously speculative," "a caricature of a caricature," and "limited and superficial." His
critics give as good as they get, and Gould's views and claims are condemned as "uninformed," "nonsense," "a travesty," "systematic and
hilarious inversions of the truth," "spectacular distortions," and "bodies of fiction," and Gould is described as "a man whose ideas are so
confused as to be hardly worth bothering about" and as motivated by
"self-aggrandizement rather than the careful and charitable pursuit of
the truth."[2] Science is not for the faint-hearted!

Such academic wrestling matches are not confined to a few in the
upper echelons of science. In the social psychology and relationship
science conferences I attend each year, there is one sure-fire way of
generating a rip-roaring argument at any conference dinner table or
social occasion – bring up evolutionary psychology. Fundamentalist
religious zealots believe that Darwinian evolutionary theory is entirely
fallacious (as well as evil), and so of course they oppose it. Scientists, on
the other hand, overwhelmingly accept the centrality and validity of
Darwinian evolutionary theory (including all whose words I have quoted
in the preceding paragraph). Yet the central wellspring for the contentious (and dangerous) status of Darwinian evolutionary theory is the
same in both cases; namely, the application of Darwinian theory to ourselves – *Homo sapiens.*

In this chapter I offer a brief review of Darwinian evolutionary theory
and its possible application to the psychology of intimate relationships.
One immediate question is, why bother? Presumably, one could develop an entire psychology of relationships, paying attention only to
the proximal-level causes involved – indeed, this is exactly the strategy
adopted in a good deal of the scientific work on intimate relationships
over the last 30 years or so. The main advantage of considering the
origins of the intimate relationship mind is that it informs our understanding of the proximal-level cognitive and affective machinery (as well
as vice versa). It accomplishes this in two main ways. First, by analyzing
the functions that our intimate relationship mind was designed for (via
evolutionary processes) clues can be provided about its functions within
contemporary settings. Second, an evolutionary analysis can help uncover important facts about how the proximal-level relationship

51

processes work. The best arguments I can give for these claims are scattered throughout the book in terms of the many illustrative examples I will compile.

In considering our evolutionary origins I will not ignore the role of culture. However, culture does not operate independently of the constraints provided by our evolutionary origins. Indeed, evolutionary processes and cultural processes are interwoven. The nature of the connections between evolution, genes, and culture is one of the thorniest topics in contemporary psychological science. However, I chance my arm on this topic occasionally, and I also refer to the cross-cultural and anthropological literature where appropriate. Marvelous treatments of Darwinian evolutionary theory, in all its guises (both biological and psychological) already exist in profusion, and little of what I will argue in this chapter is new. However, it is important to sketch out the basic issues and critical questions involved, as well as to stake out my own position.

Darwin's Idea

A confusion sometimes made in criticisms of Darwinian evolutionary theory (especially by creationists) is between the fact of evolution and the theory of evolution that explains the underlying mechanisms of evolutionary processes. The enduring persuasiveness of Darwin's famous original evolutionary treatise can be tied to both factors. Darwin was certainly not the first to promote the view that life on earth has evolved, but in the *Origin of Species* he presented a meticulously detailed and organized array of evidence that essentially rendered the fact of evolution inescapable. Darwin's masterstroke, however, was to also hypothesize mechanisms that could plausibly account for the facts of evolution.

The Darwinian engine-room of evolution comes down to three indispensable elements: variation, inheritance, and selection. First, there must be variation in the characteristics of the organisms making up a given species. Second, some of these variations must have the capacity to be inherited; that is to be reliably passed on to offspring. The third aspect – selection – specifies that environmental elements (e.g., competing animals, access to food, weather conditions, diseases, and so forth) determine the extent to which particular individuals survive and reproduce successfully. In contrast, those individuals who are comparatively less well adapted tend not to survive and reproduce so successfully, and, thus, are gradually culled out of the species. Hence, selection controls which variations survive and regulates changes in species over eons of time. Taken together, these three elements provide a powerful mechanism that explains why many species are well adapted to the environments in which they live, and why it is estimated that as many as 99% of the species that have ever lived are now extinct – evolution is assuredly a grim reaper![3]

The critical point to note about biological evolution is how utterly blind it is. When discussing and describing Darwinian evolution it is natural to talk about the functions, or goals of the evolutionary process, and it is abundantly clear that organisms are often designed to fit their environments. But the way in which organisms are designed is not intentional or planned by the organisms. Darwin's concept of "natural selection" is intended to catch this point although Darwin himself came to dislike the term because it invited the incorrect assumption that there was a selector (aka God) at work, and he suggested privately that "natural preservation" might have been a more apposite title.[4]

Although elegant and plausible, Darwin's basic account was beset by a host of problems and lacunae, most of which Darwin was only too painfully aware of. Indeed, Darwin's genius was not only in providing the basic evolutionary thesis, but also in supplying some important elaborations of the basic theory that have helped provide the launching pad for the continuing growth of evolutionary biology and psychology; especially (as we shall see) with respect to understanding the human intimate relationship mind and associated behavior.

Darwin's initial proposal (still widely accepted today) was that geographical isolation of groups from the same species was one key element needed to split one species into many over millions of years, leading to the branching tree of life that has become an icon of evolutionary theory. His examples of the closely related but distinct species that existed on the Galápagos Islands (such as finches and giant turtles) provided compelling illustrations of this argument. Thus, the myriad different species existing at any given snapshot of time are the products of a long series of intermediary stages or species that have themselves become extinct.

Darwin proposed two distinct ways in which the forces of selection functioned. The first dealt with the factors that increased the chances of survival (e.g., success at obtaining food and defense against predators).

According to this general theory, any variation that enhanced the chances of survival, and thus reproduction, would tend to be selected for. The second evolutionary account (termed sexual selection) was fully outlined by Darwin in his book in 1871 (published 12 years after the *Origin of Species* appeared) titled *The Descent of Man, and Selection in Relation to Sex*. This "second" evolutionary theory was devised mainly to explain why male and female animals are so often different in appearance and behavior (sometimes to the point that they have been mistakenly assigned to different species).

According to Darwin, sexual selection processes are fundamentally generated by mate choice – typically with females choosing males. In many mammals, males compete vigorously with one another to increase their chances of being chosen as a mate by the females, or of gaining access to fertile females, which leads to the development of male weapons (such as antlers in deer), and increased physical size and power (relative to females). A difference in size between males and females is termed *sexual dimorphism*. In addition, male features that females favor will tend to evolve into an increasingly exaggerated form (and sometimes relatively rapidly it turns out) – whether it be the redness of the band around a woodpecker's leg or the showy tail of the peacock.

Why do females concentrate on particular features of males in choosing their mates? For example, many species of female birds get all of a twitter about the bright color of portions of their mate's anatomy, while others are attracted to the size and magnificence of their mate's tails. Yet, being brightly colored or dragging round an enormous tail, on the face of it, seem likely to increase the chances of being attacked by predators, and thus to decrease the chances of survival and subsequent reproductive success.

Darwin's explanation was simply that there was no accounting for taste or fashion in either humans or in peahens. Evolutionary biologists, however, have not given up on the notion that taste or fashion in females might be directed via Darwinian adaptational logic. An increasingly popular and ingenious theory exploits the idea that big tails, bright colors, and the like, are indeed likely to handicap the survival of the males; thus, males who can afford to maintain such exaggerated impediments signal to the female that they are especially healthy specimens of good genetic stock. Support for this theory has steadily mounted. For example, it has been found that peacocks that possess elaborate tails actually do produce both more offspring and healthier offspring than do their tail-challenged male counterparts.[5]

Scientific developments and vastly increased knowledge since Darwin's day have cemented Darwinian evolutionary theory into place, while, paradoxically, doing nothing to quash scientific debates over its proper applicability to humans. As already mentioned in chapter 1, by 1906 it was realized that the discovery of radiation provided an internal source of heat in the earth, a discovery that finally swung physics into line with geology and enormously extended the probable age of the earth to easily allow enough time for the slow march of Darwinian evolution. Based on Mendel's theory of the gene (Mendel was a contemporary of Darwin) – and the discovery of the molecular structure of the blueprint of life in 1953 (DNA) – modern theories of inheritance are also elegantly consistent with, and increasingly tied into, Darwinian evolution.[6]

It is important to understand a few basic facts about the relationship between genes and DNA.[7] DNA molecules can attain gigantic size, with billions of atoms. If the DNA in a single human cell were rolled out into a straight line it would be about 7 feet (2.13 m) long; yet it is crammed into the miniscule nuclei in most of the millions of cells in the human body. When DNA was initially discovered it was thought that genes would simply map onto separate hunks of the molecule in a straightforward way. Research has revealed a much messier reality. It has turned out that perhaps less than 2% or so of DNA in humans is ever decoded and used, the remainder often being termed "junk" DNA. Scientists are undecided to what extent the unused DNA is really functionless junk, but it appears to represent the genetic detritus of our long evolutionary history.

Genes are to DNA something like cognitions are to neurons. That is, genes are units of information that map onto DNA in complex ways that scientists currently do not fully understand. This is why we know how much DNA humans have, whereas estimates of the number of human genes vary considerably. The latest estimates from the Human Genome Project (as this book goes to press) range from 30,000 to 50,000, a much lower figure than originally expected. It is also one reason why being able to map the entire human genome does not guarantee anything like a full understanding of how genetic inheritance works.

Genes typically operate in complex ways, in interaction with, and in the context of other genes. The discovery of single genes that cause diseases and developmental problems – such as breast cancer, Hunting-ton's disease, and so forth – are regularly announced in the media. Such genes may certainly play critical causal roles in the links between the genotype and the adult organisms finally produced, but this does not mean that identifying a critical gene gives anything close to a complete genetic account of normal development.

If I slightly altered the design of an airplane so that one simple com-ponent failed (say the regulation of fuel in the jet engines) this may prevent the plane from flying, but it would not make sense to say one had discovered how planes fly. Similarly, if there were 150 genes that together provided the genetic recipe for the development of adult ro-mantic love, a mutation on only one of the genes might effectively cripple the development of normal adult love. Yet, to say I had found the gene for love would be wrong, given that the normal expression of this gene would still rely on the other 149 genes.

The development of Mendelian genetic theory, in relation to Dar-winian natural selection, in the mid-nineteenth century, in turn, en-couraged a development in evolutionary theory that has had a profound impact on many domains including the psychology of intimate rela-tionships – the so-called "gene's-eye view" of evolution. The most well-known proponent (and indefatigable popularizer) of this approach is Richard Dawkins.[8] In Dawkins's approach genes are replicators – things that have a single blind aim in life; namely, replication. Organisms are simply vehicles for the genes designed to perform the genes' mission in life, which is written into every gene of every creature (from viruses to humans) – "Replicate me." Thus, gene's-eye proponents are fond of pronouncements like "Elephants are the genes' way of making more elephant genes." Let me give just one example of how such a gene's-eye view of evolution encouraged influential theoretical developments in evolutionary theorizing, and one that is especially relevant to inti-mate relationships.

William Hamilton and others in the 1960s provided an elegant solu-tion to a problem that Darwin originally thought was both insuperable and fatal to his entire theory; namely, how can natural selection explain the way in which individual organisms in some species willingly sacrifice their own potential for reproduction. Such altruism reaches its biological apotheosis in worker ants or bees that are sterile. Darwin's entire theory rests on the variable reproductive success attained by individual organ-isms – how on earth could ants or bees that cannot even reproduce evolve?[9]

Hamilton's gene's-eye solution was in terms of what he terme clusive fitness." That is, because genes are shared among family bers, behaving altruistically toward family members will tend to increase the chances of ones' own genes being passed on. Indeed, from this viewpoint, individuals should be quite concerned with promoting the survival of their siblings, given that two siblings share the same percentage of genes as a parent and child (50%).[10] If Fiona's sister has a child (Fiona's niece or nephew) then this child will possess about 25% of Fiona's genes, compared to a 50% gene inheritance for Fiona's own offspring. Thus, from an inclusive fitness standpoint, two nieces or nephews are equivalent to one offspring for a given individual. I reiterate that this evolutionary process carries on independently of any personally held goal or intention of either ants or humans. It just so happened that in the human species genetic variations that promoted the establishment of special bonds with kin were selected for by the inexorable and mindless logic of the evolutionary algorithm.

Darwin's ideas on sexual selection were not taken particularly seriously in comparison to the mighty theory of natural selection in relation to survival.[11] This may have been, in part, because of male biologists growing pale at the thought that the female of the species – by generally exercising the most choice in mate selection – thereby controlled and directed both the evolutionary direction of the male and the species. However, research and theoretical developments on sexual selection theory have dramatically burgeoned over the last few decades, with some profound implications for the study of human intimate relationships.[12]

To take one example, Robert Trivers developed a seminal theory in the 1970s, based on sexual selection theory, termed parental investment theory.[13] Trivers argued that the sex that invests the most resources in raising its offspring (usually the female) would evolve to be more discriminating in mate selection. In contrast, the sex that commits fewer resources to raising offspring would be less choosy, and also adopt more competitive tactics with members of the same sex, in order to gain sexual access to the more discriminating sex. Thus, Trivers explained what Darwin assiduously documented but failed to explain; namely, (generally speaking) males court and females choose.

Parental investment theory has been a major success story in predicting the nature of gender differences in mate selection across a variety of species. For humans, in whom both genders tend to commit considerable resources to rearing offspring, we should expect that both men and women would be discriminating in mate choice. On the other hand, women invest somewhat more in time and energy in having and raising children than do men; hence, we might expect men to do a little more of the courting and women to be a tad more choosy. Indeed this seems to be the case (although the story with humans is both complex and controversial, as we will see in later chapters).[14]

Sexual selection processes, as originally postulated by Ronald Fisher in the 1930s, can lead to an unusually rapid and directional form of evolution (termed "runaway evolution").[15] In this form of evolution, female (or male) preferences interact with genetic inheritance to place organisms on an evolutionary escalator. For example, a female bird who prefers male mates with red bands around their legs will both genetically endow male offspring with more brightly colored red leg-bands, and female offspring with an increased preference for males who possess such red leg-bands. A variety of evidence, including modeling simulations, has been gathered that supports the existence and importance of such an evolutionary process.[16]

Of course, as Darwin makes clear, sexual selection processes have to stop somewhere; otherwise peacocks' tails would increase in size indefinitely. However, regardless of the sheer physical constraints involved in the size and height of any body part, sexual selection should be balanced out at some point by selection for survival. At the point at which the peacock's tail becomes so bulky, tall, and visible that he becomes easy prey for predators, and his survival becomes moot, then selection for survival will take over and tail-length should stabilize.

Homo Sapiens

Near the end of his final chapter in the *Origin of Species*, Darwin speculated that in the distant future the study of psychology "will be based on a new foundation."[17] Based on the developments in evolutionary biology outlined above, and fueled by the steady flow of genetic and fossil evidence concerning human evolutionary origins, there is evidence of Darwin's prediction finally being fulfilled with massive attention over the last three decades being given to the evolutionary psychology of humans.

This work has proceeded along several fronts including theories of human culture in relation to biological development, the evolutionary origins of human intelligence and language, and human social behavior and cognition more generally. Moreover, one of the main thrusts of this theoretical and empirical program has been devoted to the psychology of human intimate relationships. Obviously, it is this last domain that is central to this book. However, the work and debate in the domain of intimate relationships cannot be evaluated, or even really understood, without placing it in a more general theoretical and empirical context.

At the beginning of the twenty-first century, fossil evidence, the development of new more accurate dating methods based on radioactive decay, and evidence from studies of genetic variation in human populations across the globe, have converged to produce two reasonably firm conclusions about the evolutionary origins of *Homo sapiens*. First, humans originally having evolved in East Africa. Second, we are a remarkably young species, evolving into our current biological state around 150,000 to 200,000 years ago, and from about 100,000 years ago migrating from Africa to every region of the earth (apart from the poles and a few small Pacific islands) by 1,000 years ago.[18]

Some of the most provocative and far-reaching findings concern the degree of genetic similarity both within and between species. Genetic variability can be used like a genetic clock, because the DNA across individuals becomes more dissimilar over time at a rate that can be assessed.[19] The findings show that *Homo sapiens* is the youngest species of primate on earth, and by a considerable margin. Thus, two gorillas (or any other ape) from the same forest in Africa (provided they are not directly related) will differ more in their genetic constitutions than would say a comparison between an Inuit and an Aborigine. The same kind of evidence has also shown that the closest relative to *Homo sapiens* is the chimpanzee, with whom we share about 98% of our genes. This latter figure translates into a common ancestor of humans and chimps of around 4 to 6 million years ago (score another hit for Darwin who suggested that humans are descended from an ancient species of African ape).[20]

Thus, the ancestral evolutionary environment, within which hominoids evolved over the last 2 million years and more, was almost certainly in Southern and Eastern Africa. This period of time (termed the Pleistocene) captures a large period of time, with many changes in habitat, species, and climate. In this environment, *Homo sapiens*, and ancestors, almost certainly lived in relatively small family-based groups of hunter-gatherers (of up to 150 or so for *Homo sapiens*). Settled agrarian cultures, with the subsequent development of cities and modern forms of culture, did not appear until after the last ice age – about 11,000 years ago – which means that over 95% of the last 2 million years of human evolution has been spent by *Homo* species living as hunter-gatherers. Thus, anthropologists and evolutionary psychologists sometimes use modern hunter-gatherer societies, such as the !Kung San (Bushmen) of the Kalahari Desert in Africa, or the Ache of Paraguay, to gain at least some idea of what life was like in our ancestral environment.

There is one indisputable fact about human nature and the workings of the intimate relationship mind that we know for a dead certainty; namely, whatever the causal origins of modern humans, such forces have produced the human animal we can see before us today. If evolutionary or cultural theories of human origins are not plausibly consistent with human nature as it exists today, then so much the worse for such theories. The thrust of a Darwinian perspective is to topple humans off their special pedestal, and to view *Homo sapiens* as products of the same evolutionary system as other organisms – as just one more species on the evolutionary tree. This is why Darwin's theory is such a dangerous idea.

Humans are animals, of course, and show clear and massive continuities with other animal species, not only in genetic and biological terms, but also in terms of cognitive, emotional, and behavioral traits. Moreover, the degree of similarity between other species and ourselves is well correlated with how recently we shared the same ancestors. Genetically speaking, our closest relatives are the other primates. Sure enough, compared to other animal species, humans are most obviously similar to the appearance, behavior (and minds) of the other primates including chimpanzees.

Yet, *Homo sapiens* is truly a remarkable animal, marked out from all other species (including other primates) by a set of characteristics that, if present at all, only exist elsewhere in the animal kingdom in embryonic or much less exaggerated forms. These include the possession of:

- an exceptionally large brain for our size, with a massively developed cerebral and prefrontal cortex;
- a fully developed language;
- a complex folk psychology, with an associated theory of how the

mind functions based on cognitive representational attributions (e.g., beliefs, desires, and so forth);

- an extraordinary facility and motivation to imitate others' behavior, and associated high levels of social intelligence;
- upright walking along with high levels of dexterity and hand–eye co-ordination, which allow remarkable accuracy in throwing objects (like spears and frisbees) over long distances;
- the ability and motivation to practice and master complex cognitive and behavioral activities of many kinds, regardless of their novelty or apparent utility (e.g., chess, music, stamp collecting, playing air guitar);
- sophisticated cultural knowledge and beliefs, which are passed on to each generation both informally and formally;
- the ability and motivation to generate complex causal models of the world, and to mentally plan far into the future, in a deliberate reflexive fashion, and often in planned and co-ordinated concert with others; and
- the ability and motivation to develop sophisticated tools, including writing, computers, atomic bombs, and all the other paraphernalia of modern technology.

This is by no means a complete list, and excludes some characteristics associated with intimate relationships, and other traits associated with art, humor, war, religion, politics, and music, that are unique to our species. But it will do for the purposes of this discussion.

Evolutionary Psychology

The main aim of evolutionary psychology can be described as understanding the cognitive and emotional mechanisms of the contemporary human mind, through understanding how such mechanisms evolved via natural and sexual selection in the ancestral environments. Disagreements among proponents of such an approach are a dime a dozen the closer one gets to the fine print of how such an aim should be unpacked. Nevertheless, there is widespread adherence to three basic principles among devotees of this approach. I will later discuss these principles in detail, in terms of the intimate relationship mind; here I simply lay them out for inspection.[21]

First, this approach is essentially cognitive, in that it attempts to understand how human cognition and emotion have evolved. Human behavior is not ignored, and behavioral repertoires do evolve, but the human mind (which directs behavior) is assumed to represent the key evolved organ, rather than a collage of specific behaviors.

Thus, one often hears objections to evolutionary psychology, such as "If the evolutionary imperative is to reproduce, then how come men are not queuing up to place their sperm into sperm banks, and women are so keen to use the birth control pill?" The answer is that evolution has not worked to instill the general behavioral strategy – I must produce offspring – into the brains of humans, or any other animal for that matter. Rather, a suite of emotional and cognitive proclivities has evolved associated with sexual behavior, mate selection, attraction to the opposite sex, and so forth, that would have had the consequence of enhancing reproductive success under the conditions that existed in our ancestral environment (which did not contain sperm banks or contraceptive pills). To understand human behavior, it is argued, we must look to the normal emotions, cognitions, and goals of the human mind, because it is they that show the imprint of our evolutionary past. Human minds and bodies are products of the Stone Age.

Second, the notion that humans have evolved as general learning machines is not considered plausible from an evolutionary perspective. Humans faced a whole host of specific problems in the ancestral environment, not one general problem. Accordingly, the mind should consist of specific modular sets of learning abilities and proclivities that have evolved to meet the problems faced in the ancestral environment, including detecting cheating, gathering food, mating, raising children, maintaining territory, and so forth. The human mind is viewed as a cognitive Swiss army knife, rather than as a general problem solver. This is termed the "assumption of modularity."

Third, an evolutionary approach is historical. It attempts to understand the selection forces that rendered specific mental modules functional within an environment that existed long ago. And, recall, that what being functional means is not that whatever was selected for felt nice, led to people leading happy lives, or even to longevity, but simply that reproductive success was enhanced. A way of thinking or feeling may be brutal and thoroughly nasty, but if it produced more reproductive success, then it was selected for in our species. Accordingly, if a common human behavior is functional in modern environments (i.e., leads to greater reproductive success) this does not mean it was functional when it counted in our ancestral past (unless it can plausibly be argued that the key features of the environment at work are the same in both environments).

Indeed, the existence of widespread behaviors in humans in contemporary environments that are hard to stamp out, and look designed to reduce reproductive success, constitute good a priori evidence of an evolutionary design that was functional long ago but is ill-fitted for life in the contemporary fast lane. Examples of such pernicious human traits (that have a plausible evolutionary history) include xenophobia, male violence toward female partners, and sexual jealousy.

Arguments about evolutionary psychology (including the open warfare that exists between Stephen Jay Gould and his critics) tend to revolve around how best to deal with the sorts of distinctive human characteristics noted previously. Because of Gould's eminent reputation, and the widespread currency of these arguments, I will discuss them in some detail. Gould levels three kinds of argument against what he terms the biological "Darwinian fundamentalism" of folk like Dennett and Dawkins, as well as the general program of evolutionary psychology. The first two arguments I think are bad, whereas the third one is on the button.

Gould's first general argument is that adaptations shaped by natural selection comprise only one of several important causal factors in explaining the origins of any life form (including humans). Evolution, in part, has been a function of random events, including catastrophic extinctions produced by comets or meteorites. In addition, as noted by Darwin, a severe constraining factor on the evolution of adaptations are the biological structures and processes that already exist, upon which the evolutionary processes do their work. Thus, there is no guarantee that animals or plants will necessarily be elegantly adapted to the environment. Evolution cannot decide to back up, if it goes down a blind alley; it must build on what already exists, and, thus, will often produce a ramshackle or imperfect engineering solution (to human eyes anyway).

A well-known example, often cited by Gould, is the panda's thumb. Panda's are descended from carnivorous bears whose thumbs were irrevocably designed for the limited movement and function well adapted for meat eating. When adaptation to a diet of bamboo required more flexibility, panda's evolved a Heath Robinson substitute for a true thumb by way of an enlarged radial sesamoid bone in the wrist.[22] It is a clumsy structure but works well enough for the manipulative needs of the panda. Adaptations also produce a plethora of incidental byproducts that are not themselves adaptive, but which may be picked up and used for evolutionary advantage at a later date. These incidental byproducts are termed "spandrels," a term Gould appropriated from its original architectural context. Spandrels are the curved triangular spaces (used for decorative purposes) incidentally created between domed roofs and supporting arches. Such spaces, common in churches, are incidental byproducts of the way in which the architect or builder is obliged to design and construct a domed roof supported by pillars.

The upshot of Gould's thesis is that the evolutionary history of any organism is complex, not easily reconstructed, and that not every body part or behavior is necessarily an adaptation (even if it possesses apparently functional contemporary uses). Moreover, Gould argues that these problems with adopting an excessive brand of evolutionary logic are especially vivid when it comes to humans: "The human brain must be bursting with spandrels that are essential to human nature . . . but that arose as non adaptations, and are therefore outside the compass of evolutionary psychology, or any other ultra-Darwinian theory."[23] Examples given by Gould include the familiar ones of written language and religion.

The main difficulty with Gould's thesis (funnily enough) is that he is correct. It is widely agreed by mainstream evolutionary biologists, and those Gould labels as Darwinian fundamentalists, that nature abounds with spandrels, adaptations of spandrels, and adaptations of adaptations, that there are many causes of an organism's structure and behavior outside natural selection, and that the evolutionary history of any organism is complex and not easily reconstructed. It is also universally agreed that considerable caution is required in labeling any aspect of an organism as an adaptation, that multiple criteria need to be used, and that cocktail evolutionary theorizing should be eschewed.

However, the fact that adaptations are piled on adaptations, or spandrels sometimes later become adaptations (e.g., some snail species use the space generated by the winding of the umbilicus inside the shell as a chamber to brood their young) seems, if anything, to emphasize the primacy of Darwinian adaptation. Gould may certainly have contributed to the recognition of the problems involved in testing Darwinian hypotheses, and to have discouraged facile adaptational theorizing.

However, his ideas, when stripped of their hyperbole, do not look very different from mainstream evolutionary biology. The conclusion remains fast that Darwinian natural selection (including sexual selection) is the only known mechanism that can effectively explain the origins of complex, functional biological design.

Gould's second major argument is that specific claims made by evolutionary psychologists about the nature of the ancestral environment that have produced adaptations of the human mind and behavior are untestable, and therefore unscientific. The reason is we have no way of ascertaining (in the absence of a time-travel machine) what small bands of hunter-gatherers actually did in Africa 1 or 2 million years ago. The testability problem is a common charge leveled against evolutionary psychology.[24] It is the kind of allegation that relies on an approach to science that I have previously discussed – and repudiated – in which the evaluation of theories is reduced to the confirmation or disconfirmation of predictions or claims simply through observation. If one adopts a model of science that uses multiple criteria for evaluating theories (previously described in chapter 1) the untestability charge fails.

Let us take the example of language. How do we know that (verbal) language is not a biological adaptation but a spandrel? Indeed, there is a school of thought that has argued that language is likely to be a byproduct of human cleverness, which has itself evolved for reasons that were little to do with the functions of language.[25] However, consider the following features. Language is a universal ability, found in all cultures. It develops in childhood in a particular developmental sequence that is the same in all cultures. It possesses certain basic features (such as syntax) that are universal. Language is dependent on a set of specific biological features that are unique in humans; namely, the ability to regulate breathing while talking, the development and lowering of the human larynx so that humans cannot breathe and eat at the same time (which often leads to choking on food), and the localization and development of brain areas (usually in the left hemisphere) that are specifically related to the production and comprehension of language. In short, there is a swathe of evidence that, collectively, points toward language as an adaptation.

It can be cogently argued that the postulate that language is an adaptation scores highly in terms of the criteria for theory evaluation I discussed in chapter 1; namely, its internal coherence, the way it unifies disparate empirical findings, simplicity, and the way in which it coheres with other well-entrenched theories (especially Darwinian evolutionary theory).[26] The spandrel theory, in contrast, assumes that the co-ordinated appearance of the different facets of language is an illusion, and it faces the daunting task of explaining the existence of each of the features of language taken separately. The suggestion that language is a spandrel is about as plausible as the proposition that the human eye is a spandrel. I will argue, in due course, that the same kind of cases can be made for counting several kinds of relationship phenomena as evolutionary adaptations (including love and mate-selection criteria).

More generally, it is important to note the diverse kinds of evidence that can be considered when evaluating evolutionary claims, including those about the intimate relationship mind. These include testing predictions from evolutionary psychology using standard experimental and correlational techniques, gender differences, cross-cultural evidence, neurophysiological evidence, fossil evidence, genetic evidence, natural experiments in which human groups have attempted to set up local subcultures (e.g., religious cults, Israeli kibbutz), comparisons of humans with other species, and computer simulations.

The notion that evolutionary psychology produces untestable claims almost always reduces to the naïve positivist position that the only way of testing an empirical hypothesis, such as *a* causes *b*, is to observe the events in question. If such a notion is accepted, then theories that make claims about past causal events, such as Darwinian evolutionary theory, are thrown out of science as untestable – along with physics and astronomy, and indeed any science that postulates the existence of unobservable constructs and causal processes to explain what we do observe. But, if we accept a less simplistic and stringent criterion for what "testable" means (as presented in chapter 1), then evolutionary theories and hypotheses are eminently testable.

Gould's third argument concerning evolutionary psychology also constitutes a problem considered on occasions by evolutionary biologists and psychologists, but one which I believe is on the money and presents some difficult questions for an evolutionary account of human behavior. This issue concerns one of the key ways in which humans are unique animals; namely, humans possess sophisticated cultural knowledge and beliefs, which are passed on to each generation both informally and formally. This form of transmission is non-Darwinian, as it involves the transmission of acquired knowledge, beliefs, or skills, to the next generation that is not accomplished through genetic inheritance. Such cultural knowledge can be (and often is) altered or even rejected by individuals, and the shared beliefs and knowledge of any given culture are capable of massively more rapid change than is true for biological evolution.

Based on a provocative theory initially floated by Richard Dawkins, some have argued that cultural development can also be understood in terms of the basic Darwinian algorithm.[27] Recall that Darwinian evolution requires three elements: variation, inheritance, and selection. There is certainly plenty of within-culture variation in terms of people's beliefs and behavior. There also exist loads of transmission of cultural beliefs and practices both intragenerational (e.g., talking to others, sending e-mails) and intergenerational (raising and teaching children). And finally, there seem to be a plenitude of consequences and environmental presses available to establish the relative survival of beliefs and ideas. But to be genuinely Darwinian we need a unit of selection like the gene. Richard Dawkins coined the term "meme," which is essentially a cognitive unit that lives in people's brains. The class of memes is immense and polyglot; it includes simple beliefs like the world is round, melodies, games like chess, scientific or political theories, not too mention beliefs and lay theories about intimate relationships.

I do not doubt that cultural change is, to some extent, a trial-and-error process that might be termed Darwinian. But memetic and genetic development are so different, that using biological evolution as a metaphor for cultural "evolution" is hopelessly flawed. The historical pathways by which culture develops over time are quite different from those of biological evolution. Biological evolution cannot back up and start again; once a specific adaptation has become extinct in a species, it is typically gone forever. In contrast, memes can disappear from a culture, then easily be rediscovered and flourish spectacularly. However, perhaps the most fundamental difference between genes and memes is that biological evolution is blind through and through, and is never intentionally directed toward adaptive goals. It is just a fact that some genetic variations survive while others are culled. The proliferation of memes is often not blind, but intentional and deliberate. People hatch plans and develop strategies, typically in concert with others, in order to intentionally both spread their own favorite memes and to eliminate those they dislike. Hitler, Darwin, Einstein, and their followers worked for lifetimes to effectively spread their particular brand of memes in a focussed and intentional fashion. If biological evolution worked in the same fashion then animals and plants would get together in committees, decide what sort of biological adaptations they would like to evolve, then arrange their own reproductive behavior and patterns in order to accomplish such goals. Needless to say, this is not how biological evolution works.

The ability of humans to learn, and to deal with novel problems, combined with the massive role played by cultural transmission of knowledge, can make it difficult to distinguish between culturally learned cognitions or behaviors and strict genetic adaptations. The fact that particular behaviors, skills, or beliefs are universal might mean that every culture has independently discovered and developed them in a similar way. The anthropologist Donald Brown has assembled a large range of traits present in all known human cultures, including the use of punishment, regulations concerning sexual activities including forms of marriage, and a division of labor between the genders.[28] But are such activities widespread because they represent adaptations caused by genetic dispositions, or because successful cultures that have survived until recently have hit upon similar solutions to problematic domains of life, encoded them in cultural rules and knowledge, and transmitted them to each successive generation? Of course, these possibilities are not necessarily either-or options. Cultures could either exaggerate the effects of the genes or work to minimize them.

I do not believe that one cover-all answer can or should be delivered to this difficult question of the respective causal roles of biological or cultural transmission. Instead, one must examine each putative adaptation in turn, and give the best answer one can based on the available evidence and the scientific criteria available. Sometimes the answers are reasonably clear-cut, one way or the other, but sometimes they are not. I will analyze an extensive range of relationship phenomena including love, selecting mates, relationship violence, marriage, and so forth, and give my verdicts in due course.

Our genetic endowment is bound to have had a huge influence on all human cultural practices. Even if they are products of culture, the division of labor and the regulation of sexual activities are nevertheless rooted in the fact that humans come in two biological genders and reproduce sexually. If humans were hermaphrodites, then things would obviously be very different. To make matters more complicated, the likely existence of proto-cultures in our recent ancestors means that cultural developments probably influenced our genetic endowment. To give a speculative illustration, if some bright *Homo erectus* back in the Pleistocene persuaded his or her family members to form larger alliances or bands (from say 30 to 60 plus) for self-defense or for more effective hunting and this was effective enough to be culturally sustained through generations, then this would have increased selection pressures for the evolution of higher levels of social intelligence (and associated brain size).[29]

A more recent and less speculative example concerning the effects of culture on genes is related to the widespread variability among humans in the tendency to produce the enzyme lactase as adults, which is needed to digest the sugars (lactose) in unprocessed milk. Everyone possesses a gene that produces this enzyme (located on chromosome 1) but in many people, as with most mammals, this gene switches off during infancy. This is understandable: Why bother to produce an enzyme to process milk past the age when milk is consumed? Some folk, however, have inherited a mutated control gene that fails to switch off the lactase gene in childhood. This genetic variability seems to be mainly a function of how one's ancestors lived in the last few thousand years.

Those individuals descended from cultures that have a long history of herding cows or goats, and consuming associated dairy products, are generally lactose tolerant as adults. The opposite is true with individuals from cultures that did not herd animals or consume milk products from those animals. Thus, in Africa, 90 to 100% of Tutsi populations (who are milk-dependent pastoralists) are lactose tolerant throughout their lives, whereas none of the hunter-gatherer !Kung are lactose tolerant as adults.[30] About 70% of Western people have acquired the mutation, which has allowed them to drink milk as adults.[31]

Arguments concerning the respective causal roles of culture and genes do not, or should not, reduce to claims that human nature is completely a product of one or the other. No one in their right mind would argue for such a position (except perhaps for the odd postmodernist). The cultural pole of the argument (termed the "standard social science model" by its evolutionary critics) posits that evolutionary processes have produced an animal more or less free of instincts, an all-purpose intelligent learning machine that learns to be human according to the culture in which it is immersed. Exponents of such a model usually happily admit to the existence of basic biological constraints, and related gender differences, that are part of human nature. Obviously, women (not men) have babies, and are equipped to suckle them, and women are not as physically big or as powerful as are men. The sort of standard gender differences we find across cultures, such as women gathering food and looking after the children while men hunt, or the widespread male dominance found across cultures, are typically explained as stemming from such basic biological differences.[32]

The psychological evolutionary end of the argument, in turn, does not typically deny that culture has an impact on people's behavior, or that humans are an exceptionally bright species. However, as previously described, it stresses the way in which both cultures and the human mind and behavior (and associated gender differences) are products of human evolution, and rejects the notion that humans are born as *tabulae rasae*. Evolutionary theorists also keenly reject the charge that human genotypes determine the adult end product (the phenotype) in a direct and simple fashion. Instead, it is (correctly) noted that the way in which genes are expressed is typically flexible, and operates in terms of the interaction between the organism and the environment. This, in turn, implies a focus on the way in which individual humans, or other organisms, develop over time.

Developmental flexibility can reach spectacular proportions in animals and plants. The arrowleaf plant develops leaves that look like arrowheads when it grows on land, like lily pads when it grows in shallow water, and like seaweed ribbons when submerged in deeper water.[33] If the male orangutan grows up in the vicinity of full-grown male adults, it becomes stuck at an adolescent stage of development, often for years. These "Peter Pan" orangutans look so different from the regular-sized males that biologists have sometimes mistakenly assigned them to different species. The females prefer the full-grown males; thus the undersized versions adopt a sneak/attack strategy and attempt to rape female orangutans, regardless of whether the females are sexually receptive or not.

If the dominant male in the area disappears, the Peter Pan orangutan will suffer an infusion of testosterone and rapidly grow into the full-grown version, wandering the forest emitting long calls and fighting off competition. At this stage fully adult males mate in a languorous, prolonged fashion with sexually receptive females in a happily mutual fashion.[34] The developmental flexibility in these cases is built into the *same* genotype of each individual plant or animal. There is evidence, as I will cite in later chapters, that the same kind of developmental plasticity can be found in humans in terms of intimate relationships and mating strategies.

The role of genetic and environmental influences in an extensive range of abilities and traits (including some specifically related to intimate relationships) has been extensively investigated using both adopted children and twins. The logic and methods are different in the two kinds of study, but both produce estimates of the extent to which the genes versus the environment account for variation in any given trait that is measured (extroversion, intelligence, attachment styles, or whatever). In either case, such estimates are possible because we know what the genetic overlap is between parent and child (50% on average) or between siblings (100% for identical twins and 50% on average for fraternal twins). Such studies, for example, have suggested that about 50% of cognitive abilities are inherited from parents. Such estimates need to be treated with considerable care, partly because of the slippery nature of the concept of genetic inheritance.

What these heritability estimates mean is that 50% of the variability in individuals, in say, intelligence, is accounted for by genetic inheritance from their parents. Such estimates must not be equated with the stronger claim that 50% of intelligence is caused by genes and 50% by the environment. Indeed, a heritability estimate of 0% is possible even when the characteristic in question is completely a product of genetic inheritance. The reason is that many characteristics have evolved to the point where there is little or no variability involved – almost everyone is born with two hands, two feet, and two eyes. In such cases, whatever variability exists is not inherited. But the fact that such organs mostly come in twos is because this feature is genetically encoded and passed on faithfully generation after generation.

It is important to avoid arguments about the causal role of cultural or genetic forces becoming snarled by arguments about causality and free will. In my view, there is no contradiction between the existence of human freedom or free will and the postulate that all human behavior is caused.[35] Indeed, the concept of human agency is *dependent* on the assumption that human behavior is caused.

If I decide to ask Mary out for a date, or get married, or get divorced, such decisions are, of course, conditioned and influenced (caused, if you will) by a variety of factors (genetic, environmental, contextual, quality and quantity of in-depth cognitive processing, my relationship theories, and so forth). But this assumption does not necessarily remove the agency or freedom to make such decisions and judgments. Indeed, the opposite is the case. Imagine if one's mental life suddenly failed to causally mesh at all with one's behavior, or that mental decisions and desires occurred randomly, simply popping into one's head with no causal history – scary possibilities that are scarcely consistent with the notion of human agency or freedom.

We should resist phrasing the debate in terms of whether human cognitions, emotions, and behavior are caused or not. Of course they are. Rather, it is the nature of the causal theory imposed that can legitimate or dispose of lay concepts of human freedom and individual autonomy. Behaviorist or sociological approaches, that view humans as helpless pawns in the grip of the environment or the culture, are inconsistent with the idea that humans have free will. However, the approach expounded in this book is elegantly compatible with the idea that humans are (to some extent) autonomous organisms capable of resisting or channeling the wellsprings of human behavior – to resist the "tyranny of our selfish replicators (genes)" to use Richard Dawkins's colorful phrase.[36]

Back to the Intimate Relationship Mind

The social cognitive model of the intimate relationship mind presented earlier is agnostic about the origins of relationship thinking and emotion. Nevertheless, it is important to provisionally assess the extent to which this model is consistent with an evolutionary account, or might raise difficult questions in terms of either cultural or evolutionary origin accounts. In the model proposed the intimate relationship mind is split into three kinds of overlapping stored theories: general social theories, general intimate relationship theories, and local intimate relationship theories.

Although there is some domain specificity involved, I also argued that lines of influence are likely to operate among all three categories, which will tend to keep them roughly in synchronization. For example, explaining why Mary left Fred will influence Fred's general theories about intimate relationships, reading an article in a magazine about intimate relationships (scholarly or pop) can influence Fred's local relationship theories, and Fred can use his understanding of a restaurant script to impress his partner on a first date.

Cognitive psychologists hold that such stored knowledge structures are constantly available, being pressed into action and conditioning our cognitions, emotions, and behaviors often unconsciously and automatically. This notion nicely squares with both evolutionary and cultural origin accounts. For example, in evolutionary approaches nascent rules and tendencies encoded genetically need to operate in exactly this kind of omnipresent background way, ready to exert their influence when the developmental and/or environmental context call them into action.

The distinction drawn in my model between unconscious/automatic processing and conscious/controlled processing raises some thorny issues with respect to evolutionary psychology. In particular, it is the nature and power of human conscious and controlled cognition that makes humans so distinctive in the animal kingdom. In the intimate relationship domain this activity is revealed in many ways, including the way in which humans talk about such relationships, explicitly theorize about the causes and effects of specific relationships (including their own), consciously forge long-term relationship plans and predictions, consciously adopt strategies to solve relationship problems, and so forth.

As noted previously, evolutionary psychology assumes that human cognition and emotion is modular; that humans evolved to develop hundreds if not thousands of cognitive and emotional rules or strategies specifically designed to solve the problems faced in the ancestral environment, including the myriad problems faced in the intimate relationship domain.

The concept of modularity was pioneered by Jerry Fodor who used it to refer to cognitive or perceptual capacities that are hard-wired and automatic, such as visual or auditory perception.[37] In an oft-cited example, he pointed out that a visual illusion still remains potent, even when we know that what we are looking at is wrong. The visual system is, thus, insulated against the influence of other cognitive systems, such as higher-order knowledge or beliefs, and proceeds in an automatic and encapsulated fashion. On the face of it, the idea that conscious and controlled cognition is controlled by thousands of if-then programs that operate in an insulated and automatic fashion (like the visual system) adds up to a rather stupid organism, rather than a flexible and intelligent organism.

Indeed, Fodor believed that higher-order human cognition is not fundamentally modular. Conscious, in-depth cognition appears to be highly permeable, open to suggestion and influence from all quarters, and actively nonmodular in its operation. The development of scientific theories, for example, almost always involves the deliberate and imaginative comparison between two or more domains, as does the everyday use of metaphors and similes. The ability to generate highly abstract and hypothetical knowledge structures (e.g., logic and mathematics) that are context-free, and can be applied across domains, also seems inherently nonmodular.

The nonmodularity of the intimate relationship mind is represented in the following aphorism that one sees occasionally emblazoned on T-shirts – "A woman needs a man like a fish needs a bicycle." Understanding what this means, and why it is funny, relies on the human ability to compare and understand relations among disparate domains (fish, modes of transport, and sexual relationships). A highly modular mind would be dumbfounded at such an expression. Indeed, language itself is a device that appears wonderfully adapted to nonmodular, cross-domain cognition.

One useful way of approaching this issue is to concede that the human mind possesses both modular and nonmodular features.[38] Consider the intimate relationship mind in this light. I will compile evidence throughout the book that the intimate relationship mind is shaped and composed of a range of distinct phenomena that have specific biological features, developmental trajectories and causal etiologies, and that often operate in modular ways (automatically, and relatively independently of other traits and processes) – these include romantic love and other relationship emotions, sexual passion and behavior, mate selection, physical attraction, and sexual jealousy.

Men sometimes claim that their penis has a mind all of its own – I believe the same is more or less true of some pivotal relationship phenomena, including ways of thinking and feeling. This proposal places me in the evolutionary camp and against those, who argue, for example, that all gender differences in intimate relationships flow from one or two basic biological differences, such as women (not men) have babies, and women are physically smaller than men. The view that humankind's long evolutionary history has produced a few obvious physical and biological differences, but has wiped out all remnants of gender-linked psychological differences in relationship contexts is implausible. It is also inconsistent with the available evidence, which I will detail in due course.

On the other hand, the intimate relationship mind is clearly not insulated from other psychological and life domains that evolutionary theorists often put into different baskets, including language, theory of mind, status concerns, food gathering, and so forth. Because humans have the capacity for conscious self-reflection and sophisticated causal model building, they have the power to understand and to exploit possible connections among such domains. Because human intimate relationships are central in people's lives, they often represent a battleground of conflicting tendencies, emotions, and cognitions that often need to be self-consciously and perhaps rationally reconciled. Cultures represent this cognitive melting pot writ large. Thus, in many cultures marriages are controlled by parents in order to establish and maintain political alliances, or to generate wealth for the family.

One suggestion made by various authors is that automatic cognitive and emotional processes are likely to be under a firmer evolutionary genetic leash than is the case for conscious/controlled processing.[39] There is merit to this view, and I will explore it in detail in places. However, the temptation to trace the extraordinary human capacity for learning solely with the development of the conscious/controlled end of cognition is a mistake. This is because all the psychological analyses of human expertise in any given domain including chess playing, music, reading minds, or whatever, make it clear that the development of such abilities is just as much, if not more, rooted in the development and use of automatic processing, as it is in the wise and efficient use of conscious planning.

Every conscious and controlled aspect of cognition, from speaking, to making a good impression with a date, to designing a bridge, is undergirded and guided by a myriad of automatic cognitive processes working in parallel. If humans are the masters of the animal world at learning and problem solving, then this is clearly rooted in their expertise at both ends of the cognitive processing continuum.

Conclusion

Having argued a provisional case for the role and power of evolutionary theorizing in understanding the intimate relationship mind, I turn to its first real trial and application in the next chapter – love and other relationship emotions.

Chapter 4

Love and Other Emotions in Intimate Relationships

IT'S SEVEN whole days since I
have seen my lover. A sickness
pervades me. My limbs are lead.
I barely sense my body.
Should physicians come,
their drugs could not cure
my heart, nor could the priests
diagnose my disease.
Should they say, "Here
she is," that would heal me.
Her name would restore me.
Should her messengers
come and go, that
is what would revive my heart,
More potent than medicine
my lover is to me.
More powerful too is she
than books of medicine.
Her arrival from outside
is my amulet. At the sight
of her I regain my health.
She widens her eyes at me,
and my body becomes young.
She speaks and I am strong.
I embrace her. She banishes
the sickness from me. But she
has left me for seven whole days.
Fowler, 1994 (3,000-year-old Egyptian poem)

One general criticism that readers may have of my treatment, to this point, is that relationship cognition and behavior all sound rather too cerebral for comfort. Certainly, individuals develop relationship theories that they use to predict, control, and explain relationship events, and they possess goals and strategies. However, a critic may argue, surely a key feature of intimate relationships is that they are shot through with powerful emotions including love, anger, jealousy, and even hatred. Moreover, relationship cognitions are typically not dispassionate intellectual judgments, but are "hot" cognitions, suffused with positive or negative feelings (or "affect" as it is called in the trade).

I plead guilty. The cognitive treatment so far requires buttressing regarding the role of emotions. Indeed, who can doubt that emotions play a central role in understanding intimate relationships? However, this claim can also be reversed to the effect that to understand emotions, in some general sense, requires a grasp of the psychology of intimate relationships. The reason is that intimate interpersonal relationships constitute the crucible within which emotions are expressed, learnt, and used both in infancy and throughout life. Consider basic emotions like anger, love, hate, jealousy, guilt, and shame. These are largely social or interpersonal emotions, and are almost certainly experienced and expressed most frequently within the contexts of intimate relationships. As will be seen, however, understanding how emotions function within intimate relationships by no means implies that we can or should disregard the role of cognition.

I previously raised a distinction that importantly applies to this domain; namely, that people possess lay psychological second-order theories that apply to first-order phenomena. Such second-order theories cannot be ignored, even if they are nonsense, because they will exert causal influences on psychological processes and behavior. However, such lay second-order theories can also be critically evaluated for their wider scientific value or credibility. In this case, the first-order phenomena constitute the experience and expression of emotions in intimate relationships. The second-order theories constitute folk or common-sense theories about what emotions are, how we know when we are feeling them, how they are typically expressed, and so forth.

This common-sense (second-order) theory of emotions, I will term the *Star Trek* theory of emotions. This name is derived from the two characters (Spock and later Data) who were central figures in the long-running science-fiction series *Star Trek*. Neither Spock nor Data apparently experienced emotions, and both possessed completely logical (rational) minds. Spock was half human and half Vulcan, thus raising the suspicion that he suppressed any (human) emotions he might have had. Spock regarded emotions as impeding the goals of an orderly and rational mind. Data, on the other hand, was an advanced robot and genuinely felt no emotions. Data was portrayed as being baffled about emotions in humans (unless he plugged in his emotion chip) because he could not experience emotions for himself.

The *Star Trek* theory of emotions, thus, embraces two themes about emotions that are lifted straight from folk psychology. First, emotions typically get in the way of rational thought and action. Second, we attribute emotions to ourselves in much the same way in which we perceive the differences between tables and chairs, or know the difference between basic sensations like pains and sounds. That is, we project an introspective searchlight into the furniture of the mind, and identify which emotion we are experiencing. Emotions like love, anger, jealousy, and guilt simply feel different. If someone informs you about an emotion they are experiencing (say "anger") try asking them how they know. You are unlikely to get an informative answer. They will probably say they just "know" or they "feel angry." If you press the question they are likely to become even angrier. In the folk model of emotions it makes as much sense to ask people how they know they are experiencing a particular emotion as it does to ask them how they know they are looking at a table rather than an elephant. I believe (as do many psychologists) that folk psychology, along with *Star Trek*, have got emotions more or less wrong on both counts. The basic reason is that the clean split between cognition and emotion in folk psychology is a fatally inaccurate depiction of the mental machinations involved in adult emotional experience, emotional self-attribution, and emotional expression.

How Do People Know When They Are Feeling Anger or Love or Jealousy?

Think back to the last time that you felt angry with your partner in an intimate relationship. What caused you to feel this way? What physiological experiences did you have? What urges did you have? What behavior did you actually perform? What did you feel like afterwards?

To the extent that you expressed the emotion what did your partner say or do? To what extent did you blame your partner? How much control did you have over the emotion? How predictable was the emotion?

Researchers, such as Julie Fitness and Beverley Fehr, have asked exactly these kinds of questions (and many more) of large samples about a range of emotions that people experience in intimate relationship contexts.[1] The results have shown that different emotions are distinguished by a set of characteristics that cohere into core themes or scripts. For example, if you responded according to the prototypical script for anger revealed in participants' reports, you would have said that your partner triggered the emotion by treating you unfairly, that you felt a good deal of muscle tension and felt a strong urge to express yourself (which you probably did), that your partner responded in kind (angrily), that despite the short-lived nature of the anger you felt tense or depressed afterwards, that you perceived that you had reasonable control over yourself and the situation, and finally that it was mainly your partner's fault.

Similar thumbnail sketches of emotions like jealousy, hatred, love, and guilt are provided by the same research. Each emotional prototype has the same general scriptlike form that unfolds in a particular way, with the raw feeling being enveloped in a set of perceived causes and effects, and with appropriate accompanying states and behaviors. In short, the self-perception and expression of emotions involves a lot of cognition, and, in intimate relationship settings inevitably drags in both general and local relationship theories of the sort I have previously described. If Mary's husband buys her a bunch of roses she may experience love toward him, or anger if she knows, that he knows, she is allergic to flowers.

This cognitive approach has several key explanatory strengths (apart from being true). It is consistent with the way in which emotion concepts are fuzzy, overlap, and can shade into each other at their borders; hatred and anger, for example, share more prototypical features than do, say, jealousy and guilt, which reflects the similarity between these emotions.

This approach also solves a particularly nasty problem implicit in the *Star Trek* or folk model of emotional self-attribution. As pointed out, such a model implies that we directly (internally) observe our own emotions and simply report what we observe. If this model is correct, then the problem arises as to how we can reasonably attribute emotional states to others, given that we do not directly observe others' internal emotional states of anger, jealousy, and so forth. This is known in philosophical circles as the "other-mind" problem. A social cognitive approach solves this problem parsimoniously, and elegantly, by postulating that we attribute anger or jealousy to others in much the same way as we do to ourselves – through application of the same scriptlike mini-theories.[2]

Imagine that Fred embarrasses his partner in public, his partner becomes tense and flushes, and later she suggests that it was entirely Fred's fault. Fred can safely assume that she is angry, and is likely to react by either getting angry in turn or apologizing to her (a prototypical anger script). To take a different example, imagine that Gary's partner is brooding and detached on the way home from a party, and Gary gathers that the cause of his partner's behavior was that he had spent time talking with an old flame at the party, and that his partner blames this old flame for shamelessly encouraging Gary. Gary can reasonably conclude that his partner is jealous, and is likely to reassure his partner and express his love for her (one prototypical jealousy script). The upshot of this discussion is that if Data, of *Star Trek* fame, really did have a fantastically powerful brain, and amazingly good software, then he would be pretty good at both appropriately attributing emotions to others and feigning emotions of his own in the appropriate circumstances. If all Data's emotion chip provided were the raw emotional experiences, and omitted the necessary detailed cognitive information, his emotional intelligence would resemble that of a two-year-old toddler; unless Data also had access to the functional scripts and prototypes specifying the typical causes and consequences, and associated interpersonal scripts, associated with each emotion (as do adult humans).

The social cognitive approach just sketched also explains how people are able to convincingly feign emotions in relationship settings in order to obtain various goals. Susie deliberately reacts in a mildly jealous fashion to her partner's flirting with someone else, in order to induce guilt, so her partner will agree to going on a holiday (actually, Susie is amused rather than upset by her partner's behavior); Gertrude pretends to be angry about her partner being late, to punish him for forgetting her birthday; Samantha smiles and pretends to celebrate her partner's good fortune, when privately she is gagging with envy, because she does not wish to appear curmudgeonly to her friends who are present.

Admittedly, the feigning of emotions tends to produce the experience of the emotion itself (as any actor knows). It is difficult to act flying into a rage or behaving in a loving fashion, without inducing something like the appropriate experiences. Nevertheless, feigned emotional experiences are intentionally induced and expressed (rather than being automatic and uncontrolled) in order to obtain specific goals that may be quite different from those that the emotions were originally designed to achieve as evolutionary adaptations. Humans do a good deal of this sort of co-opting of evolutionary adaptations – a fact that creates difficulties for evolutionary psychology, as previously observed. The ability to feign emotions in this way also illustrates the practical mastery attained by most adult humans of the cognitive psychological architecture of emotions.[3] To reiterate, possessing massive knowledge and expertise, in both expressing emotions and identifying them in others, does not necessarily equate to possessing a decent second-order theory about how such feats are managed. Most people know how to ride a bicycle, or talk, but few could tell you, accurately or convincingly, how they do it.

The precursor of a social cognitive approach to emotions was developed by Stanley Schachter and Jerome Singer in the 1960s.[4] They proposed that internal experiences are certainly necessary for emotions to be attributed to the self, but that they represent undifferentiated and malleable states of arousal of the peripheral nervous system (increased heart and respiration rate, increased adrenalin secretions, and so forth). The social context and other information then enable individuals to attribute the appropriate emotions to themselves.

In the classic experiment conducted to test their two-factor theory (published in 1962) Schachter and Singer injected male participants with a supposed vitamin supplement called Suproxin, which was in reality adrenalin. When the participants were told to expect some side effects of the drug, they did not attribute their subsequent arousal to any particular emotion. However, when the participants did not expect any side effects of the drug, they proceeded to attribute emotions to themselves, but different emotions according to the social context. When participants were placed with another participant (actually a stooge of the experimenter) who became angry over completing the endless questionnaires, the real participants also behaved angrily and attributed anger to themselves. However, when the stooge started behaving in a euphoric manner and horsing around (making and throwing darts and so forth), then participants also became euphoric and attributed elation to themselves. A control group of participants who had injections of saline water did not experience or express either anger or euphoria, no matter what the stooge did.

Thus, this experiment confirmed that two factors appear to be necessary for people to "know" what emotions they are experiencing – undifferentiated internal arousal and information from the social context.

Schachter and Singer's model of emotional attribution was subsequently picked up and applied to the attribution of passionate love by Elaine Hatfield who proposed that simply increasing arousal (no matter what the source) should increase the tendency for people to (mis)attribute their experiences to increased love or attraction.[5] For example, scaring the daylights out of your date on turbulent rides at a fairground visit might leak over to heightened feelings of passion or love. In a particularly cute experimental demonstration of the tendency for fear and attraction to be confounded, Donald Dutton and Art Aron had a female confederate approach men and ask them to complete a questionnaire. The men were about to cross either a short, low bridge or a narrow, long, wobbly, suspension walkway hanging high above a river with rocks and shallow rapids. Half of the high-bridge (presumably fearful) men later called the woman, but few of the low-bridge men did.[6] The results from this field study have also been replicated within more stringently controlled laboratory studies.[7] Adrenalin does appear to make the heart grow fonder.

It is clear, based on recent neuropsychological evidence, that Schachter and Singer's approach exaggerates the extent to which emotional states are labile and indistinguishable from one another, when described at the bodily and neurophysiological level. Feelings of love and affection, for example, are specifically associated with the release of oxytocin and vasopressin, produced in the hypothalamus.[8] Feelings of lust and sexual excitement, in contrast, are principally influenced by androgens (such as testosterone) that are released by the adrenal glands (next to the kidneys), and in the testes in men or the ovaries in women.[9]

Moreover, different basic emotions (e.g., fear, anger, disgust, happiness) have characteristic patterns of nonverbal facial behavior that are produced automatically and universally across cultures, and are recognized and appropriately labeled as distinct emotions in all cultures.[10] Paul Ekman showed, for example, that members of cultures that had experienced virtually no contact with Western cultures (such as the Fore and Dani of New Guinea) correctly recognized emotions, and told related appropriate emotional stories when shown photographs of Western faces portraying basic emotions like happiness, surprise, disgust, and anger. Moreover, photographs of the New Guineans displaying the same emotions were similarly correctly identified when shown to American undergraduate college students.

On the other hand, there is considerable disagreement about exactly which emotions have specific and identifiable neurophysiological patterns and associated nonverbal behavior – the so-called basic or primary emotions. Proposed lists of basic emotions vary considerably (from 5 to 17) and few lists include love as a basic emotion.[11] For example, Keith Oatley and Philip Johnson-Laird proposed the following list of basic emotions: anger, disgust, fear, happiness, and sadness.[12] Ira Roseman's alternative list comprised anger, disgust, fear, sadness, contempt, dislike, frustration, guilt, hope, pride, regret, relief, shame, surprise, joy, distress, and *love*.[13] I will argue in this chapter that Roseman is correct in that love can and should be counted as a basic emotion. The central caveat, which I will unpack in due course, is that love is also much more than a single emotion, and applies to several distinguishable behavioral/cognitive/affective systems that can work together or function independently.

More generally, the point holds fast that the experience and self-attribution of emotions is malleable, and can be readily altered according to the social context and associated cognitions. Indeed, the neurophysiological evidence is utterly consistent with a social cognitive model in which cognitions interact with raw affective experiences to produce the end product of emotions and associated self-attributions. Various organs or regions of the limbic section of the brain are thought to be centrally involved in generating basic emotions and hedonic tone, including the cingulate gyrus, the hippocampus, and the amygdala. However, these organs are also involved in a constant interchange of information with the cerebral cortex.[14] Thus, the neuropsychological evidence is nicely consistent with the proposition that causal influences between affect and cognition constitute a two-way street.

In relationship contexts, as previously argued, the role of both local and general lay theories will play a critical role from the word go in determining which specific cascade of internal neurophysiological and hormonal processes, associated with particular emotions, will occur. If June's partner alludes to her sexy appearance while they are having a coffee with friends, her resultant emotion will depend on what June thinks her partner's attitude to her appearance actually is. If June believes her partner thinks she is overweight, she may interpret his remark as a cruel barb, and become angry. If June believes her partner thinks her body is great, she may interpret his remark as a genuine compliment and feel a surge of love.

Once an emotion has been engendered, both lay relationship theories and online cognitive processes will continue to profoundly influence the course of the emotion, and subsequent behavior. A small stab of sexual jealousy, if ruminated upon and cognitively elaborated, can turn into a full-blown bout of suspicion and sexual jealousy. The classic literary example of this process is Othello's agonizing and prolonged bout of sexual jealousy, inexorably leading to the murder of his (innocent) wife.

It is granted in folk psychology that we can and should exercise control over our emotions (witness the popularity of "anger management" courses). However, it is only too easy to slip into the facile assumption that because emotions involve internal characteristics such as genes, hormones, and neurotransmitters, that the occurrence of the emotions themselves is determined by forces beyond our control. In fact, as we have seen, the causal flow is often reversed with intentional decisions or actions switching on the complex internal emotional dance of body and brain. We control our emotions as much as they control us.

I hope the discussion so far has raised doubts concerning the common-sense second-order theory that we attribute emotions to ourselves by the simple act of observing the raw emotional experiences in our own heads or bodies. Given the subtle and complex connections between emotions and cognitions, the groundwork has also been laid for questioning the notion that emotions always impede rational thought or action. I complete my attack on folk psychology (regarding the two propositions in question) by turning to a discussion of the functions of relationship emotions. What are they for?

The Functions of Relationship Emotions

The general functions of emotions in intimate relationships are no different from the functions of emotions in any context. First, they attract our attention – something unexpected or unusual has occurred, something important and possibly dangerous is going on, and it is in our interests to be vigilant and to be ready for action. This explains why general arousal of our nervous system (increased flow of adrenalin, heart and respiration rate, increased availability of glucose, increased secretions of various neurotransmitters that focus and excite the mind) is a common feature of many emotions – we become primed for action. Second, emotions provide both information and motivation. Information is vital in terms of helping organisms decide what to do in situations where more than one course of action is possible.

Do you flee, fight, or have sexual congress with the bear? Consult your emotions! If you are a human being, then fear will almost certainly tell you to flee (although if you have more specialized knowledge about bears you might quell your instincts and stay perfectly still). If you are another bear, then any of the above actions might be appropriate depending on the context and which emotion is engendered (fear, anger, or lust). Emotions also provide copious doses of motivation to make decisions that enhance the chances of experiencing happiness and joy, and decrease the chances of experiencing distressing emotions like guilt and depression. Professional sportsmen are motivated to win important games as much by the fear of losing as by the desire to win. In a similar fashion, in adult intimate relationships, everyone (well, almost everyone) wants to attain love and intimacy but to avoid grief and disappointment.

As Darwin first documented, in his book *The Expression of the Emotions in Man and Animals,* the expression of emotions also has a range of social and communicative goals that are of massive importance (in humans as with other animals).[15] By expressing anger Brian might be attempting to intimidate and therefore control another person, or to indicate that he is holding his ground and expects an apology or some change in behavior. Expressing anger is a prime way of asserting oneself (indeed, as I shall later document, and against the conventional wisdom, the expression of anger in intimate relationships does not necessarily have negative consequences). By expressing love, Suzanne might be communicating a desire for sex or affection, or simply the desire for continued company. In short, emotional expressions are routinely used for several social purposes, including intimidation, supplication, and the gaining of approval or status.

Antonio Damasio has argued persuasively that emotions are indispensable for motivating people to make rational decisions and to behave rationally.[16] Damasio bases this argument partly on case studies of individuals who had suffered localized forms of brain damage (to regions of the prefrontal cortex) that specifically incapacitated their ability to experience emotions, but left other abilities and functions intact. These case studies show that lack of emotion is not associated with more logical or rational behavior, but rather the opposite. In particular, social intelligence and interpersonal relationships in such cases become badly dysfunctional. Damasio's explanation for the crippling effects of such deficits is that the absence of emotion removes an essential element that people routinely use when making choices among different actions or activities.

Damasio's theory has the ring of truth when applied to relationship settings. Imagine making decisions and judgments in relationship contexts while experiencing no emotions or feelings. If you were to meet a few people at a party, which one do you phone up for a date? If you go on a date with someone, how do you decide whether to go out on another date? How do you respond when your partner tells you he or she loves you, or that he or she wants to go to bed with you? If you do decide that your partner can be trusted or not trusted, is warm or cold, is patient or bad-tempered, how do you act on those judgments? Without any emotions or affective tone to go on, I suspect we would become like rudderless ships – indeed, just like the individuals described by Damasio who suffered from specific damage to regions of the brain centrally involved in emotions and affect.

The point I am making here is *not* that we make decisions or judgements (including emotional attributions) in relationships without complex cognitive processes in train (as I have strenuously argued) – it is that such cognitive processes are thoroughly intertwined with emotions and feelings. Dominic decides to date Elizabeth because he likes her – the automatic and conscious processing that underlies such a judgment may be complex, but it is likely to be the resultant hedonic feel to Dominic's interaction with Elizabeth that he uses as the final output in making some sort of decision. It is the lack of introspective access to the complex cognitive and neurophysiological machinery at work, which informs and produces emotions like "love," that is (I suspect) the reason why people often pronounce love as inscrutable.

An influential neurophysiological-cum-evolutionary model of the brain developed by Paul MacLean, known as the Triune Brain, has perhaps encouraged an incorrect (Freudian) view of higher-order cognition in humans as perched on top of, and as vainly trying to control, our primitive, seething, emotional demons.[17] In the Triune Brain, the most primitive system (the reptilian system) in the brain comprises the motor system. Next comes the limbic system (containing the cingulate gyrus, the hippocampus, the amygdala, and a few pathways), which is responsible for the emotion system. This system, and accompanying emotions, MacLean argues evolved in mammals partly to promote attachments or bonding between parents and offspring. The third brain layer, which reaches its zenith in *Homo sapiens*, comprises the development of the neocortex and higher-order cognition.

As Steven Pinker argues, MacLean's description of the brain may be substantially correct, but the way in which evolution works is not to simply slap one system on top of another, without tinkering and altering what already exists.[18] The human brain needs to be understood as a system, or more accurately as a myriad of systems, working in conjunction with the biological systems of the body, the genetic programs, and in constant interaction with the physical and social environment.

I have stressed the point that in the emotional/cognitive systems sometimes cognition can drive emotions, but I do not wish to deny that cognition can also be the tail wagged by the emotional dog. Indeed, one of the paradigmatic examples of emotions taking over and channeling behavior and cognition is romantic love, a theme constantly expressed in literature, movies, and songs (and, I confess, has occurred in my own experience).

An evolutionary psychological approach suggests that different emotions have evolved to deal with different problems, and therefore should have special (and universal) characteristics. Indeed, (universal) basic or primary emotions must have particular evolutionary histories, with specific associated functions; otherwise it is hard to see why they would exist in some sort of encapsulated form in the first place. As I stated before, I believe "love" certainly deserves the status of a basic emotion, even though it is not usually given that status by emotion theorists. Phillip Shaver, Hillary Morgan and Shelley Wu have laid out a convincing case for the view that love is a basic emotion, a case from which I will borrow heavily.[19]

Social constructionists and postmodernists have often (absurdly) claimed that romantic love is an invention of European culture, with one popular analysis by de Rougemont dating its inception to the twelfth century.[20] However, as illustrated by the 3,000-year-old Egyptian poem cited at the beginning of the chapter, there is considerable evidence for both the antiquity and the universality of romantic love.

One popular pre-European legend of the Te Arawa tribe of Maori in New Zealand recounts the story of Hinemoa and Tutenekai, a tale strongly resembling that of Shakespeare's *Romeo and Juliet*. Hinemoa and Tutenekai came from different tribes and were forbidden to marry because of the low status of Tutenekai.[21] Every night Hinemoa would hear the haunting sound of Tutenekai's flute across the lake from the island where he resided (Tutenekai was both handsome and a talented musician), but she could not gain access to a canoe as her father had ensured they were pulled well up on the beach. Finally, Hinemoa decided to swim to Tutenekai's island, a hazardous plan, but one she accomplished using calabashes as floats. They finally fell into each other's arms and lived happily ever after.

It turns out that Maori and Western cultures are not alone in terms of the presence of romantic love. An analysis by William Jankowiak and Edward Fischer found good evidence (based on folk tales, ethnographies, evidence of elopement, and so forth) of romantic love existing in 147 of 166 cultures.[22] This is a conservative figure, given that in 18 of the 19 love-absent cultures the ethnographic accounts were uninformative rather than definitive. In only one culture did an ethnographer claim that romantic love did not actually exist.

Romantic love has other features that mark it out as a basic emotion. The stereotypical behavior associated with being in love is familiar to us all. Imagine observing a young couple sitting on a public bench in a fond embrace and gazing into each other's eyes. They walk slowly away, holding hands, still maintaining eye contact. She breaks away, and they indulge in some horseplay accompanied by laughter and giggling, followed by a passionate embrace. No prizes if you were to guess the pair were "in love." Moreover, as pointed out previously, romantic love and bonding have attached distinctive physiological events, including the release of hormones such as oxytocin and vasopressin, and are triggered off by predictable and specific interpersonal contexts.

Finally, there exists a plausible evolutionary account that specifies the functions that love evolved to meet. In a nutshell, it runs as follows. Compared to other primates, humans have exceptionally large brains and thus heads, which necessitates them being born at an unusually undeveloped stage (for a mammal) in order to achieve egress though the birth canal. In addition, humans are dependent on their parents and other relatives for an exceptionally long period of time before attaining adulthood (compared to other animals including primates) and also require a tremendous amount of informal and formal education from their parents to attain the social, cultural and practical knowledge necessary for survival and reproductive success. Accordingly, as brain size and childhood length steadily increased over the last million or so years of *Homo* evolution, there were strong selection pressures toward the development of (relatively) monogamous pair bonding.

Love is, thus, an evolutionary device to persuade couples to stay together for long enough to give their children a good shot at making it to adulthood. Reproductive success only counts if your progeny make it to adulthood and pass on your genes (in turn) to their offspring. The existence of a stable monogamous couple in a hunter-gatherer lifestyle also allows for a potentially valuable division of labor, with the male being the dominant provider and the female being the dominant caregiver (although in hunter-gatherer cultures both genders typically perform both functions). In brief, in our ancestral environment, two parents were better than one.

This sort of evolutionary account is plausible, and it is also consistent with much of what we know about both the physiology and social psychology of "love" in contemporary cultures. For example, it explains why the most important set of ideals across cultures (for both men and women) for long-term relationships consistently concern a partner's warmth and loyalty (not attractiveness or status/resources).[23]

However, although adult (romantic) love can rightly be considered as a basic emotion, the underlying psychological and related evolutionary processes are more complex than I have so far presented; namely, I will advance the hypothesis that what we call "love" is based around three distinct basic evolutionary adaptations and related psychological components of love. In an influential theoretical analysis (and brilliant associated program of research) Phillip Shaver and his colleagues (especially Cindy Hazan) have conceptualized adult romantic love in terms of John Bowlby's pioneering (evolutionary) treatment of attachment systems in humans.[24] Bowlby argued for the existence of three basic behavioral systems that bond dyads together: attachment, caregiving, and sex. Thus, Shaver et al. write that saying "I love you" can mean any or all of the following:[25]

- *Love as attachment*: "I am emotionally dependent on you for happiness, safety, and security; I feel anxious and lonely when you're gone, relieved and stronger when you're near. I want to be comforted, supported emotionally, and taken care of by you. Part of my identity is based on my attachment to you."

- *Love as caregiving*: "I get great pleasure from supporting, caring for, and taking care of you; from facilitating your progress, health, growth, and happiness. Part of my identity is based on caring for you, and if you were to disappear I would feel sad, empty, less worthwhile, and perhaps guilty."
- *Love as sexual attraction*: "I am sexually attracted to you and can't get you out of my mind. You excite me, 'turn me on,' make me feel alive, complete with my sense of wholeness. I want to see you, devour you, touch you, merge with you, lose myself in you, 'get off on you.'"

One can see in the above descriptions, the indispensable role played by various emotions in Bowlby's love trilogy. Recent social psychological research, which has examined the underlying dimensions of lay judgments of love in adult relationships, has revealed a remarkably similar tripartite pattern to those postulated by Bowlby; namely, intimacy (attachment), commitment (caregiving), and passion (sexual attraction).[26]

Tellingly, social psychologists who have carried out this work have done so quite independently of, and with no reference made to, either evolutionary psychology or to Bowlby's work. Moreover, it is important to note that the emergence of such an underlying structure does not mean that laypeople are necessarily aware of this tripartite structure of love, or that it exists as part of their second-order theories. The methodology used in the social psychology research relies on self-reports, but typically proceeds by first getting each participant to provide independent ratings on a multitude of items (such as excitement, honesty, and loyalty). Participants either rate the meaning of "love," viewed hypothetically, or directly rate the extent to which items describe their own relationships on numerical scales (1–7 point scales are the most popular). This set of ratings is then subject to a statistical procedure, known as factor analysis, which reveals the underlying way in which the items fall into distinct groups. The factor analysis results are the same, regardless of which kind of rating task is completed, and are mathematically generated as a function of the ratings provided by the raters. Research participants are not actually asked to group the items, or to report whether they think the individual items are related.

The similarity between adult-to-adult love and adult-to-child love is exactly what an evolutionary approach would predict. The attachment and care-giving behavioral/affective systems are ancient, present in all mammals that care for and protect their offspring for lengthy periods of time, and precede the emergence of primates and *Homo sapiens* by millions of years. These two specific affective and behavioral systems were clearly designed to increase the odds that vulnerable infants would survive to adulthood. If pair-bonding and love between human adults (or adults of any species) was to emerge as an adaptation, then evolution would assuredly tinker with the serviceable attachment systems that were already in place – no need to invent something completely different. Thus, the basic commitment and intimacy components of adult human love are likely to have been directly lifted from the same systems that promote adult–infant bonding.

But, romantic love has a critical feature lacking from parental love; namely, lust. Romantic love is rendered complete, and more frenetic and breathless, with the additional component of sexuality and passion. No wonder romantic love can lead brave men and true to abandon their wives and children, encourage single women to have scandalous affairs with married men, and motivate young people to defy traditional sanctions or the heartfelt wishes of their parents.

The existence of separate hormonal and neurophysiological systems undergirding the three different components of love supports the view that love is based on biology, rather than simply invented by Western culture. To recap, passion is associated with the sex hormones (such as testosterone) juiced up by the peripheral arousal systems. Commitment and intimacy seem to be promoted by hormones like oxytocin and vasopressin. Consistent with their purported role of enhancing bonding, the same hormones are released by women when giving birth and when breast-feeding. They are also produced during sexual intercourse and after experiencing orgasm by both men and women.

Examining the way in which adult intimate relationships unfold over time, and the varieties of adult love, gives clues about how these three components (intimacy, commitment, and passion) can become entangled, but also can adopt independent trajectories. The empirical evidence, in line with common sense, suggests the following patterns are common.[27] In flings or one-night stands, passion can run high, whereas intimacy and commitment are probably low. However, in relationships that develop past a few dates, high levels of passion typically follow the

91

development of intimacy, and high levels of commitment (such as in a marriage) lag further behind again. In many relationships, especially in full-blooded romantic affairs, the three components operate in unison. As relationships mature over several years, the passion component usually fades, often leaving behind high levels of intimacy and commitment.

Of course, some relationships that maintain high levels of romance and passion endure over many years. My casual observations of such couples who are proud of maintaining romance and passion in their relationships is that they expend a considerable amount of effort in keeping up the pace. Keeping up a sustained flow of surprise gifts, small romantic notes, candle-lit dinners, back rubs, and compliments, seems to be the recipe to follow. Not surprisingly, most couples settle back into a more comfortable and less arduous regime after a few years – or even months.

The tendency for passion to fade is not only true in Western cultures, but is probably widespread across cultures. While watching a recently married couple from the !Kung culture horsing about together, another !Kung man commented spontaneously to the anthropologist Marjorie Shostak, "When two people are first together, their hearts are on fire and their passion is very great. After a while the fire cools and that's how it stays. . . . They continue to love each other but it's in a different way – warm and dependable."[28]

Commitment may also tail off for a variety of reasons, often leading to the demise of the relationship. However, individuals can and do maintain that they "love" their partner even though passion and commitment have both disappeared. For example, in marriages where one partner is an alcoholic, the passion (sexual attraction) and commitment (caregiving) modules may be running on empty, but the intimacy (attachment) module might still be up and running.

Commitment can also attain astronomical levels, even in the total absence of behavioral interaction, such as in the (usually painful) cases of unrequited love. In one infamous case of unrequited love, John Hinkley shot President Ronald Reagan in an attempt to impress Jodie Foster. In a bizarre twist, Jodie Foster had starred in a movie (*Taxi Driver*) in which an older male (played by Robert De Niro) planned an assassination attempt on a local political figure to impress the character played by Foster in the movie. Hinkley became obsessed with both the movie (which he reputedly watched more than a dozen times) and also the actress Jodie Foster. He scrawled her the following letter two hours before he shot Ronald Reagan:

Dear Jodie,

There is a definite possibility that I will be killed in my attempt to get Reagan. It is for this very reason I am writing you this letter now.

As you well know by now I love you very much. Over the past seven months I've left you dozens of poems, letters and love messages in the faint hope that you could develop an interest in me. Although we talked on the phone a couple of times I never had the nerve to simply approach you and introduce myself. Besides my shyness, I honestly did not wish to bother you with my constant presence. I know the many messages left at your door and in your mailbox were a nuisance, but I felt that it was the most painless way for me to express my love for you . . .

Jodie, I would abandon this idea of getting Reagan in a second if I could only win your heart and live out the rest of my life with you, whether it be in total obscurity or whatever.

I will admit to you that the reason I'm going ahead with this attempt now is because I just cannot wait any longer to impress you. I've got to do something now to make you understand, in no uncertain terms, that I am doing all of this for your sake! By sacrificing my freedom and possibly my life, I hope to change your mind about me. This letter is being written only an hour before I leave for the Hilton Hotel. Jodie, I'm asking to please look into your heart and at least give me the chance, with this historical deed, to gain your respect and love.
I love you forever
John Hinkley[29]

Hinkley's letter illustrates the yearning and frustrated passion that can accompany a virtual relationship. It also embodies the timeworn strategy of attaining status through some heroic act and, thus, attracting the attention (and perhaps love) of the desired person. The only real madness in Hinkley's case was his decision to attempt an assassination of the president, in order to demonstrate his love and prowess. If the plan of assassinating Ronald Reagan was replaced (in the above letter) with joining the foreign legion or becoming a missionary, then the letter might strike one as foolishly romantic rather than insane.

Love and Marriage Go Together Like a Horse and Carriage – or Do They?

One might question how the account presented so far squares with arranged marriages, or the existence of polygyny (one man married to more than one women) in many cultures. It could also be objected that the bonding mechanism of love obviously does not function particularly well, given that extramarital liaisons are so common, and that divorce is so prevalent in Western countries and in many other cultures. I will consider some of these topics in depth, especially in relation to gender differences, later in the book. However, it is important to establish a few general facts at this point.[30]

The universal nature of marriage and the incest taboo

One of the most remarkable (but typically unremarked upon) universals is that marriage is found in all known cultures, often with an associated set of rituals, and always with associated duties or expectations on both sides. Moreover, although the field of eligible candidates one is permitted to marry varies across cultures, incest taboos are virtually universal, with an occasional exception in brother–sister marriage for royalty or special groups (such as in ancient Egypt or in pre-European Hawaii). Admittedly, what counts as immediate family varies across cultures. For example, in some cultures marriage among cousins is permitted, whereas in others it is strictly forbidden. However, with the few curious exceptions noted above, mother–son, father–daughter, and brother–sister sexual relations are universally banned, with infringements being typically severely punished.

Edward Westermarck, who was an enthusiastic Darwinist, initially proposed the most plausible and commonly accepted explanation for why incest is avoided among humans (and many other animals) in 1891.[31] His proposal was simply that individuals who grow up together naturally develop a sexual aversion to one another. In modern parlance, such familiarity experienced during childhood switches off the genes responsible for sexual attraction (but leaving love experienced as attachment and caregiving intact). Indeed, the very idea of having sex with a brother or sister in adults is likely to generate strong feelings of disgust. Thus, according to this thesis, cultural taboos reinforce an evo-

94

lutionary adaptation. Sigmund Freud vigorously challenged Westermarck's hypothesis in 1910, and proposed his exotic theory that young children experience strong sexual feelings toward their parents and siblings. Thus, Freud argued that cultural incest taboos are required to repress natural and universal sexual feelings between children and their parents and siblings. Freud's theory became the standard view for many years, but in more recent times the consensus (sensibly) has swung decisively against Freud and in favor of Westermarck.

Some of the most compelling evidence in favor of Westermarck's theory has come from the kibbutzim in Israel, in which unrelated children grow up and live together in close proximity in family groups. Joseph Shepher and his colleagues found that among 2,769 marriages of young adults reared in this environment, not a single one was between members who had lived together from birth.[32] The genetic evidence is also compatible with an evolutionary thesis that incest avoidance is fundamentally instinctual; namely, consistent with folk stereotypes, inbreeding tends to sharply increase the probability of producing offspring with genetic defects. The problem lies in the existence of recessive genes, which can result in death or cause crippling defects, such as dwarfism, mental retardation, deafness, and so forth.

Recall that in sexual reproduction, 23 chromosomes come from each parent to form the 23 pairs of chromosomes in the child. Typically, in genetically unrelated parents, the recessive problematic genes (from one parent) will be paired with dominant genes on the same sites in the chromosomes inherited from the other parent; such recessive genes will, thus, not be expressed. In contrast, for a sister impregnated by her brother, both of whom share 50% of their genes, the chances of the same recessive genes from the same locations on the two sets of chromosomes being paired together (and, thus, being expressed) are sharply increased. For example if the sister has two lethal genes (about the average in humans) there is a 20% chance that the fetus will die. Even if the child survives, there is a tenfold increased risk of suffering from other genetic defects.[33]

Arranged marriages

Marriage in many cultures is firmly tied into economic and political concerns, often to the point where marriages are arranged principally to provide wealth or status to the families (especially for the men).

However, in traditional cultures that practice arranged marriages, brides (and grooms) are typically given some choice in the matter. For example, in arranged marriages in Sri Lanka men and women who like one another (or fall in love) usually let their parents know their choices in advance through indirect channels.[34] Moreover, families often use similar criteria that the individuals themselves might use if they had a free choice, including matching on attractiveness or socioeconomic status. The classic example is the Jewish custom of having a matchmaker arrange a suitable match.[35] In India, Hindu children are taught that love should follow an arranged marriage. A study carried out by Usha Gupta and Pusha Singh in Jaipur, India, found that levels of self-reported love gradually increased in arranged marriages over time, until they superseded levels of love in marriages that were freely entered into (which followed the standard Western pattern of sadly heading downwards in the years after marriage).[36]

Even in cultures in which marriages are strictly arranged, and romantic attachments are forbidden, romance has a tendency to erupt. In China, foot-binding of young women had been used for 1,000 years (presumably) to prevent them from fleeing from their husbands. There are also many Chinese stories (some ancient) that illustrate the nature and power of love and its potential to rent asunder the social fabric. As Helen Fisher concludes in her analysis, "Taboos, myths, rituals, myriad cultural inventions coax the young around the world into arranged marriages. Yet where these marriages can be dissolved, as in New Guinea, on atolls in the Pacific, in much of Africa and Amazonia, people regularly divorce and remarry mates they choose themselves."[37]

Monogamy and polygamy

First some definitional bugaboos to clear up. *Monogamy* and *polygamy* refer to the practice of marrying one partner or many partners respectively. Gender is not at issue so this can mean one man and several women, or one woman and several men. The term monogamous is also (confusingly) used to refer to couples or individuals that are sexually faithful and, thus, do not indulge in extramarital sexual relations, but I will reserve the term "monogamous" to refer to a one man/one women relationship to avoid ambiguity. The term specifically applied to one man marrying more than one woman is termed *polygyny*, and the term for one woman marrying more than one man is defined as *polyandry*.

A whopping 84% of known cultures allow polygyny, and some men carry harem-building to excess.[38] According to the *Guinness Book of World Records*, the harem champion was an emperor of Morocco, with the unlikely name of Moulay Ismail the Bloodthirsty, who purportedly sired 888 children from his many wives. However, it has been estimated that only about 5 to 10% of men in cultures that allow polygyny actually have more than one wife,[39] the majority of marriages being monogamous. In cultures that allow polygyny the wives often complain and suffer from bouts of jealousy, and, genetically speaking, there is not much in it for the women. They may certainly attain a share of the status or wealth of their husband, but will probably have to compete for such resources with the other wives. From the male point of view there is the distinct genetic advantage of siring more offspring, but on the other hand, considerable resources and wealth may be required to maintain more than one wife, and the task of ensuring spousal fidelity may become difficult, if not exhausting.

The existence of polyandry is exceedingly rare, in both humans and other species. The evolutionary reason is obvious. Women can only bear a limited number of offspring, so their reproductive success is not enhanced a great deal. Men are decidedly worse off, reproductively speaking, given that they may not be genetically related to the children they are expending considerable resources in helping to raise. However, in special circumstances polyandry can crop up as an option, such as when women are scarce or when women possess considerable economic power.

In summary, the vast majority of marital relationships, across both Western and traditional cultures, are monogamous. It is also instructive to note what occurs when so-called free love is practiced. Like many of my age-group, I went through a period in the 1970s in which free-wheeling sexual relationships and open marriages were presented as an ideal, and sexual jealousy was thought to be a function of insecurity and weakness. The results, from my casual observation, were a rash of broken marriages and the reassertion of more traditional relationship formats. The fate of cults in which free love has been attempted dramatically illustrates the point. The Oneida community was started in 1847 by John Noyes, an avant-garde religious zealot. In this community (which at its height had 500 men, women, and children) romantic love was banned, and men and women were expected to copulate with each other – often. Like many cults, Noyes and his immediate family held the whip hand, attempted to rigidly control reproduction (using

97

withdrawal as means of birth control), and Noyes and his son had first call on the pubescent girls. It did not work. Men and women constantly fell in love and formed clandestine intimate relationships with one another. The ancient love systems have an inexorable logic of their own.

Extramarital liaisons and divorce

How powerful are the bonds of love? The divorce rate in the USA and other Western countries has steadily increased since the 1940s, but has leveled off in the last two decades in most Western countries. The USA still retains the lead with current estimates that about 50% or higher of marriages are likely to break up. This rate is almost double that of most European countries, Australia, and New Zealand.[40] The widespread perception that divorce rates have become outrageously high in the USA and other Western countries, compared to all other cultures, is a fallacy. Traditional hunter-gatherer cultures, such as the !Kung, have comparable divorce rates to those now seen in Western countries, as do many Arab or Muslim countries along with preindustrialized Japan. The peak period for divorce in the USA is currently running at about four years after getting married, and Helen Fisher has shown that this peak period for divorce is also common across many cultures.[41]

Of course, there is massive diversity in the divorce rate across cultures and such diversity is causally related to many factors. One major factor at work is the economic and political equality of women with men.[42] In cultures that are relatively egalitarian in terms of sex roles, such as hunter-gatherer cultures in Africa or in contemporary Western cultures, the divorce rates tend to be higher because women (as well as men) have the power to leave the relationship. Indeed, in Western countries women outnumber men in initiating divorce or separation.[43] It is certainly true that fewer people are becoming married in Western countries, such as New Zealand, and they are getting married and having children later in life. In New Zealand, which is typical of Western countries, from 1971 to 1998 the marriage rate per 1,000 of population has halved, while the divorce rate has doubled over the same time period.[44] Meanwhile, the median age for getting married has steadily increased in all Western countries. For example, in New Zealand, from 1971 to 1998, the age at marriage for men went from 23 to 28 years, and for women from 21 to 27 years (very similar figures to the USA).

These striking trends in Western countries have been driven by the huge population bulge of the baby boom, and the associated aging of the population, as well as the increasing divorce rate itself. In New Zealand one in six marriages in 1971 involved the remarriage of one or both partners, whereas this figure had shot to one in three by 1998 – one major reason why the mean age at marriage is increasing. Most individuals in Western countries, including the USA, who get divorced eventually remarry (from 80% to 90%). The same pattern is found across most cultures.[45] In short, where divorce is relatively common in cultures, it is not replaced by celibacy or promiscuity, but by serial monogamy.

Finally, one major reason for the steadily lower (official) marriage rate in Western countries is the increasing acceptance of de facto marital arrangements. In New Zealand, for example, it is now more common for young people to live together in de facto arrangements than in a legal marriage, and about 25% of men and women (aged from 15 to 44) live together without legalizing their union.

It is not as easy as it may appear to accurately estimate divorce rates. The usual measure of divorce adopted is to compare divorce rates, in any given year, with either per 1,000 population (a crude figure) or per 1,000 estimated existing marriages in the population (a more appropriate figure). However, this latter comparison also runs into trouble in situations in which relatively rapid demographic shifts are taking place (as has been the case in Western countries). For example, when marriage has become less popular over the years, as has happened in Western countries including New Zealand, calculating the divorce rate in the standard fashion will tend to exaggerate the true divorce rate. A cohort analysis of the couples who married in New Zealand in 1981, followed up 18 years later, revealed that 83% were still together. Moreover, it has been estimated that for about two-thirds of this total sample, death, not divorce, would end their marriages.

Adultery

Extramarital sexual activity is common in Western countries, and its existence has also been documented in many cultures. Surveys in Western countries have produced variable results, but generally indicate that somewhere between 20% and 50% of people admit to having had extramarital affairs.[46] Anthropological work in traditional cultures is more anecdotal, but suggests, likewise, that adultery is not uncommon.[47] I will examine this topic thoroughly in later sections of the book, but will punch out a few relevant points here. It is not difficult to propose plausible evolutionary arguments for extramarital sexual activity. For males, it looks like a way of having one's cake and eating it too. Males can spread their genes around, with the hope that some progeny will make it to puberty, while also ensuring that their own children are well cared for in the primary relationship. For women, extramarital sex can enable them to obtain some top-quality genes while also retaining the support of their husbands (who, one hopes, blithely assume they are the father).

Of course, extramarital liaisons carry risks and costs. They normally need to be carried out in a clandestine fashion, put the primary relationship at risk, and, if discovered, in many cultures carry legal penalties or socially sanctioned physical attacks from the sinned-against partner (especially by men against women). Moreover, it is not as if the neuroendocrinal, cognitive, and behavioral "love" systems turn off in extramarital affairs. Thus, sexual activity that goes beyond a one-night stand always carries the risk of developing into full-blooded (and potentially life-wrecking) romantic love. How often does it happen that a casual extramarital fling, carried out through boredom or simply because it becomes available, turns into a passionate affair, with oxytocin, vasopressin, and testosterone liberally flowing? I suspect, without any evidence apart from anecdotal to offer, it is a common occurrence. Love is a dangerous emotion.

Summary

To summarize, it is clear that humans (both men and women) are programmed via evolution to court and mate, to fall in love, to bond and commit to another person, to nest, and to raise a family. The divorce rates in Western countries can be seen as a glass either half full or half empty. In most Western countries there has been a considerable dismantling of legal obstacles against divorce, a no-fault divorce system is now common, negative social attitudes against divorce have weakened considerably, and many women are no longer economically tied to the marriage. Yet 50 to 75% of couples in most Western countries apparently choose to live together for most of their lives. This unadorned fact is inconsistent with the *Playboy* philosophy that humans are essentially promiscuous beings, squeezed and socialized into an ill-fitting monogamous straightjacket.

On the other hand, like almost every other monogamous species known, humans have an unfaithful streak. Having illicit sex or an extramarital affair is often exciting, and can relieve the comfortable boredom of a (long-established) marriage. Extramarital affairs also often represent an attempt to find an alternative partner because the current one is perceived as inadequate. Finally, women use sex in many cultures to obtain favors or gifts or money. When Nisa, a !Kung woman, was asked by the anthropologist Marjorie Shostock why she had taken so many lovers, she replied, "There are many kinds of work a woman has to do, and she should have lovers wherever she goes. If she goes somewhere to visit and is alone, then someone there will give her beads, someone else will give her meat, and someone else will give her other food. When she returns to her village, she will have been well taken care of."[48] The existence of extramarital sex, and the different motives that can accompany it, is yet another example of the way in which the three love systems (intimacy, commitment, and passion) are capable of acting independently or in concert.

Conclusion

The warp and woof of human love illustrate two key points. First, that evolution works by tinkering with what already exists, so that evolved adaptations often have a ramshackle quality about them. Human love is like this. It consists of a hotchpotch of cognitions, emotions, and behaviors that obviously have a genetic basis, but which unfold in a flexible fashion depending on the cultural and social environment and the goals of the individual. Second, striking universalities or strong cross-cultural similarities indeed suggest that love and related emotions represent specific adaptations that have associated functions in humans (related to reproductive success in the ancestral environment). On the other hand, the fascinating variability in the way humans build love and sex into their intimate relationships, both within and across cultures, speaks powerfully to the existence of flexible mating strategies and goals that can be adjusted according to the social context and associated demands of the situation.

Part II

The Development of Intimate Relationships

Chapter 5

Reading Minds and Personalities in Intimate Relationships

Love sees not with the eyes, but with the mind;
And therefore is wing'd Cupid painted blind.
William Shakespeare

The notion that intimacy and love inclines individuals toward hopelessly inaccurate and rose-tinted views of their partners, and associated acts of stupidity (such as getting married) is a common belief in common-sense and scientific psychology alike. William Shakespeare certainly believed it, judging by the number of times this theme appeared in his plays (I could have chosen from dozens of Shakespearean quotes in selecting the one to head the chapter). But is it true? How accurate are folk in assessing the personalities of their partners and relationships? Are people in relationships better at reading their partners' minds than objective outsiders? Are intimate relationship minds rooted in reality, or do people build relationship castles in the air? These are the questions I will deal with in this chapter.

The issues and problems in this domain are thorny and complex, comprise a mixture of methodological and theoretical issues, and have sharply divided psychologists for decades. As a friendly exegetical device I begin with a debate between two hypothetical street-smart scientists who know the literature and the arguments well, but who fundamentally disagree about the underlying lay motives involved. Professor X holds that people in relationships are motivated by the need to feel positive and optimistic about intimate relationships, typically produce inaccurate relationship judgments, and work hard at constructing their relationship theories to be positive, regardless of reality. Professor Y argues that people in relationships are basically motivated by the desire for truth and accuracy, typically produce accurate relationship judgments, and develop relationship theories that largely mirror reality. An intelligent, articulate advocate, who knows the arguments and evidence backwards, can mount a convincing case for almost anything. Thus, one of the best ways of discerning the truth is to study opposing arguments, presented by such folk. The arguments, and buttressing evidence, are genuine, but the professors do not represent real individuals. In this debate I am the chair.

Professor X: First of all, I object to my views being mischievously characterized in the opening remarks by the chair. It is true that I think the motivation to maintain a positive view of the world is primal. Indeed, one cannot help but be struck by the extent to which relationship judgments are positively biased and inaccurate. Nevertheless, I would not claim for one minute that people's relationship theories are merely castles in the air. Clearly, to some extent, reality builds some constraints into the process – relationships are molded and exist in the real world. I am no postmodernist I assure you. Nevertheless, Professor Y's approach is frankly extreme and untenable.

   Let's begin with the self. There is an ocean of research in social psychology that shows that people have a basic need to view themselves in a positive light. This powerful motive leads people to exaggerate their own positive attributes, to exaggerate the control they wield over social outcomes, and to be unduly optimistic about future events.[1] Moreover, these Pollyannaish tendencies are associated with a range of benefits including greater personal happiness, improved relationships, higher motivation and persistence, and superior mental health.[2] Now, as the chair himself has claimed in past publications, people's theories of themselves are inextricably intertwined with their partner-relationship theories. Accordingly, any overoptimistic gloss for the self will naturally migrate to theories of the partner and the relationship. The fate of the self and one's intimate relationships go hand in hand. If one's partner goes mad or loses his/her job, or one's relationship goes down the tubes, the self suffers. Such dire psychological and practical costs for the self, associated with relationship problems, maintain the tendency to look for the silver linings in the relationship clouds.

Professor Y: Unlike Professor Panglossian (oops, I mean X) I think the chair got my views exactly right, and they are exactly right. Let's

106

start with the self. Professor X is certainly correct that there is an ocean of research that purports to show that people are hopelessly Pollyannaish and inaccurate in their judgments and theories about the self. I say "purports" because (as Professor X knows full well) this research is hotly disputed in terms of its correct interpretation. The view that perceptions and judgments of the self are irrationally optimistic certainly had a hold on social psychology in the 1970s and 1980s, but that view has been challenged and has weakened considerably in recent years.[3] A flurry of evidence over the last decade has shown there is a dark side to high self-esteem. People with very high self-esteem can have poor social skills,[4] are disliked by others,[5] tend to be aggressive,[6] and engage in high-risk behavior.[7] The Panglossian view that the self should possess boundless optimism is probably an artifact of the gung-ho, individualistic nature of North American culture. It is certainly not true in Japan, for example.[8]

Professor X: I will ignore the cheap crack. Well, we could argue about the self all day, but I am getting some dark looks from the chair. Let's come back to relationships. As relationships develop along standard trajectories (casual dating, to serious dating, to cohabitation or marriage, to having children) the psychological and practical costs of relationships failing grow to massive proportions. Rationally, most people know that their marriages have about a 50% chance of long-term success (at least in the USA). Yet people persist in getting married in large numbers and having children. Making a decision to increase the level of commitment in a relationship requires a leap of faith and a level of confidence that are frankly difficult to justify rationally. Accordingly, the psychological pressure to produce charitably positive judgments of one's partner and relationship is overwhelming.

Professor Y: Maybe so. However, from an evolutionary perspective one smells a rat with the proposition that people are driven by the need to feel good about their relationships, come hell or high water. Evolutionary adaptations are blind products of the drive toward reproductive fitness – they are never aimed at personal happiness or bliss. Evolution has not equipped us to taste everything as nice, hear every sound as pleasant, or to perceive everyone as honest and trustworthy. If we did, we would not survive, let alone be happy. Why should evolution have designed our brains to always perceive our relationships and partners as wonderful? Indeed, it doesn't make sense –

Professor X (interrupts): I hold little truck with evolutionary psychology. But, one answer, from an evolutionary perspective, is that love's cognitive blinkers comprise an evolutionary device designed to keep parents together for long enough to give their children a good shot at making it to puberty and, thus, passing on the parents' genes. Thus, love, it could be argued, provides the intimate relationship mind with a positive and over-optimistic default setting.

Professor Y: Have you finished? I admit this argument sounds convincing. However, there surely must be limits to such an adaptation. I am reminded of a quote by Thomas Huxley – "the great tragedy of Science [is] the slaying of a beautiful hypothesis by an ugly fact."[9] In this case the hypothesis is the presumed pervasiveness and dominance of the relationship-enhancement motive; the ugly fact is that the vast majority of romantic relationships eventually break up. Evidently, the psychological processes that maintain love and trust in the face of doubt and conflict have their limitations. More generally, lay relationship theories provide powerful cognitive tools to achieve goals such as the need to predict, explain, and control relationships. If lay relationship theories become divorced from reality, then they are hardly likely to be very effective or accurate in terms of prediction, explanation, or control. Indeed, the consequences of people steadfastly maintaining optimistic and positive relationship theories that become detached from reality can be brutal; namely, one's partner (who unfortunately might not share one's own sanguine relationship theory) might suddenly and – apparently out of the blue – start talking about divorce or just leave.

From an evolutionary perspective the human mind has been molded to ascertain the truth about our social world – no matter how bleak and depressing – in situations in which it would be dangerous or extremely costly to do otherwise. And, human intimate relationships can be both dangerous and costly. There must exist powerful natural contingencies that encourage people to seek the accurate, although possibly bleak, truth about their partners and relationships.

Professor X: To repeat your words, it sounds convincing. But let's look at the empirical evidence. Sandra Murray and John Holmes have pursued an extensive and methodologically sophisticated program of research in this area.[10] They have found that people routinely fight off doubts, which can corrode levels of commitment and trust, by restructuring or rewriting their intimate relationship theories. For example, if dating partners are persuaded to believe that open disagreement and conflict resolution are the routes to relationship nirvana, then they simply rewrite their memories of the relationship to stress their level of disagreement, or they rationalize the failure of their partners to argue by stressing how wonderful they are in other ways. Let me quote some examples from their research:

"On many occasions, I could tell that a problem existed, but she refused to talk about it, almost afraid of an argument . . . on the other hand, she is very receptive to my needs, and willing to adapt if necessary. This is beneficial to our relationship." Or,

"My partner never really starts an argument but knows that if something bothers me enough, I will bring it up. However, my partner has come to realise in the past few months that the development of intimacy is important to me and he seems to be more willing to negotiate problems that occur."[11]

Other research has consistently revealed that as love's blinkers grow stronger and more opaque, individuals inaccurately idealize their partner and exaggerate the level of similarity between themselves and their partners; and, they simultaneously report being happier, more in love, and more committed. Some research by Tara MacDonald and Michael Ross makes essentially the same point.[12] This study compared the predictions of relationship stability by university students in dating relationships with predictions by roommates of the daters, and parents of the daters. The dating couples assessed their relationships more positively than the outsiders, made more optimistic predictions, and were more confident in their predictions. However, daters were less accurate in their predictions of the fate of the relationship than predictions advanced by their friends or parents.

Professor Y: Well, I hate to nitpick, but some of this research could be interpreted in other ways. Take the study you described by Murray and Holmes which showed that, like revisionist historians, people simply rewrote their local relationship theories to fit the "good relationship" stereotype. It is equally plausible to view what the participants were up to in this study in rational terms. The cognitions that were engineered by the researchers to become imbalanced were something like the following: "Our relationship works well and is successful," "Open disagreement and conflict resolution is important for producing successful relationships," and "Our relationship is relatively free of open disagreement and conflict." Bringing local relationship theories and general relationship beliefs into balance is an eminently rational and scientific procedure. A scientist who noted some inconsistencies between the behavior of a star or a volcano, and the prevailing general scientific theory about stars or volcanoes, would be woefully irrational if he or she ignored it.

The same point can be made about the evidence that the more people are committed and in love, the more they exaggerate the extent to which they are similar in things like intelligence, emotional security, empathy, warmth, emotional sensitivity, and so forth. These are not exactly easy judgments to make. It turns out that a common belief (among laypeople and psychologists alike) is that increased similarity between partners produces higher levels of relationship happiness and success. It is a perfectly rational step to deduce that you are probably fairly similar to your partner on any given dimension (particularly if there is some guesswork involved) if you happen to be in a happy and successful relationship.

Finally, let me come back to the research by MacDonald and Ross, which I happen to know quite well. The dating partners' explicit predictions might not have been so hot, but they did not blindly produce Panglossian judgments of their relationships regardless of how they functioned. Rather, the dating partners' levels of satisfaction and commitment with their relationships predicted relationship longevity *better* than the predictions of the outsiders (family members and roommates).

Professor X: I am sure that if you cherry-pick the research findings and try desperately hard to reinterpret every single finding to fit in with your theoretical biases, you could succeed (which is ironic given the position you are adopting). But, a scientific approach mandates that we examine all the evidence, not just some of it. And, you would surely not dispute that the evidence shows that the more people are committed and in love, the more they systematically bias their judgments about their partner and relationship in a positive direction. Moreover, I throw out the challenge that this applies almost regardless of the criterion you choose to compare individuals' judgments with. In some of Murray's research, for example, a positive bias is defined as one partner (say the man) perceiving his partner's intelligence, honesty, and so forth, as even more positive than the woman independently rates herself. Love and intimacy lead people to make inaccurate judgments. Period.

Professor Y: No, no, no. I agree that people are systematically positively biased in their judgments, the more they are committed and in
love. This is consistent with the evolutionary argument that love
provides the intimate relationship mind with a positive and over-
optimistic default setting. But, this does not equate to claims about
accuracy or inaccuracy. Bias and accuracy are different animals. To
understand the difference, imagine that Mary, who loves John to
distraction, rates John on four personality traits – intelligence, warmth,
attractiveness, and ambition – using 1–7 scales where 7 = "describes
John very well," and 1 = "does not describe John well." Mary rates
John on the four traits thus – 5, 6, 6, 7.

We then acquire accurate assessments of John's personality on the
same traits using a mixture of John's self-reports, observational data,
and expert opinion, which we use as criteria (assume in this thought
experiment that the objective ratings are 100% accurate). John's objective personality ratings turn out to be 4, 5, 5, 6. Mary is certainly
positively biased, but she is also accurate in that her ratings track
John's objective personality traits exactly – all her ratings are exactly
one unit above John's personality. On the other hand, she could
have revealed the same amount of overall positivity bias, but have
been totally awry in her personality judgments with the following
pattern – 7, 5, 7, 5. Finally, Mary could have revealed no bias at all,
but could also have been completely inaccurate, as in her possible
ratings of 7, 3, 7, 3 (note that the mean level of positivity in this case
is the same as the mean positivity of John's actual personality).

In short, bias and accuracy are not only *not* the same things, but
they can, and often do, operate independently. Actually, Sandra
Murray and John Holmes, in a recent empirical study, make the same
point.[13] They found that individuals who viewed their partners in a
more charitable and rose-hued fashion were no less wise or accurate
in their judgments of their partners' personalities. Accurate and perceptive judgments of intimate relationships are not irreconcilable with
love, faith, and commitment.

Professor X: Well, OK, but this depends on how one measures accuracy. I agree that bias and accuracy can operate fairly independently.
Still, compare the following ratings that Mary might make of John:
Case One – 5, 6, 6, 7; Case Two – 4, 5, 5, 6. We would say that Mary
was more accurate in Case Two than Case One, wouldn't we? Mary
has made four direct hits in this case. But, using your definitions, the

only difference is that Mary is biased in Case One but not in Case Two. Thus, if one is biased (positively or negatively) this implies there must exist some level of *in*accuracy.

I can't help feeling that your general case is destructive rather than constructive. What positive evidence do you have that people actually make rational, accurate judgments, or ever seek the unvarnished truth, about their partners?

Professor Y: OK. Good point. The chair is giving me threatening looks, and wants me to wrap up – the audience is getting restive with this methodological stuff. Let me pick up your challenge. The evidence from research in relationships shows four clear findings. First, couples almost always have quite similar relationship evaluations.[14] Second, positive relationship evaluations are reasonably highly correlated with positive behavior evinced during conflict-solving interactions (as observed and measured by external observers).[15] Third, negative relationship evaluations predict the break up of relationships quite well, sometimes years in advance.[16] Fourth, Sally Planalp and Mary Rivers found that when important and unexpected events happened in people's intimate relationships they did things like gathering more data by talking to others, testing hypotheses by altering their interaction with their partners, thinking about past behavior for clues, and developing explanations that resolved the contradictions.[17] In short, people resembled scientists, rather than Pollyannaish twits.

These facts and findings all show that the intimate relationship mind is locked into the observable intimate world, and does not float above relationship reality like foam on the ocean waves.

Chair: Thank you for the lively debate. As chair I have the final word. I believe both sides are correct. That is, the two kinds of goals and mind-sets (esteem-maintenance and truth-seeking) are both central motivational forces that characterize humans in relationship and other social settings. Sometimes the two motivational sets will be in conflict, and sometimes not. Which motivational set is dominant in relationships should depend on a host of conditions including the following:

- Some people may have cognitive styles that are more cerebral and scientific than others.
- Relationship interactions that are especially threatening are likely to increase the accessibility and power of the esteem-maintenance

goals, and to subvert the goal of producing accurate attributions about the partner.

- Different stages in the relationship seem likely to increase the accessibility and power of different sets of goals. For example, it is plausible that the need to produce accurate empathic judgments becomes paramount when individuals are making important decisions about the relationship, such as: Should we move in together? Should we get married? Or, should we have a baby? On such occasions, the degree of commitment to the relationship is exactly what is up for grabs, so that a simple relationship-enhancing motive may cease to be important. On the other hand, when couples are settled into a comfortable maintenance phase of the relationship, esteem-maintenance goals may be automatically applied.

- When relationships are characterized by high levels of passionate love, then judgments and decisions are probably going to be more strongly driven by affective processes, and esteem-maintenance concerns, than by the goals of accuracy and truth-seeking.

This account is more or less speculative in the relationship domain, although there is good evidence that esteem-maintenance and truth-seeking motivations operate in nonrelationship contexts in the fashion I have postulated.[18] The best evidence, to date, for this proposal in relationship contexts has been provided by Faby Gagné and John Lydon.[19] They found that when individuals in dating relationships were in an accuracy-motivated mind-set, they predicted when and whether their relationships would end a lot more accurately than when they were producing such predictions in an esteem-maintenance frame of mind. However, variability in the accuracy of partner and relationship judgments is clearly a lot more complicated than simply whether people are motivated to seek the truth or cling to comfortable perceptions of reality.

Explaining Variability in the Accuracy of Social Judgments in Intimate Relationships

To answer this general question, David Kenny and David Funder have attempted to outline and measure the key components that determine the accuracy of social judgments.[20] Consider, for example, what might determine the level of accuracy attained when Bill makes an assessment of just how extrovert Mary is:

- It might depend on what one uses as the criterion for accuracy – one could use Mary's self-report of her own level of extroversion, or obtain peer-reports of Mary's extroversion, or measure Mary's behavior in some way, or do all three.
- It might depend on how easy Mary is to judge. Some people are easier to read than others.
- It might depend on how much information Bill has to go on and the quality of the information. This will depend (among other things) on the nature of the relationship between Bill and Mary – are they good friends, lovers, or strangers?
- It might depend on the ability of Bill to make such judgments. Is Bill intelligent and socially perceptive or unintelligent and socially inept?
- It might be a function of the kind of judgment being made – making assessments of extroversion, for example, might be more accurate than making judgments of honesty. Extrovert behavior is hard for an introverted person to exhibit, and the relevant behavior itself is out there for all to see. The trait of honesty is harder to judge, given that dishonest people are often experts at appearing honest, and that it is difficult or even impossible to tell whether an individual is being honest or dishonest on any given occasion.

Most research in social psychology over the last two decades has tested the role of such factors by examining how accurate people are in making personality judgments. This research is often based on strangers observing rather thin slices of a target's behavior (such as targets telling a group a few basic details about themselves, like their name, where they live, and so forth). Not surprisingly, this work has produced strong evidence that resultant accuracy is higher if the target provides more diagnostic behavior (and is thus more readable).[21] Moreover, in accord with the example described previously, accuracy is also related to the kind of personality trait being assessed. For example, it turns out that people can produce surprisingly accurate judgments of strangers' levels of extroversion, after just watching them for a few minutes interacting in a group. In contrast, judgments of neuroticism based on such information achieve chance levels of accuracy. The reason is simple – traits such as extroversion are more closely linked to observable behavior, whereas traits like neuroticism are much better hidden and less obviously expressed in everyday behavior.[22] David Funder confessed to me (personal communication) that he was concerned about his clear experimental demonstration of this explanation, in case he became known as the psychologist who showed that more visible and observable personality traits are . . . well . . . more visible and observable.

Consistent with common sense, the evidence also reveals that increased levels of acquaintanceship enhances the accuracy of trait judgments, although relatively little research has examined accuracy in intimate relationship contexts – acquaintanceship in prior research tends to stop at platonic friendship.[23] Investigation of the effects of the judge's ability has been less informative. Some have even argued that it is hardly worth investigating, given the evidence that suggests individual differences in such abilities (let us call it social intelligence) does not even exist.[24] I believe such judgments are premature.

There are several reasons for the failure to find compelling evidence for the existence of social intelligence as an individual difference variable. First, there is no point using designs of the sort that have been popular in social psychology, in which strangers make judgments based on observing thin slices of behavior. This kind of design means that the behavior of the target is almost certain to be the major factor in influencing subsequent judgments. Second, researchers ideally should get research participants to make judgments of more than one person, so they can assess their levels of consistency across targets. Third, it is advisable to make the task difficult and prolonged (but not impossible), rather than overly easy and assessed in a one-shot fashion. If chess-playing ability were being assessed, then the researcher would not get a sample of chess players to solve one simple chess problem (most people would do very well). Instead, the players would be posed several chess problems varying from moderately to extremely difficult. These three features have rarely been present in prior research on social intelligence. Hence, it is hardly surprising that evidence of individual differences in social intelligence has been hard to come by.

One thing researchers do know is that it is a waste of time asking people to report how good they are at judging others. Such self-reports of ability have a terrible track record at predicting the accuracy of social judgments – the average correlation between self-report measures and actual performance is close to zero.[25] So, if you have had the sneaking feeling (as I have always had) that people who confess that they have a special ability at reading and judging others are probably not the Einsteins of the social world, then trust your intuitions. Why this should be so is an interesting puzzle. The answer has, in part, been provided by William Ickes who has listed some of the reasons why people make lousy introspective judgments of their own abilities in judging others.[26] Taking his list, and adding one or two of my own items, here are some of the reasons:

- We make such judgments all day, every day, yet we receive almost no substantive, detailed feedback as to how well we are really doing.
- We often make such judgments without communicating them to the target, thereby preventing the possibility of feedback.
- Even when we do get feedback, it is not necessarily of high quality.
- People who are genuinely exceptionally high in social intelligence probably understand only too well the difficulty and subtlety of reading others. Accordingly, they may not rate themselves as fantastically good on self-report scales.
- Many judgments we make of others, and much of the underlying psychological processes, are automatic and unconscious.

The account so far is useful but limited. The reason is that documenting the amounts of variance associated with each causal category (e.g., the judge, the target, and the relationship) is not massively informative about the nature of the underlying causal processes involved. For example, if it turns out that there are no individual differences in the ability of people to read others, this would mean that the cognitive processes are essentially the same across individuals when controlling for the other causes involved (i.e., the readability of the target, the nature of the relationship between target and judge, and the nature of the judgment being made). However, this result would not mean that the cognitive processes are unimportant. To give an analogous example, even if we found that differences in the octane rating of gasoline did not influence the power output of the internal combustion engine, this does not mean that we could sensibly ignore the role of gasoline fuel in understanding how an internal combustion engine works.

In addition, the theoretical and research attention has been devoted to the attribution of traits or personality attributions. But a quintessential human social cognitive activity, especially in intimate relationships, involves the reading of each other's mind – the constant flux of emotions and thoughts as they occur online. How accurate is mind-reading in relationship contexts?

Reading Minds in Intimate Relationships

In a scene from Woody Allen's movie *Annie Hall*, Alvy and Annie, recently met, are having a conversation in Annie's apartment. They are obviously attracted to one another, but have not as yet started dating. Suddenly, their real thoughts and feelings appear as subtitles on the screen, as they carry on small-talk banalities (thoughts are in brackets):

Alvy: So, did you do those photographs in there, or what?
Annie: Yeah, yeah, I sort of dabble around, you know. (I dabble? Listen to me – what a jerk.)
Alvy: They're wonderful. They have a quality . . . (You are a great-looking girl.)
Annie: Well, I would like to take a serious photography course. (He probably thinks I'm a yo-yo.)
Alvy: Photography's interesting because, you know, it's a new form, and a set of aesthetic criteria have not emerged yet. (I wonder what she looks like naked.)
Annie: You mean whether it's a good photo or not. (I'm not smart enough for him. Hang in there.)
Alvy: The medium enters in as a condition of the art form itself. (I don't know what I'm saying – she senses I'm shallow.)
Annie: Well to me, it's all instinctive. You know, I mean, I just try to feel it. You know, I try to get a sense of it and not think about it so much. (God, I hope he doesn't turn out to be a schmuck like the others.)
Alvy: Still, you need a set of aesthetic guidelines to put it in social perspective, I think. (Christ, I sound like FM radio. Relax.)

Inspired by *Annie Hall*, Geoff Thomas and I have been investigating the causes and consequences of accuracy in mind-reading in intimate relationships. When people ask how on earth we measure the accuracy of mind-reading, I typically respond wryly (but accurately) – "with great difficulty." We first get couples in intimate heterosexual relationships to have ten-minute discussions of important problems in their relationships.[27] These discussions are videotaped and two copies are made. Then, each partner independently replays the videotape with a remote control, stops the tape when he or she can recall experiencing a thought or emotion, and writes it down. Most people stop the videotape about 12 times. These times are then swapped, and each partner goes through the videotape again, except this time they give their best guess as to what his/her partner was thinking and feeling at the time points indicated.

Using pairs of raters to assess the similarity between the pairs of statements from the two partners, it is possible to derive scores from each person that represents his or her accuracy in judging the partner. For example, if Miranda said she was angry at a given point on the videotape and Bernard (her partner) thought she was thinking what a nice fellow he was, then that would be counted as a complete miss. If Bernard thought she was feeling bad, that would be a ballpark hit. To score a bull's-eye, Bernard would have to report that his partner was angry.

Reviewing the videotape by the partners operates as a powerful mnemonic. The technique works well, providing the videotapes are reviewed immediately after the discussion takes place, participants are encouraged not to construct new thoughts and feelings when they review the tape, and they are assured that their partners will not get to see what they write down about their innermost thoughts. Of course, introspective reports are not infallible, will often be biased, and individuals do not have access to the unconscious flow of cognitive and affective activity. Nevertheless, honest self-reports of online cognitions and emotions (collected under appropriate conditions) provide reasonable ballpark descriptions of consciously experienced emotions and thoughts.

We have used this technique with samples of both married couples and dating couples.[28] In the dating study, we added a few novel features; namely, we also showed the videotapes to friends of the original couples, and a group of strangers, who did their best on the mind-reading task. Finally, we got everyone (dating couples, friends, and strangers) to do the same mind-reading task on some videotapes (and associated self-reports) of married couples discussing problems (that we already had available from some previous research). This design enabled us to ask and answer some questions that have hitherto not been dealt with in the relationship domain. For example, taking Mary and

Fred, if Fred is very accurate in mind-reading Mary, is this because Mary is easy to read, because Fred has natural ability at mind-reading, or because they have a happy relationship?

The central findings from the two studies (one using dating couples and one using married couples) can be summarized thus:

- Partners averaged close to a 50% accuracy hit rate in assessing what their partners were thinking and feeling.
- Friends of the dating partners were less accurate than partners in their mind-readings (41%), and strangers were the least accurate (39%).
- Individuals who did not know the couples they were mind-reading relied on the targets expressing their thoughts and feelings clearly in their verbal and nonverbal behavior, in order to obtain good levels of accuracy.
- In contrast, the mind-reading accuracy of the dating partners with each other was unrelated to how clearly individuals expressed their innermost thoughts and feelings in their verbal and nonverbal behavior.
- The longer couples were married, the worse their mind-reading became, but the more confident they became.
- The closer that people tracked and paid attention to each other during the discussion, the better they did. The reason that married couples who were married a long time did worse than younger married couples, was because they paid less attention to each other during the discussion.
- Individuals who were better at mind-reading someone they knew (partner or friend) were also better at mind-reading couples they did not know (with correlations across the mind-reading tasks of .32 to .73). This suggests some people are simply better at mind-reading than others (i.e., the existence of a social intelligence factor).
- Well-educated people did better at mind-reading than less well-educated folk.

Some of these findings can be understood from a social cognitive perspective. Strangers are relationship outsiders. When strangers try to assess the transient online thoughts and feelings of interacting partners, they must rely on general all-purpose stereotypes and theories about

119

relationships. Partners or friends of the couple, in contrast, are relationship insiders and have rich relationship and partner local theories that can help drive their own judgments. The fact that the relationship partners were the most accurate of the insiders was impressive, given that the couples were discussing important relationship problems that activated anxiety and negative thoughts. We know from analyzing the self-reports of cognitions and emotions produced in such problem-solving discussions, that people do get stirred up. The content of the private cognitive flow is typically a melange of dark thoughts and emotions – considerably more pessimistic and emotionally charged than the observable behavior, which tends to be sunnier and more positive. The typical pattern conjoins a slight furrowing of the brow, a subtle shift in the seat, and maybe a slight edge to the tone of voice, with a thought like "He always does that – it is so incredibly annoying."

Consider two of our findings together. First, individuals who did not know the couples they were mind-reading relied on the targets expressing their thoughts and feelings clearly in their verbal and nonverbal behavior, in order to obtain good levels of accuracy. Second, the mind-reading accuracy of the dating partners with each other was unrelated to how clearly individuals expressed their innermost thoughts and feelings in their verbal and nonverbal behavior. These two findings are exactly what one would expect to find *if* the insiders' judgments were theory-driven by local, specific theories and knowledge about the partner and the relationships. This does not mean that insiders use ESP to do their mind-reading. Of necessity, they rely on behavioral cues to make their judgments. However, when we know other people well, we become aware of idiosyncratic but diagnostic behaviors that outside observers are likely to miss. For example, a slight lowering of the eyes or a vein throbbing in a temple might reliably tell us that our partner is about to blow, or is especially angry. In long-term relationships a private and idiosyncratic message system (mainly nonverbal) might develop that is inscrutable to outsiders. Outsiders observe the same behavior but are likely to miss its diagnostic value.

Our findings of strong individual differences in mind-reading ability are intriguing in light of the widespread pessimism about their importance. A top-flight mind-reader is a person who is well-educated, has a high IQ, and is socially intelligent. Being a woman (rather than a man) also helps. These findings are consistent with research that has dealt with the accuracy of making personality attributions.[29] When combined

120

with situational factors, these attributes of the person explain a lot of the variance in mind-reading accuracy. An intelligent woman doing some mind-reading of her partner in problem-solving discussions should be able to achieve close to 70% accuracy. An unintelligent man would do well to break the 55% level in the same situation. An intelligent woman should be able to mind-read a couple who are complete strangers (an exceptionally difficult task) at above the 45% mark. An unintelligent man would probably dip well below the 30% accuracy level trying his hand at mind-reading strangers (even if he tried hard). The difference between 30% and 70% accuracy in mind-reading is vast – it is the same as the difference between a professional tennis player and a hack.

Social intelligence was assessed in the mind-reading studies by using a scale called the *Attributional Complexity Scale*.[30] This scale asks questions along a simple–complex continuum that assesses components like the level of motivation to explain human behavior, the tendency to infer complex rather than simple explanations, the tendency to infer causes from the distant past, and so forth. For example, it has statements that raters indicate their agreement with such as: "I am really curious about human behavior," "I enjoy getting into discussions where the causes for people's behavior are being talked about," and " I seldom take people's behavior at face value." Previous research with this scale has showed that higher levels of social intelligence do indeed predict increased levels of accuracy in making attributions of personality traits or attitudes to other people, but only under certain conditions; namely, when the task is reasonably difficult, the raters are highly motivated, they have plenty of time, and they have enough information available.[31] Moreover, scores on the Attributional Complexity Scale are unrelated to IQ.[32] Note that this scale, although a self-report instrument, does not directly ask people to estimate how accurate or good they are at making judgments about other people. Hence, it does not contain the same fatal flaw as do the scales assessing empathy.

The Connection between Mind-reading Accuracy and Relationship Evaluations

The nature of the link between the accuracy of judgments in intimate relationships and relationship evaluations, such as relationship satisfaction, is contentious. Some psychologists have argued that couples who

121

are in happier, more successful relationships must be more accurate in the way they read each other's minds or personalities, because this will enhance communication.[33] Others argue that the happier couples are, the more they will suffer from illusions and render inaccurate Pollyannaish judgments of another. Moreover, both sides can call on research findings to support their case. Some research finds that higher levels of relationship satisfaction, love, commitment, and so forth are related to higher levels of accuracy, whereas other research finds the exact opposite. The findings on mind-reading in intimate relationships are no exception, with the results going in both directions.

One of the Thomas et al. studies, which used married couples in long-standing relationships, found no relation at all between relationship satisfaction and mind-reading accuracy. The second Thomas et al. study I described, which used dating couples, found that couples who evaluated the relationship as closer and happier were more accurate. A third study by Jeffry Simpson, Bill Ickes, and others, using the same technique to assess mind-reading as previously described, had participants rate the attractiveness of rather gorgeous members of the opposite sex (who ostensibly were available and on campus) and then discuss their ratings while their partners were present.[34] To juice up the threatening nature of the task, and to hide the real purpose of the research, couples were told that the researchers needed ratings of the physical attractiveness of the photographs as part of some other dating research and the researchers wanted to match people properly (i.e., the photographs were of people on campus who were presumably available for dating). To add to the deception, participants were not initially aware that their discussions were being videotaped. The results showed that the couples who reported being closer and more intimate produced more *inaccurate* mind-readings than couples who were not as close (at least in the highly threatening situations).

These competing results can be understood by considering the different samples and contexts in which these three studies took place, and how they were likely to interact with two key motives: seeking the truth or maintaining positivity. In the Thomas and Fletcher studies, couples were discussing relationship problems that produced anxiety and defensiveness. However, in these studies couples were given the task of resolving the problems. For the married couples, the motivation to carry out in-depth processing to get at the truth would probably be lower than for the dating sample. The married couples in this particular sample had mostly been married for several years, their relationships were stable, and they had often already dealt with, or had come to terms with, their serious marital problems. The dating couples had commitment decisions yet to make, and may thus have been more inclined to slip into a truth-seeking mode. Thus, for the married couples, perhaps the two motives (seeking the truth versus maintaining positivity) cancelled each other out, whereas for the dating sample, the accuracy motive won out.

Of the three studies, the Simpson and Ickes study provided the most directly threatening context for the couples. Perhaps not surprisingly, partners in highly committed and intimate relationships are strongly motivated to avoid attributing lusty desires for alternative partners to their mates, even when such lascivious feelings and thoughts are in fact flitting through their partners' psyches. Thus, in this specific study, the committed, close partners were motivated to produce inaccurate mind-readings, the truth being just too psychologically disruptive to fully countenance.

My interpretations are speculative. But the general point is entrenched and powerful; namely, that causal connections between cognitions, emotions, and behavior are not straightforward, but twist and turn as a function of interactions between other psychological and contextual variables. Understanding those twists and turns is to understand the intimate relationship mind.

Conclusion

Social psychologists have often commented on the flawed or inaccurate nature of lay social judgments. But consider, for a moment, how many hurdles have to be clambered over in making accurate judgments of other people's personality traits, or of their ongoing emotions and cognitions, in intimate relationship contexts. The awkward conversation (and associated private thoughts and feelings) between Alvy and Annie Hall described earlier exemplifies the severe difficulties involved. First, behavioral information has to be available (which it often is not). Second, the information (when available) needs to be a reliable, diagnostic indicator of the trait or mental item in question (which it often is not, as when, e.g., an individual feigns being upset in order to elicit sympathy and guilt). Third, perceivers have to pick up and appropriately use the information. Given that such information is often fleeting and comes packaged among a swarm of related behaviors, this is no easy task. To be effective, this stage often relies on the perceiver having special local knowledge of the target, or it might depend on the judge possessing high levels of social intelligence.

In short, I am struck not by the inaccuracy of human social judgments, but by how accurate they are in relationship contexts. The glass can be viewed as either half full or half empty. I view the accuracy glass as half full, given the apparently mundane yet almost miraculous ability of humans to make judgments of intimate others based on a welter of information (or virtually no information at all) while automatically accessing elaborate and complex stores of information and theories, often during the course of a complicated social interaction. The abilities of humans to make such social judgments is, however, not a miracle, but an understandable outcome of a being that has a powerful brain, kitted out by evolutionary forces to function effectively within an intensely social and intimate human landscape.

It is virtually inconceivable that Shakespeare could be completely wrong about anything. But he is not infallible. Love is in the mind, but it is not always painted blind.

Chapter 6

Communication and Relationship Success

Research indicates that communication problems are the major source of interpersonal difficulties. For example, most marital and family problems stem from misunderstanding, from ineffective communication, which results in frustration and anger when implicit expectations and desires are not fulfilled.
Okun, 1997

The notion that good communication helps produce successful and happy relationships is both widely expounded and accepted in Western cultures, right up there with beliefs that punishment deters crime or that regular brushing prevents tooth decay. It is a maxim remorselessly expounded by the snake-oil relationship merchants, as well as by a phalanx of respectable clinicians and marital counselors (as exemplified in the above quotation from a widely used counseling text). Yet, three decades of scientific research and theorizing have left this proposition in a decidedly shaky position. What this sustained research and scholarly effort has revealed, in its place, is the subtlety and complexity of communication in relationships, and an appreciation of why such unadorned claims about the power of good communication are muddled at best.

I begin with the twin concepts of "good" communication and "successful" relationships. It is, unfortunately, only too easy to slip into defining and measuring the two concepts purely in terms of one another, so that they become empirically related as a matter of logical necessity. Some of the earliest research investigating the role of communication fell straight into this trap. A study by Leslie Navran published in 1967 reported a huge positive correlation between good communication and marital happiness of .82.[1] This is close to the sort of correlation obtained by the same people completing the same scale on two separate occasions. Navran obtained this correlation by getting participants in relationships to complete two separate scales, ostensibly measuring good communication and marital satisfaction respectively. However, on closer inspection, the marital satisfaction measure included a good number of items that were carbon copies of the items used to assess communication (e.g., "Do you confide in your mate?").[2] Thus, a strong positive correlation was a guaranteed product between scores from the two scales.

I confess that this kind of problem commonly crops up in relationship research that has relied on self-report questionnaires in determining what predicts relationship or marital quality.[3] One basic problem is that commonly used self-report measures of marital quality (developed 30 to 50 years ago) include a potpourri of items. For example the Dyadic Adjustment Scale, developed by Graham Spanier in 1976 and since used in over 1,000 studies, contains a broad array of constructs ranging from perceived happiness or satisfaction to self-reports of behavioral interactions involving the frequency of quarrels, the number of shared activities, the extent of agreement on important issues, and problems with sex or affection.[4] Clearly, one should not use the Dyadic Adjustment Scale alongside self-report measures of constructs like communication, arguments, intimacy, or sexual activity (although such use has been common).

The golden rule – I learned many years ago – is never to take the title conferred on any given scale by the scale designer at face value. The meaning of the scale items should always be checked to assess how narrowly or broadly they apply. Fortunately, this problem has repeatedly been pointed out in academic publications over the last two decades, and alternative scales to those described above have been developed to measure perceptions of relationship quality that largely avoid such problems. These alternative measures of relationship quality are confined to asking a few questions on simple global evaluative scales, such as levels of satisfaction, commitment, and happiness. Such scales can then be correlated with self-reports of things like conflict or sexual activity, without running into the problem of item-overlap. Moreover, a substantive body of research has accumulated that measures constructs like communication, arguments, and intimacy by observing and measuring couples' interactive behavior, rather than relying purely on self-report scales.

So, how should the quality of communication and relationships be

126

defined and measured? Relationship scientists typically define successful relationships in two ways – the extent to which relationships survive (stability) and the perceptions of relationship quality by partners in on-going relationships. One could quibble with both methods of measuring relationship success. A couple may be relatively happy with the relationship, whereas the relationship may appear to an outsider as long past its use-by date. Nevertheless, these two criteria of relationship success make intuitive sense. Moreover, both factors can be readily and reliably measured, and are important variables to assess in their own right, even if relationship success is construed in some broader fashion.

The construct of "good communication" suffers from more serious definitional problems than does "relationship success." It is possible, of course, to use the standard "insider" criterion; namely, how the relationship participants themselves perceive the quality of their communication. The empirical results of such an exercise show that those who are comfortably ensconced in happier and more satisfying relationships faithfully report that they also communicate more positively and effectively (typically producing correlations in the .40 to .60 range, depending on the exact nature of the question asked).[5] This result is obtained even when the shoddy practice of asking almost identical questions about relationship happiness and communication – as described previously – is carefully avoided. But how should such a result be interpreted? Given that almost everyone believes that good communication produces good relationships, and vice versa, and the associated vagueness of the term "communication," such a result may not be terribly informative. One can almost hear research participants thinking: "My relationship is wonderful, so I guess our communication must be good" (or vice versa).

The relationship scientist could switch tactics and assess different behavioral components of relationship functioning that could be objectively observed, and come up with a "good communication" index. Consider, for a moment, the difficulties in accomplishing such an exercise. Your partner lies to you when you ask him if he likes your new hat. Is this good communication (he is being kind and avoiding hurting your feelings) or bad communication (he is being dishonest)? Your partner goes to the mall when he is angry with you in order to calm down. Is this good communication (he is controlling his anger) or bad communication (he is withdrawing and not dealing with the problem)? Your partner sometimes fakes orgasms – is this good communication (she doesn't want to puncture your fragile sense of masculinity) or bad

127

communication (she is misleading you)? If you find such questions tricky, it may be some consolation that relationship scientists are divided (and sometimes nonplussed) when they attempt to objectively define and measure the nature and quality of "good communication."

On the plus side, there is general agreement that the way in which couples deal with the inevitable conflict or problems that crop up in relationships, and how they communicate their subsequent thoughts and feelings to one another, is a critical element (many have suggested *the* critical element) in determining the success of intimate relationships. However, this is about as far as the consensus extends, with different theoretical accounts offering a puzzlingly inconsistent set of relevant research findings.

Conflict and How to Handle it

Our partners can be irritating, obnoxious, insensitive, and downright impossible. Our own relationship behavior, if we are in an expansive or brutally honest frame of mind, can also occasionally leave something to be desired. Almost everyone experiences dark or uncharitable emotions and thoughts in intimate relationships. Two competing theories have been advanced by relationship scientists specifying how individuals should best deal with such mental events: the *good communication* model and the *good management* model.

The good communication model is based around three empirical postulates, describing what couples in successful relationships are supposed to do with their negative thoughts and emotions. First, they frankly express their negative feelings and cognitions (albeit in a diplomatic fashion). Second, they deal openly with conflict – they don't stonewall, withdraw, or go shopping. Third, they honestly attempt to solve their problems. If the problems are not dealt with, then it is believed they will stick around and eat away at the foundations of the relationship over time, or return at a later date possibly in a more corrosive and lethal form.

The good management model is also based around three empirical postulates. First, the regular and open expression of negative thoughts and feelings is posited as corrosive for relationships. Second, it is proposed that exercising good communication skills often involves compromise and accommodation to the partner's behavior (and not shooting from the hip with uncharitable emotions and cognitions). Third, relationships always have problems or issues that cannot be solved. People in successful relationships supposedly recognize them, accept them as insoluble, and put them on the cognitive backburner. They don't get obsessive about them, or fruitlessly struggle to solve them.

Both models possess some intuitive plausibility. Moreover, each has a body of research evidence to call upon in support. Buttressing the good communication model, studies by John Gottman and others have found that expressing anger and disagreement is actually associated with increases in marital satisfaction over time.[6] Other studies have reported that avoidance of conflict and increased stonewalling are associated with lower levels of satisfaction and increased breakup rates.[7]

In a recent study, Geoff Thomas, Russil Durrant, and I tested the good management versus the good communication model by getting observer raters to examine videotapes of 56 married couples each engaged in ten-minute problem-solving sessions. These observer raters also had access to reports from the couples of their own emotions and cognitions, which the married partners had independently furnished previously (immediately after the interactions) while reviewing the videotapes, and in which they had also noted the exact time each thought or emotion had occurred (the time in seconds was electronically embedded in the videos). The observer raters coded the extent to which each person's negative cognitions or emotions were expressed in both their verbal and nonverbal behavior.[8] The results showed that both men and women in happier marriages expressed their negative emotions and thoughts *more* frequently in problem-solving discussions.[9] Thus, the good communication model was supported.

In support of the good management model of relationship success, an extensive program of research by Caryl Rusbult and her colleagues has reported that people who have more successful relationships tend to sacrifice their own personal interests and needs, swallow hard, and ignore or respond positively to their partner's irritating or negative behaviors.[10] In addition, studies of problem-solving behavior by Thomas Bradbury, among others, have shown that partners in happier relationships are more likely to ignore their partner's negative behavior or to respond to it in a benign fashion.[11]

Resolving the paradox

So what is the poor individual in a relationship to do when his or her partner does something bad – swallow hard and say nothing or communicate furiously? How can these competing models, and the relevant supporting research, be resolved? The first step toward unraveling the Gordian knot is to return to my prior discussions that dealt with relationship emotions and cognitions. One crucial point here is that the way in which people appraise, interpret, and explain problems or negative events in their relationships plays a prime role in producing subsequent cognitions and emotions (and behavior). In some circumstances the behavior itself can be interpreted as either positive or negative – as in my prior example of June's partner alluding to her "sexy" appearance while having a coffee with friends. If June believes that her partner thinks she is overweight, June will interpret the remark as a cruel barb, but if June believes that her partner admires her body, she will interpret it as a genuine compliment.

Even if the partner's behavior is unambiguously negative, the way in which it is interpreted will play a decisive role in which emotions and cognitions are produced. Bill's partner is short with him. If Bill is feeling disillusioned about the relationship, he may attribute insensitivity to her, blame her for what he perceives as an unfair response to his polite inquiry, and become angry. On the other hand, if Bill's local relationship theory is in good shape, he is likely to attribute her remark to a cold she is suffering from, and experience mild annoyance rather than full-blown anger. In the former case, Bill yells angrily at his partner that she is an insensitive so-and-so. In the latter case, Bill frowns, and offers solicitude and a lemon drink for her cold.

If an observer (a stranger in both cases) were to watch the dyadic behavior of Bill and his partner in the two cases, without knowing anything of the hidden cognition involved, he or she might well jump to some wrong conclusions. In the former case it might appear to an observer as if Bill is responding according to the good communication model, and expressing his feelings openly and honestly. In the latter case, it will look to an observer like Bill is following the good management model, because he is not expressing his anger openly. In reality, the behavior in both cases is calibrated consistently with the underlying thoughts and feelings – in both cases, Bill is communicating his mental states accurately and openly.

One issue this example illustrates is that researchers (or counselors for that matter) need to take into account lay relationship theories and related cognitive processes when assessing the good management versus the good communication models – they cannot just go on the observable behavior. In studies that have attempted to tease apart the behavior from the underlying cognition and affect, good support has been found for the good communication model.[12] However, there are some intriguing gender differences that have been replicated across studies; namely, men are happier if their wives follow the good management model, whereas women are happier if their husbands follow the good communication model.[13] These findings are remarkably (and perhaps uncomfortably) consistent with folk stereotypes about gender differences in intimate relationships.

Another possibility is suggested by the proverb "moderation in all things." On this account, it is not healthy to routinely conform to either model. If individuals automatically and routinely squash their own negative feelings in the interests of harmony and of keeping their partners sweet, this may ultimately prove disastrous. One's partner is unlikely to appreciate or understand the sacrifice involved, and may simply come to see one as a doormat. On the other hand, if an individual scrupulously insists on complete honesty, and openly expresses every passing cognition and emotion (with little regard to the state of the relationship or the feelings of his or her partner), this may prove equally problematic. If every married couple started communicating openly and honestly, the divorce rate would be likely to climb alarmingly (consider such revelations as "I wish your penis was bigger," "I always liked your sister more than you," "I stole some money from you years ago," "I have always hated the shape of your nose," and so forth). In spite of its plausibility, little research has explicitly tested this hypothesis (to my knowledge).

Another plausible idea, often floated by relationship scientists, is that it may depend on the compatibility between partners rather than on the style of communication itself. Thus, if both partners adopt either the open communication model or the good management model, they should have a stable and happy relationship. On the other hand, if one partner is working off the good communication model while his or her partner is adopting the good management model, this should be a recipe for confusion and heartache. This notion has some empirical support. For example, there is evidence that in relationships in which one individual is vainly attempting to discuss a problem (most often the woman) while the other partner withdraws and stonewalls (most often the man), this is associated with both short-term and long-term unhappiness.[14]

Consistent with the notion that compatibility matters, John Gottman claims to have identified three basic types of couples who are able to form stable and (relatively) happy relationships.[15] Gottman's taxonomy is similar to one developed by Mary Fitzpatrick who also divides couples into three categories.[16] Combining aspects of the two schemas (and associated empirical work), and putting my own spin and labels on the resultant taxonomy, I posit the following thumbnail stereotypes as characterizing the three most common relationship styles that are both stable (unlikely to break up) and reasonably happy (according to the self-reports of the participants).

Type 1 is the *good communication* relationship. Individuals in this style adhere to the good communication model. They approach conflict, discuss problems in an open and honest fashion, and they sometimes communicate about the relationship itself – where it is going and whether it is helping them to grow as individuals. The individuals in these relationships tend to have liberal views, and are typically well educated. They consciously think about their relationships a lot, and enjoy talking about their relationships with their partners and friends. They also nurture their relationships, and express their love and admiration for one another frequently, but they value their individuality and freedom to grow. Good exemplars of these relationships are portrayed in Woody Allen movies (at least in their more angst-free stages).

Type 2 is the *good management* relationship. These folk avoid conflict, and seldom talk about their relationship or where it is going. They do not talk to each other about how hard they have to work on the relationship. They openly accept their closeness and dependency on one another, without becoming obsessive about their loss of individuality. They tend to be affectionate and warm with one another, but retain a rather rigid and traditional structure. These couples are happy with ultrapredictable and stereotyped interactions. In short, these relationships resemble those of my own parents. Other exemplars from movies and TV (which might be more helpful) are *The Brady Bunch* parents, and the parents of John-Boy from *The Waltons*.

Type 3 is the *volatile* relationship. These couples do not appear to fit either the good communication or the good management prototypes. They bicker and argue a lot over apparently minor things. They are feisty and assertive. They say what they think, when they think it. They are also more likely than the other two groups to resort to physical violence. However, they also enjoy passionate make-up sex, and can express love and affection in an uninhibited fashion. These relationships are not boring. Exemplars I can think of are George's parents in *Seinfeld*, Jack and Vera in *Coronation Street*, or perhaps Homer and Marge Simpson in the cartoon TV series *The Simpsons*. Working-class marriages in Britain, Italy, or in the USA (as they are portrayed in movies at least) often conform to this model.

Research on these different types of stable and happy relationships is limited, and, like all stereotypes, they are cardboard cutouts. Reality is messier, so that only a minority of relationships will neatly fit a particular prototype. Still, the fact that such different, and apparently successful, kinds of relationships exist should give pause to the legions of pop-psychologists and marital counselors who insist that relationships in trouble should be molded to fit only one model – namely, the good communication relationship.

So, where are we left at this point? The analysis so far illustrates the complexity and subtlety of the process and concept of communication. The related research is voluminous and informative, but only takes us so far. Almost everybody in relationships routinely, and often automatically, controls the expression of negative emotions and cognitions, up to and including ruthlessly repressing them. On the other hand, the trick in successful relationships seems to be how and when to control this process. True, in our own research, we have found that more happily married couples were more likely to express their negative emotions and thoughts. But, couples in this research were given the explicit goal of discussing and resolving a relationship problem. In other relationship contexts (e.g., working together to achieve a common goal, such as planning a holiday or organizing a dinner party), such findings could well be reversed.

The same point applies to the expression of anger, a controversial topic in the relationship literature. That is, the expression of anger or irritation (within bounds) seems to be mildly beneficial for relationships, when couples are in conflict-resolution mode. In this context, anger communicates to the partner that (1) I am not a doormat; (2) this is important to me, so listen to what I am saying; (3) I care enough about the relationship to bother exhibiting my concerns; and (4) will you "please" alter your behavior! On the other hand, the expression of

133

even mild anger and irritation in contexts when the partner needs support and soothing is particularly corrosive for relationships. Consider, for example, how you might react if you were desperately and obviously tired, you had an important and difficult meeting the next day, and your partner exhibited irritation (rather than sympathy or support) when you asked him or her for some advice. In such a context, the expression of mild irritation or anger communicates that (1) I don't care for my partner, or (2) I do not love my partner, or (3) I cannot be counted on when the chips are down.[17]

Thus, it may well be the ability to adjust communication strategies and behaviors according to the contextual demands that is critical in maintaining close and successful relationships. Partners who adopt either the good communication or the good management strategy as a consistent default option, across time and across social contexts, will have fewer psychological resources to cope with the inevitable relationship hurdles thrown across our paths. Of course there are two people to consider in intimate relationships, so the way in which couples negotiate and harmonize their individual communicative styles will be an important ingredient in determining relationship success. However, one relationship size does not fit all. There exist a range of relationship communication styles that all appear to be successful, but which are strikingly different from one another.

Communication style might be important in predicting relationship success (although the story is obviously a complex one), but it is clearly not the only potentially important factor. What are the roles of such factors as personality, similarity of attitudes, age at marriage, or the amount of money coming into the family? And, how well is relationship longevity and happiness predicted by such factors? A large body of research that answers such questions has accumulated over several decades.

Predicting Relationship Success

Research documenting the best predictors of relationship success has uncovered a similar set of factors for both dating and marital relationships (at least in Western cultures).[18] The most recent authoritative review of the marital literature was published in 1995 by Benjamin Karney and Thomas Bradbury who analyzed 115 separate studies (representing some 45,000 marriages, mainly in the USA) in a meta-analysis that examined marital relationships over time. A meta-analysis averages the size of the effects across several studies, thus, increasing one's confidence in the results. This review revealed the standard set of sociodemographic predictors of marital longevity that sociologists have known about for many years.[19] Being married at a younger age, having less money, being less well educated, being unemployed, and receiving welfare all increase the chances of the marriage dissolving. However, the effects these variables have are relatively small, ranging from zero to a 15% increased probability of divorce.

Personality factors also predict relationship success. Chances of the marriage dissolving are increased if one is an introvert, or disagreeable, or lazy, or closed to new experiences, and either depressed or neurotic. However, again, the effects this class of variables have are generally rather small. Possessing an unstable, neurotic personality has the biggest effect, producing an increased chance of divorce of 16% for men and 18% for women averaged across several studies. However, the effects of the other personality variables (just listed) on the probability of divorce are quite a lot lower, ranging from zero to 11%.

Some studies have also reported that higher similarity in partners, in terms of values, attitudes, and personality traits, increases the chances of relationship success (in terms of both staying together and of attaining higher levels of relationship satisfaction). The belief that higher similarity between partners is good for relationships is a popular one in both folk psychology and in scientific psychology. Indeed, it is a generalization that one finds frequently expounded both in academic textbooks and pop-psychology treatises. The empirical evidence, however, is less than convincing. It turns out that empirically testing the role of similarity has some methodological and statistical traps for the unwary that more than a few psychologists have fallen into.[20] A few recent studies have tested the role of similarity between partners (in relation to relationship satisfaction) more rigorously to avoid such traps, and these have uniformly found rather weak or even nonexistent links between similarity in attitudes or personality traits and perceptions of relationship quality.[21]

Intriguingly, what has emerged as a substantial and well-replicated finding is that the more that couples *perceive* themselves to be similar, the happier they are with the relationship.[22] One plausible explanation for this finding is that individuals are simply inferring such a link on the

basis of the commonly held belief that higher similarity between partners is good for relationships. These findings illustrate the power of lay
relationship theories and the way in which they can systematically color
or distort perceptions of relationship reality.

There are two variables (both psychological) that stand out from the
pack as the most powerful predictors of divorce – perceptions of relationship quality and the positivity of behavior evinced during the course
of couples discussing problems about their relationships in laboratory
settings (that are filmed or videotaped). Averaging across studies, lower
levels of relationship satisfaction or more negative behavior increase the
chances of divorce by 23% to 30% (some studies calculate their results
separately for men and women, and some calculate couple-level scores).
Research has also shown, not surprisingly, that these two factors (perceptions of relationship quality and the positivity of relationship behavior
displayed during the course of problem-solving discussions) are quite
highly correlated, typically from .30 to .50. Moreover, one recent study
I carried out with Geoff Thomas, that tracked 56 marriages over a one-
year period, suggested that perceptions of relationship happiness and a
couple's problem-solving behavior are locked together in causal loops,
each influencing the other over time.[23]

Longitudinal research, using either self-report or behavioral measures, typically ends up successfully predicting about 80% or so of which
married couples will remain together versus get divorced.[24] Such results sound impressive, and they are, but the story is more complicated
on closer scrutiny. I will illustrate taking the results from a recent study
by Sybil Carrère and others.[25] This research extensively interviewed 95
recently married couples about their relationship and partners, and the
results were coded along a variety of positive versus negative dimensions to produce a measure termed *perceived marital bond*. The perceived marital bond, in turn, correctly predicted whether couples would
get divorced from six to nine years later for 81% of the marriages. These
predictions, it should be noted, are generated via standard statistical
algorithms in computer programs, and are not made in a seat-of-the-
pants fashion by the researchers. The overall results from this study are
shown in table 6.1.

Note that the overall predictive success (81%) was not evenly spread
across the groups, with the perceived marital bond predicting those
couples who stayed together much more accurately (96%) than for those
who divorced (46%). This asymmetry is not peculiar to this study, but is

136

Table 6.1 Predicting divorce (data from Carrère et al., 2000)

	Predictions	
Actual Outcome	*Remain Married*	*Divorced*
Married = 79	64	15
Divorced = 16	3	13

Remain Married = 83%   Accuracy = 96%   Accuracy = 46%

the usual finding in such research, regardless of whether behavior or self-reports of relationship quality are used to predict breakup, and regardless of whether marital or dating couples are tracked over time.[26] That is, the predictor variables typically overpredict breakup – a finding suggesting there exist factors that keep relationships going that are not being assessed in such work. It is not difficult to guess what some of these missing factors might be, including norms and beliefs about the importance of marriage, economic factors, fear of disapproval from family and friends, beliefs that it is important to stay together for the sake of the children, and so forth. People rarely seek a divorce lightly. Almost always it is the result of a lengthy and agonizing psychological struggle with the status and nature of local lay relationship theories occupying center stage.

Notice also that in the study just described, the majority of couples stayed together (84%). If one knew the base rate in advance, then the predictive success of the perceived marital bond would be exceeded by simply guessing that every couple would stay together. Also, note that if the breakup rate was 50%, then a coin toss would produce a 50% accuracy hit rate by chance. Thus, the predictive success rate needs to take chance accuracy into account. Nevertheless, the research of John Gottman, Thomas Bradbury, and others has shown that the seeds of the fate of marriages are already deeply sown at the time couples get married.[27] Local relationship theories play a central role in determining how relationships unfold.

Psychologists began the direct observation of dyadic behavior in marital and other intimate relationships in the early 1970s. Most notably, John Gottman and his colleagues have thoroughly analyzed the various forms of dyadic interchanges that take place in marital

137

interaction (especially those that concern the way in which couples handle conflict or relationship problems). This work has highlighted the fundamental finding described already: less negative interactive behavior equals greater happiness and longevity. One might object that the average eight-year-old (not to mention one's grandmother) could have predicted this finding. My response is that it is crucial for scientists to test empirical postulates, no matter how self-evident they may appear to be. There is a long history of commonsensical, obvious claims being toppled under scientific empirical scrutiny. Moreover, this body of work has revealed some subtle features of relationship interaction that contradict some basic axioms of popular forms of marital therapy, not to mention the edicts pumped out by pop-psychology treatises.

In the 1960s and 1970s marital therapists often based their interventions on a theory of "good" relationship interaction derived from Skinnerian behaviorism. This kind of therapy attempted (vainly) to get couples to drop their own theorizing about the relationship (naturally filled with mentalistic concepts that are anathema to radical behaviorism) and to embrace a "scientific" approach. Typically, the partners signed contingency contracts in which they would agree to reinforce one another for positive behaviors and to ignore each other for negative behaviors. For example, the husband might agree to talk to and cuddle his wife in response to his wife getting his slippers and retrieving cold beers from the fridge, and vice versa. This approach was based on the behaviorist assumption that successful marriages would be characterized by partners intelligently providing each other with appropriate reinforcers when the other behaved in a pleasing or displeasing fashion.

The research results, published by Gottman and others, showed that a behaviorist approach had it precisely backwards – unhappy, short-lived marriages were characterized by individuals responding in a fine-grained quid pro quo fashion, for both negative *and* positive behaviors. In contrast, successful marriages comprised a mixed salad of positive and negative behaviors that were not produced in response to the positivity of the partner's behavior in any sort of fine-grained fashion. For years, marital therapists had attempted to get their unhappy couples to mimic the classic interactional patterns of unsuccessful, *not* successful, marriages (a good example of an apparently self-evident hypothesis being dead wrong).

Contemporary marital therapies have not ignored the flood of scientific research on intimate relationships. Straight behaviorist approaches to marital therapy have disappeared, and modern approaches typically build in some sort of attack on the attributions or cognitions that individuals hold about their relationships and partners.[28] However, research continues to throw doubt on popular maxims or techniques adopted in marital therapy. For example, the practice of "active listening" is a key element in much marital therapy. In this model the art of good communication in conflict situations runs as follows: First, one partner (say the wife) clearly states her complaint. Second, the other partner (the husband) is required to paraphrase her complaint (with no defensiveness) and check it out with her. Third, he then sympathizes with or empathizes with her concerns. In addition, individuals are encouraged to use the "I" term and to state how they feel, and what they want, rather than to attribute the problems automatically to their partners.

If anyone reading this book can confidently state that is how they and their partners discuss serious or abiding relationship problems in which emotions run high, raise your hand. I suspect few hands will be raised. When John Gottman thoroughly investigated the role of active listening in 137 newlyweds (and in another large sample) he found (to his astonishment) that it hardly ever took place, regardless of the state of the relationship.[29] Partners almost never paraphrased or summarized what they thought their partner was thinking or feeling, and they hardly ever overtly validated their partner's feelings. Instead, if the process of validation happened at all, it was conveyed subtly via head nods, grunts, and brief vocalizations.[30]

The fact that active listening does not characterize successful relationships does not mean that it is necessarily a washout when it comes to fixing relationships that are in trouble. It is possible that instigating an artificial and ordinarily difficult way of communicating may prove to be an effective circuit breaker in a troubled relationship. However, such a technique is often sold as a permanent relationship fixture, rather than as a temporary solution. The admonition to always use "I" statements in the heat of the battle strikes me as setting the bar rather too high for most folks. As Daniel Wile puts it "It is impossible to make 'I-statements' when you are in the 'hating-my-partner, wanting revenge, feeling stung-and-needing-to-sting-back' state of mind. At such a moment you cannot remember what an 'I-statement' is, and frankly, you do not care."[31]

Returning to John Gottman's more subtle findings, his research shows that it is not any old negative behavior that predicts the breakdown of

relationships but the heavy-duty negative behavior of contempt, bellig-
erence, and defensiveness. You know the sort of thing – snipes and
barbs, rolling of the eyes, belittling remarks in public, refusal to accept
any influence, attributions of stupidness and laziness, and charges of
irresponsibility, selfishness, and blame – typically accompanied with that
sort of carping, negative tone of voice that says "you are either an idiot,
or unlovable, or contemptuous." It is perhaps not surprising that many
couples call it a day after years of undergoing such a sustained barrage.

In my own research I have found evidence that people who are unhappy with their relationships tend to blame their partners for marital
problems, which in turn leads to snide remarks and other negative
behavior during problem-solving behavior. Thus, a vicious circle is completed that is hard to break.[32] In contrast, happy couples, even when
discussing relationship problems, display affection and regard for one
another. They prevent mudslinging interactions from occurring by
soothing one another, and they use humor to defuse situations. They
also seem to have the capacity to argue and to get hot under the collar
without crossing the line into character assassination and the kind of
abuse that is difficult to forget and hard to forgive. In short, they display the kind of behavior we associate with couples who love and respect one another.

There is certainly a strong case for the ready availability of affordable
effective marital therapy and counseling. There is a wealth of evidence
attesting to the negative consequences of divorce or separation.[33] Divorce or separation increases the chances of both men and women suffering from poor mental and physical health, suicide, drug problems,
mental illness, automobile accidents, and violence. The children of divorce are also likely to suffer from a range of problems including depression, health problems, problems at school, and behavioral difficulties.
However, the empirical evidence shows that the effectiveness of marital
therapy is limited. A recent *Consumer Reports* study showed that marital therapy received the lowest ratings, compared to other problem
domains, from psychotherapy clients.[34] Most couples (75%) report improvement in their levels of marital satisfaction, but long-term follow-
ups show that about 30 to 40% maintain improvement, whereas the
remainder relapse.[35]

The success rate of marital therapy has left some psychologists working in the field in a state of pessimism.[36] However, such judgments are
unduly gloomy. It is problematic to necessarily count divorce or sepa-

ration as a failure. If the process of therapy convinces one or both partners that the best course of action is to leave the relationship, and empowers them to take that course, such an outcome does not necessarily constitute a failure. Persuading a woman, who has been viciously abused and beaten by her husband, to leave her relationship seems like a successful outcome to me.

Moreover, it is difficult to exaggerate the magnitude of the task facing the psychologist or marital counselor. Producing relationship change involves two people who may well have local relationship theories that clash, and who have varying degrees of commitment to the relationship. It is frequently the case that one person in an intimate relationship decides to leave, rather than the breakup being a joint decision. Therapists have a tendency to view the problems and solutions in marriage in terms of communication skills. However, local relationship theories and judgments of trust, affection, commitment, and so forth, are based on a long history of relationship interaction, and are resistant to change on demand. Marital therapy also focuses (quite reasonably) on the relationship between the partners. But, relationship problems are often located in the personalities of each individual, along with the social and economic context. If one person in a marriage is neurotic, clinically depressed, addicted to alcohol or drugs, or is unemployed or homeless, then such problems are not likely to be remedied with a spot of marital counseling or, indeed, reading the latest pop-psychology book offering a quick-fix solution.

The success rate of marital therapies also needs to be interpreted within a broader context, in which human nature, and our evolutionary heritage, are taken into account. Humans fall in love, have extramarital sex, fall out of love, sometimes choose mates badly, and often face stressors and demands on their relationship outside of their control. Given the extraordinary social and technological environment we currently live in, the way in which we are assaulted with glossy images of attractive alternative mates, and the freedom we have in Western countries to form and dissolve long-term relationships, the number of marriages that stay the course for life is truly impressive. Given the difficult and complex nature of the task, the success with which expert psychologists and therapists can help people make decisions, communicate more effectively, and cope with distress in intimate relationships is equally impressive.

141

Is divorce in the genes?

Behavioral genetics research has regularly found that about 50% of the variability in many human traits, from personality to intelligence, is produced by genetic influences.[37] Alongside this result, the other striking finding is that the shared family background and parental influences exert negligible influences. In contrast, what is termed "nonshared" factors bulk large, suggesting that events and experiences that happen to only one sibling have a large influence on development. This research has been extended to the study of divorce, with two studies by Matt McGue and his colleagues reporting that genes are responsible for about 50% of the tendency to get divorced. There is no suggestion that there is a specific gene for divorce per se.[38] Rather, the general explanation is that genes predispose people to develop negative personality traits, like neuroticism or insecurity, that increase the probability of marital breakdown.

The findings from behavioral genetics research have gained such currency in the media, and in science generally, that I will go into some detail here. Time for some whistle-blowing. Over the last decade or so a critical chorus has been building in the academic literature, which seriously questions such claims.[39] No one doubts the proposition that many human traits are, in part, inherited. However, the percentages bandied around for the influences of genes, versus family, versus unique events or experiences, are now in serious doubt.

One standard approach, the one adopted in the divorce research, is to compare a set of identical (monozygotic) twins with nonidentical (dizygotic) twins. The critical assumption made, before any calculations are performed, is that *if* the trait in question is *completely* genetically determined, then the monozygotic twins should be twice as similar as the dizygotic twins on the trait or event in question. For example, if variability in divorce happened to be totally caused by the genes, and the correlation between the monozygotic twins in the tendency to get divorced was .60, then the same correlation for the dizygotic twins should be .10 (a difference of .50). If the difference between the two correlations is less than .50, this implies something else is causing divorce (apart from the genes). These assumptions are based on the fact that monozygotic twins share 100% of their genes, and dizygotic twins share (on average) 50% of their genes (the difference between 100% and 50% is where the .50 benchmark difference just described comes from).

The data from the twins are crunched in a complicated data-analytic model, in which the variance is distributed among three basic categories. The first category comprises the *genetic variance*, which is determined according to the assumption just outlined. Any variance left over is then placed into a second category termed the *shared environment*. This category is statistically defined as anything that tends to make the twins more similar than they should be by chance, and is often interpreted as the family effect. Finally, any variance left over, after the variance is distributed between the genetic and the shared environment, is placed in a third compartment called the *nonshared* category. This final category is defined as other events that tend to make the twins more different than they should be by chance – such events are typically interpreted as unique experiences that only one twin has (such as the effect of peers, or schooling, or mates). There is no statistical variance left over after such a statistical analysis – it all adds up to 100%.

The statistical analysis used in behavioral genetics is like a stack of cards that all depends on the original assumption that *if* the trait in question is completely genetically determined, *then* the monozygotic twins on the item in question (say divorce) should be twice as similar compared to the dizygotic twins. Unfortunately, this assumption is wrong. It is based on the supposition that genes have one-to-one effects on the trait in question (termed "additive effects") rather than interactive effects (termed "nonadditive effects"). Behavioral geneticists, along with everyone else, cheerfully admit this proposition must be wrong.

To understand why, consider an imaginary case in which the human genome contained relatively few genes (say 200) with only four genes varying across individuals. The pair of monozygotic twins would not only have the same 200 genes, but they would be in exactly the same order strung along the DNA. A pair of dizygotic twins, in contrast, would share 198 genes (the same 196 as every human possesses plus two out of the four variable genes). However, the order in which these four variable genes would be strung along the DNA is likely to be different across the dizygotic twins. Most human traits are produced by genes acting interactively – the effect of any single gene will, thus, depend on the genetic environment provided by the other genes. This genetic environment is identical for monozygotic twins, but it is different in dizygotic twins. Thus, identical twins might both be musical geniuses or mathematical wizards, because of the genetic environment in which certain specific genes are located. Now scale up the example to other humans who have anywhere from 30,000 to 50,000 genes (the true figure is currently uncertain). Because the assumption that genes have strictly additive effects is wrong, this means that if divorce (or whatever is being explained) was totally determined genetically, the monozygotic twins would be considerably more than twice as similar compared to dizygotic twins.[40]

This problem means that estimates from behavioral genetic studies have routinely produced inflated estimates of the influence of genetic factors, unfortunately by unknown amounts. The other methodology used in behavioral genetics research with twins involves the comparison between one twin and the other twin who has been adopted out and has been raised in another family. At first sight, this design obviates the problems that afflict the prior methodology described. However, such research is influenced by a different problem, which, unfortunately, also has the effect of inflating the genetic estimates. Mike Stoolmiller has shown that because twins are normally adopted into families that are screened in advance, the variability one might expect to find in random samples from the population in terms of family environments is drastically reduced.[41] He has calculated that this restriction of variability has the effect of substantially inflating the estimates of genetic influence (because of abstruse statistical artifacts that I will not go into here).

It gets worse. Because of the statistical model used in behavioral genetics research, the inflated variance allocated to the genetics category is removed from the other two categories, including the shared environment. Thus, in both kinds of twin designs, the effect of the shared environment is substantially biased downwards. Moreover, the effect of the "shared environment" is usually taken to include the shared environment of the family. But the "shared environment" is statistically defined in this approach as anything that makes the twins more similar, rather than being defined in some independent fashion. Hold the horses. This means that if two siblings experience the same event, such as their father drifting into alcoholism, and they react differently to this event (one becoming withdrawn and the other becoming aggressive), this is not counted in the shared environment, but is misleadingly dumped into the unique nonshared environment. As noted previously, any variance finally left over (after the first two steps) is then located in the "nonshared" environment. But this introduces yet another interpreta-

144

tional issue; namely, this last category includes whatever statistical noise is sloshing around, so that it is difficult to tell what is noise and what is a genuine effect.

I am sure that the potential for divorce or marital bliss is partly determined by genetic endowment. However, the apparently precise figures revealed in the research by McGue and his colleagues should be treated with skepticism. My own guess is that the additive genetic effects on complex behavioral traits, like marital satisfaction and divorce, will turn out to be rather modest, and that the interactions between genetic inheritance and the social and physical environments (including the effects of relationships) will prove to be where most of the causal action resides.

Gender Differences

Confession time. I have been putting off the task of dealing with gender differences in a concerted and focussed fashion in this book, merely noting them in passing. One reason I have done this is to help correct the unfortunate impression created by pop-psychologists like John Gray (with his notorious bestseller *Men Are from Mars and Women Are from Venus*) that the science of relationships deals almost exclusively with the differences between men and women in mate preferences, communication styles, sexuality, and so forth. However, time to grasp the nettle.

What gender differences – specifically relevant to relationship communication and relationship dissolution – have been reliably documented in Western cultures (and sometimes further afield across other cultures)? First, women tend to approach and communicate about relationship problems while men are more likely to avoid or withdraw from such interactions. Second, women are likely to talk to their friends more openly about their intimate relationships than are men. Third, women are better at mind-reading in relationships than are men. Fourth, more women decide to leave relationships than do men. Fifth, women prefer men who adopt a good communication style, whereas the opposite is true for male preferences. Sixth, women develop more sophisticated explanations for their relationships breaking up than do men.[42] I note in passing that this list is not intended to be a complete account of gender differences in relationships. I will deal with other gender

145

differences in later chapters related to such aspects as mate ideals, sexuality, and relationship violence.

This list of gender differences adds up to a picture of women being more expert and motivated relationship psychologists than men, as more active in their relationship monitoring, and as more oriented toward the maintenance and success of their relationships. Ironically, such gender differences appear to lead women to become disillusioned with their relationships to a greater extent than do men and, thus, to leave relationships more often. The size of these gender differences vary from slight (albeit statistically significant) to moderately large.

Before dealing with some explanations for such consistent gender differences, some caveats need to be made. I will succumb to the temptation of placing the first caveat in capitals to better combat the pernicious nonsense promulgated by pop-psychology. DIFFERENCES WITHIN GENDERS IN RELATIONSHIPS ARE ALMOST ALWAYS MUCH GREATER THAN THE DIFFERENCES BETWEEN GENDERS. To illustrate what this means consider the example of women being better at mind-reading than men, which is quite a substantial gender difference. This gender difference typically translates to about 70% of men possessing inferior mind-reading ability to the average women's ability, but 30% of men being *superior* to the average women's ability. For women, in turn, about 70% of women will be superior in mind-reading to the average man, but about 30% will be *inferior to* the average man. Another way of putting this is that in 70% of couples, women will have superior mind-reading to the man, whereas the man will be superior to the women in about 30% of relationships.

In short, standard gender differences are *tendencies* only, and do not translate into rigid stereotypes that apply to *all* men and *all* women. Indeed, sizable numbers of both men and women resemble prototypical exemplars of the opposite gender in terms of specific behavioral, cognitive, and emotional traits. Or, in John Gray's vernacular, many men come from Venus and many women originate from Mars.

The second caveat is that a focus on gender *differences* tends to brush over reliable findings that reveal no gender differences, which, in turn, leads to an overall impression of men and women being rather more likely to come from different planets than from mother earth. For example, men and women share very similar knowledge and understanding of emotion scripts in relationships like anger and love. Men and women are equally romantic in relationships, fall in love equally often, and have similar experiences (and similar hormonal secretions) in so doing. To presage the material in later chapters, men and women also have virtually identical styles of attachment and look for the same kind of qualities in a mate, both within Western cultures and across cultures.

Caveats aside, I have no wish to brush aside the importance of such gender differences, or to automatically explain them according to the vagaries of Western culture as postmodernists, and even some social psychologists, are prone to do. Unfortunately, evidence concerning the cross-cultural universality of the gender differences noted above is scant. However, I am prepared to place my bets (in part) on an evolutionary account; that is, genetic differences between men and women predispose them toward developing along different pathways. From an evolutionary perspective, the most plausible explanation for such gender differences is that selecting appropriate partners, and maintaining sexual relationships, had more powerful associated rewards and costs for women than for men. The reason is simply that women have relatively few shots at successfully raising their own children, and can conceive in a time window that closes off at menopause. In contrast, men can potentially sire many more children, and can do so for almost their entire lives. Such genetic predispositions that differentiate men and women can be, and are, either exaggerated or minimized across cultures, so that the size and significance of related gender differences would be expected to (and does) vary considerably across cultures.

How to explain the existence of such sizable within-gender individual differences in relationship phenomena of people who come from the same culture is a difficult question. I will postpone it to later in the book.

Conclusion

Understanding how communication operates in relationships, and what factors produce successful relationships, form two key tasks in the science of intimate relationships. However, simple bromides about the role of good communication in intimate relationships are not much help in accomplishing either task. Explaining how communication functions in intimate relationships, and its effects, requires close attention being paid to the intimate relationship mind and how it is intertwined with relationship behavior.

In the next chapter I return to the question of the origins of the adult intimate relationship mind, this time in terms of its roots in both evolutionary adaptations and in terms of the loving relationships that prefigure all others throughout our individual life spans – the relationships we form with our primary caregivers or parents.

Chapter 7

Attachment and Intimacy

A child forsaken, waking suddenly,
Whose gaze afeard on all things round doth rove,
And seeth only that it cannot see
The meeting eyes of love.
George Eliot

Human infants are born to bond. Within minutes of drawing their first breath they reveal automatic instinctual behaviors designed to locate and suckle their mother's breast (the rooting instinct) and the ability to grasp and hold fast when startled (the Moro reflex). However, there also exists a less visible but truly remarkable suite of perceptual and cognitive skills that are ready to unfold at birth. For about 24 hours, babies (and mothers) are usually calm but alert with endorphins from the trauma and pain of childbirth flooding their systems. From birth, babies can discriminate between human faces and voices and other stimuli, and they prefer faces. Within a few days, they can recognize the familiar face, voice, and smell of their mother or caretaker and prefer these to unfamiliar ones. They can also spontaneously imitate the facial expressions of their caretakers.[1]

At the other end of the relationship, mothers are biologically predisposed to bond with their infants. During labor, immediately after delivery, and during subsequent breast-feeding, oxytocin is produced in the mother's brain. Oxytocin in human females (as in other mammals) is associated with lactation. However, it also has direct effects on specific brain receptors (that human brains possess in abundance), producing a heightened state of well-being, and probably enhancing bonding.[2] After one brief contact with their infants, mothers can easily distinguish their infants from other newborns.[3] Young babies are shortsighted, so that beyond about 1 foot (30.5 cm) their world is blurred. Mothers –

149

and indeed adults generally – naturally interact with, and hold infants, at almost exactly this distance from their own faces.

Mothers (and other adults) also routinely fall into a form of language with babies known as "motherese." When using motherese, adult voices rise dramatically, their intonation becomes melodic and singsong, and their speech becomes slow and exaggerated – "Oh you are sooooo cute, when you smile, oh yes you are, ohhhhh yes you are, my liddle babykins." Babies apparently love adults talking like this.[4] It has typically been argued that the evolutionary origin of baby talk is associated with helping babies learn language. This may well be correct. However, the intriguing caveat is that at the proximal level it is the presence of two of the love systems – intimacy and commitment – that appear to trigger the use of such language. Small babies can engage these love modules in their parents, but so can other kinds of attachment targets. This explains why humans will slip into motherese when talking to their pet cats and to their adult lovers – cases that are obviously nothing to do with language tuition.

These features of human–infant attachment are universal, and seem designed (at least in part) to promote love and attachment between infant and caregiver(s). The first psychologist to firmly grasp, and to fully exploit this pivotal point, was John Bowlby. Bowlby produced a detailed version of what has come to be known as "attachment theory," which he laid out in three volumes from 1969 to 1980 dealing with the links between attachment and loss.[5] Bowlby's visionary grand theory pulled together contributions from Darwinian evolutionary theory, cognitive psychology, emotion theory, control systems theory, and ethology. This chapter presents a contemporary treatment of attachment and intimacy that is not quite so grand, but pulls together elements from contemporary social cognition, emotion theory, and evolutionary theory. I also deal with some key developmental questions concerning the origin and growth of adult lay theories of intimate relationships (what Bowlby termed *working models*).

Based on observations of both human infants and other mammalian species that were separated from their caregivers, Bowlby discovered a standard pattern of responses produced by the infant, which one sees in humans and other species including primates – protest, despair, and detachment. First, the infant will protest long and loud. If this produces no response, this will eventually lead to despair – the infant becomes passive and silent. Finally, the infant will become emotionally detached, and *apparently* begin to behave independently and normally. The evolutionary explanation produced by Bowlby is more or less obvious. Unless human babies can motivate Mum (not to mention Dad or other kin) to stay close at hand, and to provide food and protection, they will not survive.

However, Bowlby also provided a more subtle explanation for the sequence of behaviors elicited when separated from the caregiver. In what Bowlby termed "the EEA" (the Environment of Evolutionary Adaptedness) human babies would have been exceptionally vulnerable to predation, kidnapping, or injury if left unattended. Thus, kicking up a ruckus when hungry or frightened seems like it would have been an effective strategy to re-establish proximity with the caregiver. Evolution has kitted babies out with the human equivalent of a car alarm – aversive and hard to ignore – and whether you check out the problem or distance yourself from the noise depends primarily on whether or not it is your baby (or car). If protest does not succeed, Bowlby reasoned that remaining quiet, and not attracting the attention of predators, would become the best survival strategy. Finally, Bowlby hypothesized that detachment might have served the function of clearing away failed attachments, thus allowing secure affectional bonds to develop with new caregivers.

The most important elaboration of attachment theory, especially for understanding adult intimate relationships, was provided by one of Bowlby's associates, Mary Ainsworth, who developed the so-called laboratory *strange situation* in the 1960s and 1970s.[6] In this procedure a 12- to 18-month-old infant and his or her mother enter a laboratory with toys available, but with a stranger also present. The stranger engages the baby in the mother's presence, but then leaves. The mother then also leaves, and, after a brief interval, the stranger re-enters the laboratory. After a brief period, the infant's mother then returns, and the responses of the baby are monitored and recorded through a two-way mirror or videotape. This design is well suited to exploring patterns of attachment because it replicates two cues to danger that were almost certainly common in the EEA – being left alone and being exposed to a stranger.

Ainsworth expected that the infants would become distressed when their mothers left, seek physical contact when they returned, and subsequently calm down and return to playing with their toys. Indeed, this was the most common response of the American babies tested

151

(subsequently categorized as *securely attached*), but about 35 to 40% did not behave in this fashion. Twenty percent or so did not pay much attention to their mothers, were not particularly distressed when the mother left, and more or less ignored the mother on return – these infants were termed *avoidant*. The remaining 10 to 15% tended to behave in a contradictory fashion when the mother returned, whining, crying, and seeking physical contact, yet resisting and struggling at the same time – the so-called *ambivalent* infants.[7]

Subsequent research has established that infant behaviors in the strange situation are correlated with different patterns of caregiving. Mothers of securely attached infants provide secure and sensitive mothering, are highly attuned to the needs of their infants, and have warm, close relationships. Mothers of avoidant children are consistently cold and rejecting, and avoid physical contact. Mothers of ambivalent children tend to behave erratically with their infants, responding with a mixture of anger, neglect, and support. The conclusion is hard to resist that the infants have learnt specific attachment styles from the nature of the relationship with their parents. Secure infants have learnt to trust and rely on their caregiver for warmth, support, and protection. Avoidant children have learnt that they cannot rely on their caregiver for protection or love, and therefore must rely on their own resources. Finally, ambivalent children have difficulty predicting the level of support or protection available from their caregiver; however, it is sometimes available and, thus, they are encouraged to continue their demanding behavior.

The behavioral responses adopted by infants, from an evolutionary perspective, are perfectly sensible and should have enhanced their chances of survival. For example, adopting an avoidant style could enhance the chances of making it to adulthood by reducing the risk of injury or abandonment if the protest stage was persisted with. In contrast, the whining and demanding style adopted by ambivalent children may increase attention and sustenance from their inattentive caregivers (albeit at the risk of physical punishment, or verbal abuse by an exasperated parent).[8]

The application of attachment theory to adult intimate relationships is founded on the nature of Bowlby's theory, which does not just deal with infant–adult attachment, but is also a theory of personality development – in Bowlby's words, "from the cradle to the grave."[9] Bowlby was convinced that, based on early pivotal experiences with mothers or caretakers, infants develop working cognitive models of attachment (expectations, attitudes, emotional reactions, and so forth) that are carried into adulthood. These working models, he postulated, should exert profound psychological influences throughout adult life on the nature of one's intimate relationships forged with both adults and children.

However, it was not until 1987 that the first systematic (research) attempt to apply attachment theory to adult intimate relationships, titled "Romantic love conceptualized as an attachment process," was published by Cindy Hazan and Phillip Shaver.[10] This article proved to be the big bang of adult attachment research, kicking off a massive surge of theorizing and research focussed on attachment in adult romantic relationships (this one article has been cited, on average, in 128 separate research articles in scientific journals in each of the five years from 1996 to 2000[11]). How has Bowlby's approach stood up to this sustained empirical and theoretical scrutiny?

Attachment in Adult Intimate Relationships

Love and attachment between adults in some ways mirror the bonds that tie adult and child together. As I argued in the previous chapter, adult intimate love consists of three quasi-independent modules: intimacy (or attachment), commitment (or caregiving), and passion (or sexual attraction). The first two of these modules (intimacy and commitment) look very similar to the love between adult and infant. Indeed, Phillip Shaver and others have listed no fewer than 17 similarities between the two systems.[12] For example, lovers often slip into motherese when they talk to one another (nauseating though it might be for the casual observer), using favorite nicknames, and slipping into singsong cadences. Lovers have a strong need to spend a lot of time together, often caressing and kissing one another. Lovers seem fascinated with each other's physical appearance, and engage in long bouts of prolonged eye contact. Lovers become distressed if they are parted for prolonged lengths of time, and are exquisitely sensitive to each other's needs. And the list could go on.

The underlying neurophysiological processes also appear to be similar, with the same "love" hormones, such as oxytocin, involved in both adult–infant attachment and adult–adult romantic love. These behavioral and neurophysiological processes also feel much the same from inside

153

our nervous systems. I have heard individuals remark on how the process of bonding with infants feels like falling in love (but without the passion).

From an evolutionary perspective, the similarity between the attachment systems of adult–child and adult–adult relationships makes perfect sense. Why should evolution develop a completely new attachment system for adult romantic attachment when a perfectly workable, if ancient, system designed for adult–child attachment can be rejigged a little and pressed into service? Like the panda's thumb, it might not be the perfect solution, but it does the job well enough for the purposes at hand.

In their 1987 article, Hazan and Shaver initially developed self-report measures of the three attachment styles, previously described, which they derived from the work of Bowlby and Ainsworth. Participants were instructed to simply choose one of the following paragraphs that best described themselves in terms of their feelings typically experienced in romantic adult relationships:

> *Secure Style*: I find it relatively easy to get close to others and I am comfortable depending on them and having them depend on me. I don't often worry about being abandoned or about someone getting too close to me.
>
> *Avoidant Style*: I am somewhat uncomfortable being close to others. I find it difficult to trust them completely, difficult to allow myself to depend on them. I am nervous when anyone gets too close, and often love partners want me to be more intimate than I feel comfortable being.
>
> *Ambivalent Style*: I find that others are reluctant to get as close to me as I would like. I often worry that my partner doesn't really love me or won't want to stay with me. I want to merge completely with another person, and this desire sometimes scares people away.

The results from this pioneering research provided plausible preliminary evidence for this approach. For example, Hazan and Shaver found that the percentages of individuals (in the USA) who endorsed each style were similar to the figures obtained with toddlers from the Ainsworth strange situation: 56% secure, 25% avoidant, and 19% ambivalent. They also found that secure people reported more positive relationships with their parents than did avoidant or ambivalent participants. The barrage of research that followed this article has replicated these findings, but has, inevitably, complicated the attachment picture.

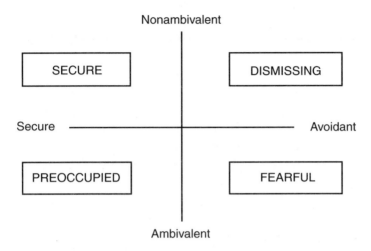

Nonambivalent

Figure 7.1 The four attachment prototypes defined by two attachment dimensions

I will start with the cornerstone of adult romantic attachment theory – the attachment styles themselves, and how to measure them.

The Hazan and Shaver measurement method assumes that people fit into either one attachment style or the other. This may seem like a reasonable assumption, but it has turned out to be wrong. Other researchers have independently developed scales using multiple items to assess each attachment style, which require participants to agree or disagree with each item (e.g., "I am somewhat uncomfortable getting close to others") by circling a number on a scale (typically 1–7) anchored by "strongly agree" at one end and "strongly disagree" at the other end. This format allows participants to rate their own styles independently across the three attachment styles. For example, using this technique it is possible for individuals to rate themselves as very high or very low on all three attachment styles. Psychometric work (using factor analysis) has consistently revealed the existence of two relatively independent attachment dimensions, regardless of which scales are analyzed: Secure versus avoidant, and the degree of attachment ambivalence (see figure 7.1).

As can be seen in figure 7.1, the existence of these two dimensions defines four kinds of attachment style (not three as in the original

Ainsworth-inspired model). These are usually termed "secure," "preoccupied," "dismissing," and "fearful." Extensive research has given us a good idea of what these four prototypical people look like. Pen portraits follow.[13]

- *The Secure Type*: Mary is secure and nonavoidant and is not ambivalent about forming intimate relationships. Mary is fairly likely to establish a long-term relationship with another secure individual. She perceives herself as warm and attractive, and is comfortable with, and enjoys, closeness. She is willing to rely on others for support and is confident she is valued by others. Mary is socially skilled in intimate relationships, and is likely to be in a happy and fulfilling long-term relationship. Mary also adopts a charitable style of explaining her partner's behavior, even when she is unhappy with the state of the relationship, or is in a bad mood. In short, she is something of a relationship Pollyanna.
- *The Preoccupied Type*: Jane is secure and is nonavoidant, but she is also ambivalent about intimate relationships. She has an intense desire for intimacy, works hard to obtain a relationship, and perceives herself as a good catch. However, she is also neurotically vigilant for signs her partner may leave her, and suffers from chronic jealousy. She tends to have on-again, off-again relationships, and has difficulty retaining a partner for long. Jane is always searching for her soul mate. But she never seems to find him.
- *The Dismissing Type*: Fred is insecure and avoidant, but is not at all ambivalent about intimate relationships. He values independence and is self-reliant, even arrogant. He likes sex, but tends to be cold and introverted. He does not like relying on others, and withdraws from stress and problems when they crop up in the relationship. He essentially does not trust other people, and seems to casually leave relationships with much less distress than other people typically experience. Fred is confident, assured, and successful, but obtaining high levels of intimacy is not his life goal. Indeed, it is doubtful that Fred would recognize an intensely intimate relationship if he fell over it. Fred is the sort of arrogant, handsome devil that legend has it women fall for, and sensitive (perhaps even secure) men may resent and envy.
- *The Fearful Type*: John has the worst of all worlds. John is insecure and avoidant; he is also ambivalent. John is anxious, depressed, and

hostile toward others (especially women). He desperately wants approval, warmth, and intimacy, but is convinced no one will really be willing to provide him with such treasures. Thus, he avoids intimacy in relationships. John is emotionally unstable in relationships, and has a chronically weak self-concept. John is not a happy person.

These descriptions are cardboard stereotypes. Reality is a lot messier, so that many people will combine characteristics across these exemplars. Still, there is enough truth in these general characterizations to remind readers of individuals they know that roughly match the descriptions. Indeed, if the readers of this book themselves are representative of the general population, then about 30 to 40% of you would have ticked off one out of the two original insecure categories initially described (ambivalent or avoidant) that Hazan and Shaver developed. And, I imagine, if you are one of those people, you may be feeling distinctly uncomfortable if not a little indignant. Fear not, because it turns out that such adult relationship attachment styles are not necessarily permanent across adulthood, nor are they unshakable structures set in concrete during childhood.

Stability and Change in Relationship Attachment Styles

Studies that have tracked attachment styles from toddlerhood (using the Ainsworth strange situation) to adulthood (18–20 years of age) were only just being published as I wrote this chapter (for obvious reasons, given that the Ainsworth strange situation was only developed in the 1970s). The findings they have produced are mixed. In four recent longitudinal studies reported in 2000 in *Child Development,* two found that attachment styles measured in toddlerhood correlated positively, from .44 to .49, with attachment styles as assessed at ages 18–21. However, the other two studies reported no evidence of any consistency across time.[14] Significantly, however, analyses in all four studies suggested that changes in attachment styles across the intervening years were not just random, statistical noise. Those who slipped from a secure to an insecure style were more likely to have experienced their parents divorcing, physical or sexual abuse, a major debilitating illness of a parent, and so forth.

One study, by Michael Lewis and others, found that 89% of the securely attached infants shifted to an insecure style if their parents subsequently divorced, whereas this was the case for only 35% of the securely attached infants whose parents remained together. A similar pattern was obtained with the infants who were classified as avoidant or ambivalent – those with divorced parents tended to remain insecure (60%) whereas those whose parents stayed together were less likely to stay insecure (32%) and more likely to shift to a secure style.[15]

Several studies have also investigated the stability of adult attachment styles in intimate sexual relationships. The findings from these studies reveal a reasonable level of consistency across periods of six months or a year (typically finding correlations of .40 to .70 across time). Such figures leave plenty of room for change, so that about 30% of individuals switch their dominant attachment style from time 1 to time 2.[16] Doubtless, some of this change is simply a matter of statistical noise. However, like the data from the longitudinal research from infancy to adulthood there is good evidence that such changes are systematically influenced by specific causes. Not surprisingly, one principal event in adulthood that shifts folk from a secure to an avoidant style is relationship breakup. One study by Lee Kirkpatrick and Cindy Hazan, that tracked 177 adults over a four-year period, reported that 50% of those individuals who reported they were originally secure, and who experienced a relationship breakup, switched to an avoidant style.[17]

In short, the evidence paints a picture of our attachment styles across the life span as being relatively stable, but as also exquisitely sensitive to external influences, especially intimate relationship experiences. Having an idyllic childhood with wonderfully supportive parents might well produce a secure attachment style. However, such a secure base can be transformed into an avoidant or ambivalent style after one has been painfully dumped a few times in succession in adult romantic relationships. Alternately, a supportive and intimate adult romantic relationship may accomplish the reverse transformation. The view that childhood experiences set attachment styles in concrete is a myth. Prolonged positive attachment experiences over long periods of time exert massive effects on our attachment styles, regardless of when they occur during the life span. The influence exerted by the social environment is further exemplified by the findings that the distribution of infant attachment styles varies considerably across cultures. Infants in Japan are virtually never classified as avoidant (they are either secure or ambivalent), whereas in northern Germany the rates of secure attachment in infancy are as low as 33% according to one study.[18] The rates in the USA and other Western countries are typically about 60% secure styles in both infancy and adulthood.

Of course, being abandoned in childhood, and perhaps being tied down to a cot (as happened with orphans in Romania during the communist era) has severe, debilitating, and long-term effects on neurological and cognitive development, not just on attachment styles. However, the evidence concerning the plasticity of attachment styles is derived from normal samples from the population, in which children were raised in normal family situations (with one or two main caretakers). This degree of plasticity in attachment styles raises some awkward questions for attachment theory.

Bowlby and Ainsworth viewed the secure attachment style, and the associated relationship between caretaker and child, as the normative prototype – as comprising an adaptation evolution selected humans to follow. According to this argument, the insecure styles (avoidance or ambivalence) should be viewed as pathological outcomes produced when things go wrong. One striking problem with this view is that the occurrence of insecure attachment styles (in children and adults) is hardly rare, occurring about 40% of the time with normal samples from Western countries.

The existence of negative or problematic attachment styles is not necessarily inconsistent with the logic of evolutionary explanations, even when related behaviors are likely to have diminished rather than to have enhanced reproductive fitness in the ancestral environment. To take a different example, sexual jealousy might sometimes have led men to kill their partners in a fit of misplaced jealous rage. However, sexual jealousy in men might also have proven to be an effective emotion that kept their female partners from sexually straying and bearing the offspring of other men. Thus, sexual jealousy helped ensure that individual men expended massive investment in sending their own genes into the future, and not (unwittingly) the genes of others. Provided the net evolutionary effects of the jealousy emotion have been to enhance reproductive fitness, the occasional pathological outcome does not mean that the emotion of jealousy itself is not an adaptation.

However, the sheer frequency of insecure attachment styles in both childhood and adult relationships (if replicated in ancestral environments) seems too much to handle for this kind of argument to be plausibly advanced. One final gambit available to the secure prototype thesis is that such figures just go to show how unfriendly modern society has become to normal family life and child-rearing. Such an argument, however, is not convincing. It implies a highly romanticized version of family life in the ancestral environment that is implausible, given what we know of family life as it exists in contemporary cultures, including hunter-gatherer societies, and making some informed guesses about life in our ancestral past.

Cross-cultural research indicates that parental investment in children (both emotional and practical) can be highly variable. The quality of child-rearing is adversely affected if effective birth control is unavailable, if the genetic father has left and is replaced by a stepfather, if there are few social supports or supportive grandparents, if the birth-spacing is too short, if the family is large, if the infants are ill or weak, and if there is poverty and hardship.[19] When such conditions are severe, this can result in children being abandoned, abused, or even sometimes killed. There is no reason to believe such factors were rare in our ancestral environment; indeed, there is every reason to think they were commonplace. Certainly, there is evidence of infanticide or abandonment of newborn babies in many cultures, including hunter-gatherer cultures.[20] Interestingly, however, Sarah Hrdy notes that when babies are abandoned to die, or killed by their mothers, it is almost always done within the first 72 hours (for both humans and other primates).[21] To do otherwise would be to allow the inexorable biological and psychological attachment systems to gain a purchase and make separation from the infant unbearable.

The approach I am building up to views evolutionary forces as having produced a relatively open-ended attachment system that is both sensitive to the nature of the relationship, and to related environmental conditions. Thus, there is no single prototype of attachment between caregiver and child that represents the single optimal adaptation. As Robert Hinde puts it:

> there is no best mothering style, for different styles are better in different circumstances, and natural selection would act to favor individuals with a range of potential styles from which they select appropriately . . . mothers and babies will be programmed not simply to form one sort of relationship but a range of possible relationships according to circumstances . . . optimal mothering behavior will differ according to the sex of the infant, its ordinal position in the family, the mother's social status,

160

caregiving contributions from other family members, the state of physical resources, and so on . . . a mother-child relationship which produces successful adults in one situation may not do so in another.[22]

This view of attachment styles – as representing optimal solutions to a given relationship and its context – is consistent with Robert Trivers' influential ideas concerned with parent–child conflict.[23] The evolutionary basis to Trivers' theory is derived from the "selfish gene" perspective championed by Dawkins and others, and notes that the reproductive fitness pay-offs between children and parents do not necessarily coincide. For example, when the mother has a new baby, she will want to wean her two- to three-year-old toddler. The toddler may well object and throw some spectacular tantrums.

From the gene's-eye perspective, such parent–child conflict is understandable given that the mother shares 50% of her genes with both children; thus, from the mother's perspective, it is in her interests for both children to survive and prosper, and each child is equally valuable (all else being equal). From the point of view of a male toddler, however, he shares 100% of his genes with himself and 50% with his sibling. If he survives and prospers, then he can pass on 50% of his genes, but his sibling will only pass on 25% of his or her genes. Hence, the toddler is bound to be more "selfish" than his mother and demand more of her investment and attention than she may be prepared to give. In short, the likelihood of parent–child conflict is built in at the biological ground level, just as it is in adult–adult romantic attachments.

Building on this view of attachment styles as providing functional solutions, recent life-span developmental theories outline how attachment styles in childhood might switch children onto different developmental pathways into adulthood. For example, Jay Belsky and others argue that the early attachment experiences of children are used to provide diagnostic information concerning what they will probably face in later life in adult intimate relationships.[24] Two basic developmental sequences are hypothesized. If a girl suffers from poor parenting and high levels of stress in the family of origin (father absence, spousal conflict, and so forth), then she will develop an insecure attachment style and associated working model. She will, thus, learn that men cannot be trusted and that relationships are often short-term. Hence, she will lean toward short-term sexual liaisons earlier in life. In contrast, if a girl develops secure attachments with both parents, her parents have a sound relationship, and she suffers low levels of stress, then she will lean toward delayed sexual intercourse and careful choice of a mate who is likely to be long-term and stable.[25]

It has often been casually noted that young teenage girls, who are the most sexually flirtatious, sexually adventurous, and likely to become pregnant at an early age, often seem to come from troubled family backgrounds or from the wrong side of the tracks. There is good evidence that such stereotypes are rooted in fact rather than prejudice. In the first classic demonstration of this effect, Mavis Hetherington in 1972 had male interviewers interview girls from intact families, divorced families (with the father absent), and girls from widowed families.[26] Girls from the divorced families sat closer to the male interviewer and behaved in a more flirtatious manner than the other two groups, including the girls whose fathers had died. These differences between the girls disappeared when they were interviewed by women. Hetherington also found that these behavioral differences were echoed in the parents' descriptions of their children. Here is the frayed description provided by one divorced parent:

> That kid is going to drive me over the hill. I'm at my wits' end. She was so good until the last few years then Pow! at eleven she really turned on. She went boy crazy. When she was only twelve I came home early from a movie and found her in bed with a young hood and she's been bouncing from bed to bed ever since. She doesn't seem to care who it is, she just can't keep her hands off men. It isn't just boys her own age, when I have men friends here she kisses them when they come in the door and sits on their knees all in a very playful fashion . . . She's smart and good-looking – she should know she doesn't have to act like that.[27]

More recent research has extended and documented the same point in relation to attachment styles. Women with less secure adult attachment styles do have more sexual partners, and are oriented to more short-term sexual partners.[28] Teenage girls from troubled family backgrounds, including divorce, are more sexually assertive, date more boys at an earlier age, and are more likely to become pregnant as teenagers or in early adulthood.[29]

Moreover, family-related stress not only seems to influence working attachment models and behavior with the opposite sex, but, remarkably, the rate of biological maturation itself. Girls who suffer from family conflict, poor relationships with parents, or an absent father reach puberty months or even years ahead of girls with intact, warm, and supportive family relationships.

Some of the best evidence for the causal role that family context plays comes from a longitudinal study by Bruce Ellis and his colleagues,[30] in which relationships between parents and their daughters were tracked over eight years, starting from when the children were four or five years old. The biological changes associated with puberty (pubic hair, breast development, menarche) occurred earlier if the father was absent, the parents had a poor relationship, and the father (if present) lacked an affectionate and warm relationship with his daughter. The correlations over time were large; for example, the extent to which fathers had affectionate relationships with their daughters (these ratings were derived from trained observers who watched the family interacting at home for four hours) was correlated with delayed pubertal development – measured eight years later – by a whopping -.43.[31] Being a daddy's girl delays the timing of puberty (the evidence shows that the relationship between mother and daughter is not as important as the father–daughter relationship in relation to the onset of puberty).

To summarize, the Belsky life-span model proposes that heightened levels of interpersonal stress and family conflict leads to an insecure attachment model, which essentially prepares individuals for an opportunistic mating strategy, geared toward early reproduction and less parental investment. Ellis has proposed that it is not general levels of childhood stress per se that count so much in terms of the timing of puberty, but the extent to which the child has extended contact with the genetic father as compared to genetically unrelated males (e.g., stepfathers).[32] His work has found that more direct interaction with the biological father during the first five years of life is associated with later puberty, whereas more years of living with a stepfather is associated with earlier puberty. What could the mechanism possibly be if this is true? One hypothesis is that our hormonal systems are sensitive to the pheromones (airborne chemical signals that may be odorless) of genetic versus nongenetic male caretakers. This may sound far-fetched, but there is good evidence from several mammalian species, such as rats, that exposure to pheromones produced by unrelated adult males (e.g., left behind in nests) accelerates female puberty.[33]

In summary, the development of attachment styles and associated working models are tied into basic developmental processes probably through the timing of release of hormones, like testosterone and estrogen, which (partly) control the onset and speed of pubertal development.

Attachment Lay Theories (Working Models)

For Bowlby, working models were internal cognitive representations that summarized the child's previous attachment experiences, both emotional and behavioral. Working models comprise beliefs about others and the self, and produce expectations and attitudes that can be used to predict consequences for future relationships. Working models provide the mechanism and the link between childhood and adult relationships. As far as it goes, Bowlby's theorizing on working models is on the money, but it can stand some refurbishment in terms of recent adult attachment research, and my previous social cognitive treatment of lay relationship theories. I will argue that Bowlby's attachment working models, suitably recast, comprise a species of lay relationship theory.

The first distinction from my social cognitive model that can usefully be applied to working models is between general attachment lay theories that gloss across relationships in an abstract fashion, and attachment models that apply to local, particular relationships. These two kinds of lay theories will not always converge: Fred may avoid intimacy like the plague with Mary, but have a generally secure attachment with Joanne (or vice versa). Mark Baldwin specifically tested this notion by asking adults to rate their ten most significant relationships according to their attachment styles; sure enough, although there was some consistency across relationships, most participants reported two or more different styles across the ten specific relationships.[34]

People will, I agree, possess global attachment lay theories that apply in some general, hypothetical fashion, and predate specific, local relationships. Nevertheless, we would expect adults (and perhaps even children) to distinguish among different classes of relationships. The three most obvious relationship attachment categories consist of parents and related kin, friends, and romantic or sexual relationships. There is relatively little direct evidence concerning differences and similarities among these classes, but I think it is plausible that people would, to some extent, keep these three models relatively distinct and update them accordingly. If Mark's wife leaves him suddenly after an affair with someone Mark has never met, his level of trust of women and his romantic attachment theory is likely to dip alarmingly to the avoidant end, leaving his friendship attachment theory intact. However, if Mark's wife were to leave him after a lengthy and clandestine affair with his best friend, then this is a double betrayal, and both his general platonic friend and romantic attachment lay theories will take a palpable and possibly permanent hit.

The quantity of research that has examined the nature and functions of working models or (romantic) attachment lay theories is far too voluminous to cover in detail here. I will pick out a few central points that will serve to integrate this material with other sections of the book. There is evidence of similarity regarding attachment styles between couples in both dating and married relationships. The most consistent finding is that both partners in relationships report similar levels of security in a relationship; if one partner is secure, then the other person is likely to also be secure. Levels of ambivalence and avoidance (in contrast) tend to be largely uncorrelated across partners.[35] However, it is extremely rare to find two highly avoidant people in a long-term relationship, a fact that is hardly surprising. Presumably, if both individuals studiously avoid attaining intimacy, the relationship is likely to be short-lived, even if it staggers off the ground in the first place. Where both individuals are insecure, the most common pattern is an avoidant individual (usually the man) and an ambivalent individual (usually the woman). This pattern is redolent of a common relationship pattern, discussed previously in chapter 6, in which the female anxiously demands and confronts the man (just like the ambivalent infant protests to its mother) and the man withdraws and avoids conflict (just like the avoidant infant does with its mother).

The fact that levels of self-reported attachment security tend to be correlated across partners (typically around the .30 level) is hard to interpret. Romantic attachment styles resonate according to relationship experiences; thus, if the current relationship is happy this will tend to produce increases in secure attachment style over time.[36] About 60% or so of university students are involved in dating or long-term intimate relationships at any given time. The standard finding obtained is that those students who are involved in an ongoing dating relationship are more likely to be secure rather than avoidant or ambivalent. However, again, we have the chicken and egg problem, given that relationship experiences can influence attachment styles; for example, as previously documented, relationship breakup tends to precipitate people toward

165

an avoidant style (although this may be relatively temporary). Based on the longitudinal evidence gathered, the most reasonable interpretation is that attachment styles and relationship experiences influence one another in a reciprocal fashion (experiments, that could offer more convincing causal evidence are, of course, out of the question for obvious ethical reasons).

In chapter 2 I outlined three major goals that lay relationship theories have – explanation (or understanding), prediction, and control (or regulation). Attachment lay theories are related to all three functions. Research by Nancy Collins has shown that when secure individuals explain negative behaviors from their partners (e.g., failing to comfort them when they were depressed), they are inclined to produce charitable, relationship-positive attributions apparently designed to hold on to their belief in the essential warmth and trustworthiness of their partner (e.g., the partner had a bad cold).[37] In contrast, ambivalent folk tend to adopt a relationship-negative pattern and emphasize their partner's indifference to their needs and lack of commitment. These findings were not produced by differences in relationship satisfaction between secure and ambivalent individuals, because Collins found that these effects remained strong after the impact of relationship satisfaction was statistically controlled for.

Bowlby suggested that attachment working models could be used by people to run through thought experiments and thus make predictions. Certainly, people's expectations about hypothetical intimate relationships do emanate from their attachment models in some fairly obvious ways. Secure people adopt an optimistic stance generally, avoidant folk expect not to be able to trust their partners, and ambivalent individuals predict (quite realistically) that they will strike problems getting anyone to commit fully and to accept the intense form of intimacy they seem desperate to achieve.[38] More generally, individuals often spend time thinking and daydreaming about the future course of specific relationships. Thus, attachment lay theories will almost certainly shape and guide such thought experiments.

Finally, there is good evidence that attachment lay theories are used to guide and regulate one's own, and one's partner's, behavior (the third leg in the function table of explanation, prediction, and control). In a pioneering piece of research, Jeffry Simpson and colleagues revisited Bowlby's hypothesis that the attachment systems should be kicked into action when infants are under stress; indeed, this is the basis of the strange situation developed by Ainsworth to uncover the different attachment styles evinced by toddlers. In an analogous fashion Simpson and colleagues set out to stress adult individuals in relationships and to observe their interactive behavior.[39] The female members of each dating couple in this study were initially shown some fearsome-looking apparatus they were about to be hooked up to, set up in a psychophysiological laboratory that resembled a large refrigerator. These women were also informed that the experiment might cause some discomfort. The chilled women then returned to sit with their partners in a waiting room, during which time the couple's behavior was surreptitiously videotaped. The story was, of course, bogus and was designed to invoke stress.

The more stressed the individual women became, the more their attachment styles (assessed prior to the experiment) seemed to influence their behavior; secure women sought support whereas avoidant women avoided seeking support from their partner, to the point of expressing irritation if their partners asked what was wrong or proffered support. Moreover, secure men offered more emotional and physical support the more anxiety their partners displayed, whereas the avoidant men became less helpful, and again actually expressed irritation. Finally, in a control group, in which neither partner went through the stress manipulation, there was no indication that the partner's attachment styles were reflected at all in his or her behavior.

In a sample videotape from this experiment that Jeff Simpson has shown me, a highly stressed, but avoidant woman, appears upset but turns her body away from her partner and studiously flicks through a magazine. Her partner asks what is wrong and puts his hand around her shoulders – she shrugs him off and tells him to leave her alone in a sharp and aggrieved tone. In short, she behaves remarkably like an avoidant infant in the strange situation. In the previous chapter, I opined that anger or irritation expressed at the partner, in contexts that more appropriately call for physical and emotional support, are likely to be particularly corrosive. Perhaps it is not surprising that high levels of the avoidant attachment style predict a greater likelihood of relationship breakup.

The final element I will borrow from my social cognitive model concerns the way in which attachment working models should operate like highly accessible relationship theories. When such lay theories are triggered off, they should automatically and unconsciously influence relationship judgments or decisions. Indeed, research by Mario Mikulincer and his colleagues have found evidence that attachment lay theories can be cognitively triggered, even when the stimulus is presented on a computer screen subliminally, so that the individual is not consciously aware of the event that initiated the process.[40]

Thus, the activation of relationship threat immediately and automatically calls up attachment theories from the mind. The nature of those attachment theories (which may be specific to particular targets) will then partly determine the subsequent emotions, cognitions, and behavioral responses. For example, individuals who are avoidant (the dismissing or fearful types described previously) have learnt, and overlearnt, that particular attachment figures cannot be relied upon for support, and may represent a threat.

Conclusion

In conclusion, it is clear that love and intimacy in adult sexual relationships are cognitively and emotionally prefigured in early childhood. Both love and attachment are based on the same evolutionary-derived set of adaptations first speculated about by Bowlby. The Bowlby war-horse has held up remarkably well against the sustained empirical and theoretical battering it has received in the last few decades. Its gradual refurbishment, however, has exemplified in stark relief the principle that to understand the intimate relationship mind requires the adoption of an interactional perspective. Traits, relationship theories, expectations, or other stored knowledge structures in the intimate relationship mind will not typically be behaviorally expressed in a simple and straightforward fashion. Rather, they will be accessed and articulated as a function of the social and physical environment. This is true regardless of whether such dispositions are primarily of genetic origin, are purely learned, or (more commonly) comprise some sort of mixture.

Throughout the last three chapters in this section of the book, I have ranged widely in discussing the various ways in which relationships develop, and how the intimate relationship mind works. In the next and last chapter in this section, I complete the picture by analyzing how and why adults select their mates and their relationships. As will be seen, however, mate selection is not just a one-shot process determined at the very beginning of the relationship.

Chapter 8

Selecting Mates and Relationships

sometimes the most extreme passion is aroused – not by real-life love objects – but by partners who are barely known . . . or who exist only in imagination.
Berscheid & Walster, 1978

In a graduate class I teach on the science of intimate relationships, I start the year's work with a demonstration developed by Bruce Ellis and Harold Kelley.[1] The 25 or so students in the class are randomly given cards with numbers on them, ranging from 1 to 10, that represent their assigned mating value. These cards are held to their foreheads in such a way that others can see them, but remain out of sight for the card-bearer (so that each individual does not know his or her own mate value). The aim of the game is to get together with the individual with the highest mate value possible (biological sex is ignored). Once a mate selection is made, the initiator indicates his or her selection by attempting to shake hands. If the individual approached spurns the handshake, then the initiator must look elsewhere. When a couple is formed, indicated by a handshake, then each individual first guesses his or her own mate value number, before taking a peek at the assigned value. As the class members mill about, individuals pair off, until a small and disconsolate group is left, standing in the middle of the room. Inevitably, this group represents the dregs of the mating market, but they too finally pair off in a crestfallen sort of way.

The numbers are then crunched on a laptop, and reported back to the class. The results typically reveal that the mating values of the paired-up partners are highly correlated (about .70 or so), but also that individuals are very accurate at guessing their own mate value after pairing off (with correlations also of around .70 between the predicted self-mating values and the actual numbers assigned). This demonstration

169

suggests two important features about choosing potential mates. First, merely utilizing the heuristic – get the best deal possible – is enough to produce assortative mating (i.e., mating in which people match highly on given characteristics) in situations where both parties exercise choice. Second, the process of assortative mating provides feedback that allows people to accurately assess their own mate value.

However, such a classroom exercise leaves many questions unanswered. Do individuals deliberately choose others who are similar to them? Are people rated according to a simple mate value dimension (good versus bad)? Do people carry round general ratings of their own mate value in their heads, or are such judgments more complex and variegated? Does a man who is good-looking, but cold, offer the same overall mate value as a man who is homely and warm? To what extent do people differ in what they want in a mate? Does the mating war between the genders really exist? What is the origin of mate ideals? Evolutionary psychologists and social psychologists have devoted much attention to such questions. However, researchers from these two domains have tended to work in hermetically sealed camps. I will illustrate in this chapter the gains that can be forged by attempting to integrate these two approaches.

Searching for the Ideal Mate

In New Zealand, the United States, Polynesian Islands, African hunter-gatherer cultures, and around the world, people focus on the same three categories in evaluating their potential mates: personality factors related to intimacy, warmth, and commitment; a second set related to passion, attractiveness, excitement, vitality and sex; and a third set related to status and resources such as influence, age, money, position, possessions, and so forth. Moreover, although there are characteristic gender differences in the importance attached to such categories, there is also remarkable agreement across both gender and cultures concerning which factors are most important in selecting mates for long-term relationships: the winner is warmth and loyalty, a close second is physical attractiveness and general vitality, and down the track is status and resources.

The evidence for this generalization comes in various forms. David Buss has carried out the most systematic, and commonly cited, analysis in which men and women ranked a range of factors in their importance for selecting mates across 37 cultures.[2] A good deal of similar research has been carried out within Western cultures with similar results.[3] However, one difficulty with this style of research is that the nature of the items presented to participants is selected beforehand, often based on the hunches or theories of the experimenter.[4] Thus, it is quite possible that such research omits important mate categories.

To deal with this thorny methodological issue, and to develop some valid and reliable scales to measure individual differences in mate ideals, my colleagues and I embarked on a series of studies.[5] Initially, we asked groups of women and men to write down all the items that described their own ideal mates. We then took the hundreds of items collected and placed them into categories, sticking as closely as possible to the actual words used. Any item that was cited by less than 5% of the sample was deleted, which left 49 items. We then had a different sample of students rate how much importance they placed on each ideal in the context of sexual or romantic relationships (using standard 1–7 scales anchored by "very important" and "very unimportant").

By using a statistical technique known as factor analysis we then unearthed the general way in which people were grouping the items together. The items fell neatly into the predicted tripartite ideal structure previously described: *warmth/loyalty* (with items like understanding, supportive, considerate, kind, a good listener, and sensitive); *vitality/attractiveness* (with items like adventurous, nice body, outgoing, sexy, attractive, good lover); and *status/resources* (with items like good job, financially secure, nice house or apartment, appropriate ethnicity, successful, and dresses well). These results proved to be the same regardless of whether the samples comprised men or women, or whether or not individuals were involved in sexual relationships. Moreover, the importance that people attach to these different categories of ideal mate standards predicts relationship cognition and behavior in predictable ways (as I will document in due course).

What this brand of data analysis (factor analysis) shows is that people differ in terms of which sort of mate characteristics they think are important, but that these differences occur across the three categories rather than within the sets of specific items that are included within each general ideal category. That is, people do not just set high or low ideal partner standards – individuals set high or low standards in ways that vary in a relatively independent fashion across the three kinds of mate

171

characteristics. Indeed, differences between men and women are considerably less extreme than differences within men and within women. Some people (both men and women) are essentially on the hunt for an exciting, passionate relationship with a gorgeous hunk; others care relatively little about passion and are preoccupied with the search for intimacy, warmth and commitment. Yet others are prepared to sacrifice somewhat on the passion and intimacy front, if they can obtain a partner with considerable status and resources.

Why do people not want it all? Why is Jane's ideal partner not incredibly kind, beautiful, remarkably fit with a wonderful body – and rich? First, such people might be plentiful in TV soap operas, but in real life they are remarkably thin on the ground. Second, even when Jane meets such a male paragon he will probably not be interested in Jane (who is not a perfect ten in every category). Third, even if Jane succeeds in striking up a relationship with such a catch, he may be difficult to retain, and Jane may find she needs to invest an exhausting amount of time and resources in maintaining the relationship. Different people favor different trade-offs and, hence, should differentially weight associated ideals – and they do.

Why do people in cultures across the world share the same core set of three concepts around which they store their mate expectations? Clearly, culture has a pivotal role in any origin account of ideal mate standards. Within Western cultures, for example, we are incessantly exposed to theorizing about the nature and functions of relationships from birth, emanating from our parents, teachers, friends, the media, books, plays, TV, magazines, music, and so forth. Such theorizing is certainly not totally coherent, but by the time people enter puberty they have become thoroughly psychologically conditioned with a shared language, in addition to concepts, beliefs, and expectations about intimate relationships. However, an answer in terms of a shared cultural heritage only goes so far. Why does Western culture, for example, contain these particular ideal standards rather than others? One could adopt a relativist approach at this point and claim that it just does – that cultures develop such theories in some sort of random fashion, or tied to historical accident and contingencies. However, such an account is not plausible, given the available evidence documented in this book.

Moreover, not only are the kinds of ideal standards universal, but also the way in which at least some of the mating criteria are cashed out. I will consider the three basic mating criteria in turn.

First, there is a wealth of cross-cultural evidence that people everywhere categorize people in terms of personality categories such as warmth, loyalty, and trustworthiness.[6] In contrast, although increased status and resources elevates mating value everywhere, the fashion in which this is done is amazingly variable. Where I live in Christchurch, men can gain status by dressing expensively, driving a Porsche, hanging around cafes talking on a cell phone, playing in a band, flashing money around, playing professional rugby, winning a drinking contest at a local dive, being a successful local politician, living in a fabulous house with a view, and the list could go on and on. The key seems to be to provide evidence of the sort of ambition, drive, and ability that signals the probability that one is, or may become, a wealthy man, or a man who can forge social connections and win respect from the group.

In our human ancestral environments, men who wished to establish their status and resource-gathering credentials did not have cafes, cars, or cell phones. Moreover, in hunter-gatherer cultures, it is not easy to accumulate much in the way of resources, given the lifestyle and the need to travel light. No matter. Political savvy, hunting prowess or fighting ability are respected and confer status in almost every culture. One obvious (evolutionary) explanation for the mate value of hunting ability is that the man will be able to supply more food to his own family. However, in contemporary hunter-gatherer cultures, anthropological research has found that the best (male) hunters often give away most of the food to friends and others in the tribe.[7] Such displays of generosity are effective advertisements of status and prowess – "Look at me, I am a great hunter." They also increase the chances of others in the group rallying around and supplying food and support in times of illness or hardship – what goes around comes around.[8]

The human desire for status and respect (especially for men) is one of the most powerful, yet most general, human traits known. The evolutionary reason is almost certainly because women (and perhaps men) find such a characteristic attractive in potential mates (or more accurately, did so during our ancestral past). Indeed, Geoff Miller has advanced the bold claim that men became locked into a mate-attraction arms race in which the need for men to be admired and respected (by women) for their mental agility, linguistic skills, musical ability, joke-telling skills, and so forth, became a crucial force in the evolution of human language and the human neocortex.[9] Thus, according to Miller, the human mind is not a computer, but an entertainment center. How come women are equally as intelligent and witty as men? Because such abilities had to co-evolve across genders in order for women to appreciate men. Being witty and amusing is not going to get you very far in the mating stakes if your intended audience is dull and lacks a sense of humor.[10]

In contrast to status and resources, vitality and physical attractiveness are judged in very much the same way both across and within cultures.[11] It is commonly, but wrongly, believed that physical beauty is judged in wildly different and unpredictable ways across cultures. The reason may reside in our exposure in Western cultures to photographs and documentaries featuring men and women from traditional cultures who look anything but attractive to our eyes. Male members (forgive the pun) of the Ketengban tribe in New Guinea who wear enormous penis sheaths, or Maori warriors with heavily tattooed faces, probably do not appeal to the average Californian woman. In the same vein, women from the Mursi (a Southern Ethiopian tribe) who wear enormous discs to push out their lower lips, or women from the Paduang (in Burma) who wear multiple brass coils around their necks, which lengthens them to the point where they can die from suffocation if they are removed, probably look grotesque to the average Californian male.

But this sort of experience is misleading, as it mixes up fashion with the more basic bodily features associated with physical beauty. Western cultures have featured many fashions over the centuries that look absurd to modern eyes, from the wigs and white faces of Elizabethan times, to the enormous bustles of the Victorian era. In contemporary Western culture it has become fashionable for young people to wear ornaments that pierce the face and body. This fashion, as fashion tends to do, has gradually become more widespread and extreme in its manifestations, so that even middle-aged men are getting their nipples and ears pierced, and the assortment of ornaments that individuals put in their ears, noses, tongues, eyebrows, cheeks, lips, belly buttons, and even genitals has become quite astounding. One gets used it, however, and what might have seemed repellent in a potential mate five years ago tends to become perfectly routine and perhaps even mandatory (depending on one's age and cultural subgroup).

Individuals in Western and other cultures differ (to some extent) in whom they find attractive. Popular magazines often feature stories that exploit this idea with men varying in terms of whether they get turned on most by women's legs, breasts, or bums; and women arguing over whether size counts, and to what extent big muscles are attractive. However, the research evidence shows that differences of opinion within Western cultures in standards of beauty and sex appeal are no greater than the differences across cultures. Beautiful or homely faces are perceived the world over in much the same way. Michael Cunningham and others had Asian, Hispanic, Taiwanese, and black and white Americans rate the attractiveness of faces from all the same ethnic groups. Individuals from the different ethnic groups overwhelmingly agreed with one another about who was more physically attractive (with correlations reported of over .90!).[12] Such results have been replicated with other cultural and ethnic groups.[13]

The universally attractive female face (for men) has a relatively child-like appearance, with wide-set, large eyes, a small nose and chin, prominent cheekbones, high eyebrows, large pupils, and a warm smile.[14] The story with men's faces is more complicated. Michael Cunningham and his colleagues have found that the universally attractive male face (compared to a woman's face) has a relatively angular appearance, wide-set eyes, and a large chin – but combined with baby-face features including large eyes, and an expressive smile.[15]

One of the major tools that researchers are now exploiting is computer-morphing programs that can alter individual digital photographs in systematic ways, or generate composite photographs based on hundreds of individual photographs. Using this technique, Gillian Rhodes created different human facial images based originally on an average female and an average male face (using both European and Chinese faces). Some of the images created represented exaggerated versions of stereotypical human female and male faces, while others became feminized male faces or masculinized female faces. The results (for both Chinese and European faces) showed that the superfemale faces were rated as most attractive by all the raters, whereas for the male faces, the feminized versions were the clear winners.[16] If you are a woman and look like Lonie Anderson you seem to be on to a winner; if you are a man, then it looks like a compromise between Tom Selleck and Leonardo DiCaprio may be the best bet.

The development of preferences for attractive faces requires little or no learning. Infants from 14 hours to 6 months old prefer looking at faces that are attractive, rather than unattractive (as defined according to adult preferences).[17] Preferences for attractive faces are not only universal, but are hard-wired and present at birth.[18]

175

What goes for faces also goes for bodies; namely, particular body prototypes are universally held to be attractive. Men who could hold down a
part-time job as a male stripper – being muscular, athletic, and tall – are
sexier than flabby, out of shape, short men worldwide.[19] Short, out of
condition, middle-aged men with potbellies can still do surprisingly well
in the mating stakes, if they hold power and prestige, or have other qualities such as high intelligence. Indeed, if there is a famine in the land, then
being overweight could be a drawing-card, given that it may signal the
presence of status and wealth. However, excessive corpulence combined
with a large protruding stomach is not regarded as sexy anywhere – what
is perceived as universally sexy in women (by men) is the classic hourglass
shape with rounded, firm breasts and smooth skin.[20]

It is true that fashion models tend toward thinness, sometimes to the
point that they resemble advertisements for famine relief. However,
when ordinary men (not fashion mavens) are asked to rate body shapes,
fashion-model thinness is not judged as physically attractive.[21] Certainly,
the fashionable degree of buxomness (i.e., the size of the breasts and
hips) varies both across cultures and over time within cultures. However, Devendra Singh has shown that, although attractive stereotypes
of a woman's body shape do vary in terms of overall size, what remains
more or less constant is the favored ratio between the woman's waist
and hip, which is about .70. Venus de Milo, Sophia Loren, or Marilyn
Monroe might seem chunky to contemporary fashion-conscious eyes.
However, all these women have (or had) waists that are close to 70% of
the size of their hips. Singh measured the dimensions of *Playboy*
centerfolds and Miss America winners over the last 30 to 60 years. He
found that the critical ratio (.70) between hips and waist remained largely
invariant over time (although overall buxomness varied).[22]

It is important to note that although judgments of physical attractiveness are automatic and deeply rooted in evolutionary adaptations,
this does not imply that such judgments operate in encapsulated and
splendid isolation from the rest of the intimate relationship mind. The
Country and Western song by Micky Gilley intones that "girls get prettier at closing time; they all get to look like film stars." Inspired by this
potential wisdom, James Pennebaker and his colleagues found that,
sure enough, as the hours passed, both men and women perceived potential mates in bars as more attractive.[23] Further research has replicated the finding for both genders, confirmed that the effect is not
simply caused by people steadily getting drunk, and shown that the

effect only occurs for those who are not involved in an intimate se
relationship (and who are thus more likely to be monitoring the bar for
potential mates).[24]

But the critical question remains. Why are these three particular categories – Warmth/Loyalty, Vitality/Attractiveness, and Status/Re-
sources – pivotal in mate selection? An evolutionary approach recently
developed by Steven Gangestad and Jeffry Simpson answers this question (along with others) by positing that each dimension represents a
different route used to obtain a mate and promote reproductive fitness
in our ancestral environments.[25]

Gangestad and Simpson argue that individuals utilize two basic kinds
of mating criteria: the possession of "good genes" and/or "good investment." By being attentive to a partner's capacity for intimacy and
commitment an individual should increase his or her chances of finding
a co-operative, committed partner who would be a devoted mate and
parent (good investment). By focusing on attractiveness and health an
individual would be more likely to acquire a mate who was younger,
healthier, and more fertile – this is the primary "good genes" factor.
And, by considering a partner's resources and status, an individual should
have been more likely to obtain a mate who could ascend social hierar-
chies and form coalitions with other people who had – or could acquire
– valued social status or resources. This last category is likely to represent a mixture of both good genes and the ability to invest in the relationship and the children.

It is more or less self-evident why a mate loaded with warmth and
loyalty, along with high status and wealth, should make an effective
provider and a good parent. But why should attractiveness and vitality
be associated with good genes? We so routinely perceive human faces
and bodies as inherently attractive and beautiful (or the opposite) that
it is difficult to step back and ask why particular arrangements of the
human body strike us so forcefully and automatically as either beautiful
or homely. Sexual selection theory provides the only plausible explanation; namely, that such features were associated in human ancestral environments with an increase in reproductive fitness. Remember the
peacock and his gorgeous tail. The most popular explanation currently
for why peahens are so fixated on this feature, when selecting mates, is
in terms of the handicap principle. That is, large and gorgeously colored
tails represent honest advertisements that indicate good health, a robust body, and high fertility (good genes). For humans, the same kind

177

of explanation entails that beautiful people with great bodies were healthier, more fertile, and bore healthier children in the past than those lower on the attractiveness scales (for both men and women). But is this true and, if so, what are the causal mechanisms involved?

Research in contemporary Western cultures has generally found positive relationships between physical *facial* attractiveness and levels of health,[26] although the most thorough longitudinal investigation over the entire life span, carried out by Michael Kalick and colleagues, failed to find a link between facial attractiveness in late adolescence and either adolescent health or health in later life.[27] It is hard to know, however, to what extent modern healthcare systems, the availability of antibiotics, childhood inoculation, and cosmetic dentistry and surgery have attenuated the links that formerly existed between good skin, clear eyes, good teeth, and robust good health. Evidence concerning the links between body shape and condition, with both health and fertility, in modern environments are more robust. Research has shown that the classic hourglass woman's figure (associated with Singh's waist-to-hip ratio of .70) is associated with good health and high fertility in women (controlling for the effects of age).[28] In short, it is not so much how fat people are that counts, but rather how the fat is distributed.

One recent theory that provides a plausible causal link between body shape or facial attractiveness with reproductive fitness exploits the concept of "fluctuating asymmetry." This term is somewhat confusing as the word "fluctuating" refers to the way in which asymmetry varies across populations, rather than over short periods of time within individuals. Imagine the human body split vertically down the middle from head to toe – highly symmetrical individuals have faces and bodies that are similar across the left and right sides. Individuals who have lopsided faces, with different-sized ears, different looking eyes, and so forth, have high levels of fluctuating asymmetry, as do those with legs, feet, arms and hands that are different shapes and lengths.

The standard explanation for why fluctuating asymmetry is related to health and fertility is that marked asymmetry is produced by genetic abnormalities, by falling prey to illness and disease during the life span, being subject to toxins or mutations, or combinations thereof. Thus, adults who are symmetrical should have an absence of genetic abnormalities, and should also possess a hardy and healthy constitution that has enabled them to remain relatively unaffected by serious disease or illness throughout the course of their development.

This is all well and good, but it is not an easy matter to accurately judge how symmetrical people are, as researchers have discovered when attempting to do it. Measuring fluctuating asymmetry in people's bodies in the laboratory is a tortured process, involving the use of sensitive calipers to measure people across multiple locations, and using two independent raters to repeat all the measurements.[29] Laypeople can effectively judge levels of fluctuating asymmetry in photographs of faces, but to obtain reasonably accurate measures, the researcher needs to average the results across quite large groups of raters to reduce the measurement error to acceptable levels.[30]

Which raises the question – if fluctuating asymmetry is difficult for laypeople to accurately assess beyond some crude level, then how can it possibly be a major factor in mate selection? Gangestad and Simpson's answer is that fluctuating asymmetry is correlated with factors that humans can readily perceive quite accurately.[31] For example, men who are more symmetrical tend to be more facially attractive, more robust and athletic, more socially dominant, and even smell more attractive – these proximal-level factors are reliable indicators of high levels of symmetry (good genes). In addition, men who are more symmetrical have more sexual partners over the lifetime, women tend to prefer them, and they are more likely to be involved in infidelities. Finally, fluctuating asymmetry has high variability among human populations and is strongly genetically transmitted, both of which make it a good candidate as a reliable indicator of good genes.[32]

As Darwin first showed, and everyone knows, an important component of mating behavior is competition among men (and among women) to get dates and mates. In a recent intriguing study by Jeffry Simpson and others, men competed with one another for a lunch date with an attractive woman.[33] Each man was asked a series of questions over a video system by a female interviewer (actually a videotaped research assistant who delivered the same predetermined questions) located in another room. After the interview was finished, the attractive woman asked each man to tell the "competitor" (ostensibly located in a different room) why she should choose him instead of the competitor. More symmetrical men were more likely to directly compare themselves with, and belittle, the competitor ($r = .49$). This research makes the point that good genes are not only expressed in terms of appearance, body shape, and athleticism, but are also connected to the use of more aggressive within-gender strategies. The good genes are housed in male

179

bodies that end up getting the girl (at least they tended to do so in our ancestral environments).

The Gangestad and Simpson approach predicts the existence of substantial differences within men, and within women, in terms of what people are looking for in a mate – the name of the mating game is to do the best one can, in light of the available pool of mates, one's own perceived mate value, and other prevailing circumstances. Our would-be ancestors who were unrealistic in terms of their ideal standards (both men and women) ended up being constantly rejected, were less likely to pass on their genes, and thus, were not our ancestors. Accordingly, a more refined and successful set of flexible mating strategies, in which expectations and ideals were tied to what individuals could reasonably hope to attain, was selected for (so the argument goes).

What then specifically causes people to attach different amounts of importance to different ideal categories? Consistent with the classroom exercise I described at the beginning of the chapter, one major factor is self-perceived mate value. In some recent research, my colleagues and I have found evidence for this proposition. Individuals who rate themselves as superior in terms of warmth and loyalty attach more importance to the same ideal standards, those who perceive themselves as more attractive and vital give more weight to the equivalent ideal category, and, finally, those who believe they have more status and resources rate this ideal category as more important.[34]

The related correlations between ideals and self-perceptions vary from .37 to .53, and are shown in table 8.1. These data are from 100 men and 100 women (all university students). Note that these findings are not produced by a general tendency simply for those who have inflated views of their own mate value to rate any old ideal standard as more important. Rather, there is clear evidence that the mental links between self-perceptions and ideal standards are funneled through these three distinct ideal categories. It is beginning to look as if this tripartite structure of mate standards is carving the intimate relationship mind at its joints.

The model presented by Gangestad and Simpson exploits a concept that I have returned to often; namely, that people flexibly alter their cognition and behavior (consciously or unconsciously) according to interactions between their stored relationship theories and a range of other factors, including personal goals, biological variables, and the relationship or social context. For example, a well-replicated finding is

Table 8.1 Correlations among self-rated mate values and importance attached to mate ideals

	Warmth/ Loyalty Ideal	Vitality/ Attractiveness Ideal	Status/ Resources Ideal
Self Warmth/Loyalty	**.53**	.26	.11
Self Vitality/Attractiveness	.04	**.54**	.23
Self Status/Resources	.10	.29	**.37**

that women prefer the smell of T-shirts that have been worn by men who are more symmetrical (the women have no idea who actually wore the T-shirts). However, the intriguing caveat is that this kind of female preference is only found when the women participants are near ovulation. In this phase of the menstrual cycle, testosterone (which tends to increase sexual desire in women) is generally at its peak of secretion just when women are also most likely to conceive.[35] In the same vein, other research has found that women increasingly prefer more stereotypical male faces (jutting jaws, angular face shape, and craggy eyes) as they near ovulation in the menstrual cycle.[36]

Short-term versus Long-term Mating: Gender Differences

Evolutionary-based models of mate selection typically frame their predictions and explanations in terms of two different goals – the search for a short-term sexual fling or for a mate who would make a suitable partner in a long-term committed relationship. These goals, it bears repeating, are not necessarily conscious, and typically find their expression in terms of emotions and desires. This distinction is exploited by Gangestad and Simpson to argue that humans can, and do, change their mating aims depending on circumstances, but that both men *and* women may adopt a characteristic mate-selection style as a function of their upbringing, personal experiences, situational contingencies, and so forth. Thus, their theory is primarily directed at explaining the substantial within-gender differences that exist. However, the same distinction between short-term and long-term mating strategies can also be fruitfully adopted in explaining the existence of characteristic gender differences in the importance of different mate standards.[37]

In short-term sexual liaisons, women need to invest heavily in any subsequent offspring resulting from such a union, but will not have the benefit of a lifelong mate and parent for the children. Thus, in this context, women should be mainly on the hunt for an attractive hunk (good genes) rather than for a sensitive and supportive mate. In short-term settings, men also should not be much interested in their mate's suitability as a long-term partner, but, if they have a choice, should go for the best genes (e.g., the sexiest woman in the bar). However, because the potential investment in subsequent offspring for the woman is vast, compared to the man flitting through town, the woman should be even choosier than the man in this context.

Research has generally affirmed this theorizing. Several studies have found that when men and women are asked about their minimal requirements in a mate for a one-night stand, men typically express more modest requirements than do women on factors associated with warmth, loyalty, intelligence, status, and so forth. Given that everyone "knows" that men are generally easier than women when it comes to rapid sexual conquests, women can afford to be much choosier than men in such a context.

This stereotype (men are easy) is no mere fiction. In a famous study Russell Clark and Elaine Hatfield had (brave) male and female confederates approach members of the opposite gender on the campus at the University of Hawaii (repeated in 1978 and 1982) and ask them if they would go to bed with them.[38] Seventy-two percent of the men agreed, whereas none of the women did. This difference was not a function of the attractiveness of the person making the request. When the same individuals softened the request to going out on a date, 50% of the women and 53% of the men agreed. Oddly, therefore, men were more likely to agree to have sex than going on a date! Even men who declined the offer of sex apologized, and explained themselves by saying they were married or already involved, whereas women responded with outrage or complaints (e.g., "You've got to be kidding").

The standards that are maintained most steadfastly across short-term and long-term relationships are concerned with physical attractiveness, and this is true for both men and women. These findings are consistent with the theory that physical attractiveness and vitality form the primary "good genes" factor – in a short-term relationship all one is getting out of the deal (reproductively speaking) are (potentially) the other person's genes.

In the long-term mating scenario, women should be exceptionally picky in terms of the factors that make for a good parent and a supportive mate – that is, warmth/loyalty and status/resources. They should also be interested in good genes (attractiveness and vitality), but they may be prepared to trade-off such characteristics against the presence of personal warmth and loyalty or money and status. Men should certainly be more interested in the woman's ability to be a supportive mate and parent than in the short-term mating context, and they should also maintain their search for a woman with good genes; after all, men make substantial investments in parental and mating effort in long-term relationships.

However, in evolutionary terms, the woman's eggs are more or less all in one basket – the success with which she can pass her genes on are dependent on her husband (and wider family). In contrast, the man has more options. He can continue to spread his genes around while he is married, and he will remain fertile with the ability to father children for many more years than women are able to muster. Thus, evolutionary logic (derived from Trivers' parental investment theory) dictates that a high level of investment by the man should be more important to the woman, than vice versa (although, in absolute terms, high levels of investment should be important to both genders in long-term relationships).

Again, there is a wealth of research that supports the existence of related gender differences. In long-term relationships men tend to attach more importance to attractiveness and vitality (than do women), and women tend to give more weight to loyalty and warmth and to status and resources than do men.[39] These findings have been found in many cultures, and have been replicated consistently within Western cultures by research using standard rating scales,[40] or by analyzing the contents of personal advertisements.[41] An important caveat is that the size and significance of such gender differences is sensitive to both how preferences are measured and to the cultural context.

Take, for example, the mate ideal category of status and resources.

When the importance given to this category of mate characteristics has been assessed using standard rating scales, using student samples from the USA and New Zealand, some studies have found no gender differences.[42] This lack of a significant gender difference in the USA and New Zealand is consistent with Alice Eagly and Wendy Wood's recent work in which they reanalyzed data from the 37 cultures surveyed by Buss in 1989. Eagly and Wood found that as women's empowerment (indexed by their earnings, their representation in legislative government, and their involvement in professional positions) increased relative to men across cultures, women placed increasingly less value on the earnings of a mate.[43] Eagly and Wood, in turn, explained this finding in cultural terms; namely, women rate resources as more important in mate selection than do men, simply because men tend to possess more resources than do women.

The finding that relative access to power and resources in specific cultures influences the importance placed on such factors in potential mates by men and women does not, per se, damage an evolutionary approach. An axiom of evolutionary psychology is that the unfolding interaction between environmental contexts and various (genetically encoded) dispositions produces behavior and cognition. However, if coming close to equalizing power and resources in a culture (as perhaps is true for university student samples in egalitarian Western cultures like the USA and New Zealand) succeeds in wiping out gender differences in mate ideals, then this creates a problem for any evolutionary-derived thesis for their existence. If evolution has built in genetically encoded sex-linked differences that tend to push men and women in different directions in terms of mate criteria, then residual gender differences should remain when the proximal cultural contexts are equalized for men and women.

One possibility that rescues an evolutionary argument is that because university students (men or women) do not have much in the way of status and resources it is hardly surprising that current wealth and power do not rate very highly when they choose mates. To test this particular gender difference, using a more sensitive and realistic measure, my collaborators and I altered our ideal rating scales assessing status and resources to include the phrase "or potential to achieve" after each status/resources item (e.g., good job [or potential to achieve]). Presto! This alteration in wording produced a dramatic gender difference in the ratings (a finding we had never previously obtained) with women students at the University of Canterbury now rating the importance of this mate ideal category as considerably more important than did the men.[44]

Perhaps the most famous, and bitterly contested, gender difference commonly cited in psychological evolutionary circles is that men, to a greater extent than women, have evolved a sexual system and set of desires oriented toward obtaining short-term sexual relationships. In Edward Wilson's words, published in the original sociobiological manifesto in the late 1970s:

> The . . . conflict of interest between the sexes is a property of not only human beings but also the majority of animal species. Males are characteristically aggressive, especially toward one another and most intensely during the breeding season. In most species, assertiveness is the most profitable male strategy. During the full period of time it takes to bring a fetus to term, from the fertilization of the egg to the birth of the infant, one male can fertilize many females but a female can be fertilized by only one male. Thus if males are able to court one female after another, some will be big winners and others will be absolute losers, while virtually all healthy females will succeed in being fertilized. It pays males to be aggressive, hasty, fickle, and undiscriminating. In theory it is more profitable for females to be coy, to hold back until they can identify males with the best genes. In species that rear young, it is also important for the females to select males who are more likely to stay with them after insemination . . . Human beings obey this biological principle faithfully.[45]

David Buss, in his subsequent influential development of Sexual Strategies Theory, has picked up on the same theme:

> What specific adaptations should be expected in the evolved sexual psychology of men to solve the problem of gaining sexual access to a number of women? One first-line solution to the problem of number can be expected in desire: Men may have evolved over human evolutionary history a powerful desire for sexual access to a large number of women . . .[46]

I will pick up and critically analyze the evidence for this proposition in the next chapter, where I deal specifically with sex and passion. However, I will take an initial pass at it here. One apparently knockdown argument often leveled at this thesis advances speculations about the likely mating environment that existed during the Pleistocene ancestral environment.[47] Consider the likely reproductive success of an imaginary ancestral Lothario, who specialized in spreading his wild oats in a succession of one-night stands. My colleague Russil Durrant has calculated that one act of sexual intercourse between two healthy, fertile adults has approximately a 2% chance of producing a baby nine months later. This may seem low, but there exists a multitude of biological hurdles to cross before sexual intercourse produces a successful birth, and the 2% figure is probably at the upper end of a reasonable estimate.[48]

In contemporary Western cultures, some attractive high-status men have been reputed to have had sex with thousands of women. Wilt Chamberlain (a renowned basketball player) claimed to have had sex with close to 20,000 women in the USA over a 40-year period, which is 1.37 women every 24 hours.[49] However, any reasonable scenario of life in prehistoric Africa would involve much more limited access to fertile women, if we accept the standard view that our ancestors lived in small family-sized groupings, in a largely nomadic hunter-gatherer lifestyle. Our mythical Don Juan would have needed to be reasonably choosy in terms of selecting women of the right age. Married women would have constituted a possible target group, but many married women in the typical hunter-gatherer culture would have been breast-feeding a child (which they may have done for up to four years after birth, judging from what happens in contemporary hunter-gatherer cultures). And, breast-feeding severely reduces fertility by suppressing ovulation.[50]

Let us also grant that our mythical male figure is a ten on all of our mating criteria (after all, a good number of women have to choose to have sex with him), and that he manages to evade being killed or maimed by jealous and vigilant husbands and fathers. Conceivably he may be able to achieve one sexual coupling with one different (fertile) mate per week, on average. This optimistic projection would produce one child every year (based on the 2% figure noted previously). However, adopting such a strategy would involve the trade-off of making minimal further investment in the child to help ensure its survival to adulthood. The one-night stand approach does not look like a particularly successful reproductive strategy for ancestral men, especially given the risks involved to life and limb.

A better strategy for our ancestral Lothario would be to reduce the number of women, but drastically increase the quantity of sexual intercourse; that is, carefully select a succession of healthy women of good genetic stock, and have three-month flings, indulging in sexual inter-course every day. Three such relationships every year could produce two or three children a year (three times as many as adopting the one-night stand strategy, and probably a lot less exhausting and danger-ous). Apart from the standard drawbacks (not being around to help raise the children and the physical risks from competition with other men or from outraged family members), another problem with adopt-ing this strategy is that one evolved system is likely to short-circuit the other. The man is in danger of falling in love, swearing undying com-mitment, and developing a powerful urge to put down roots and raise a family.

Such scenarios may seem convincing, but they fail to deliver a knock-out blow. Consider how an evolutionary psychologist might explain the short-term mating behavior of men, if she was transported to East Africa via a time machine, say 175,000 years ago. She observes that the roving and promiscuous desires of East African men do not seem to be especially adaptive in terms of increasing reproductive success in the current environment. Using standard evolutionary reasoning, she would posit that such desires and behaviors (and associated gender differences) were probably adaptive in the living arrangements of the immediate ancestors of *Homo sapiens* (recall that our species is only about 200,000 years old).

In short, the human intimate relationship mind has been evolving for an awfully long time. It is true that proclivities of the intimate relation-ship mind that imposed serious reproductive costs (without countervailing reproductive advantages) would probably have disap-peared over the last 200,000 years of human evolution. However, both costs and benefits need to be taken into account in calculating repro-ductive success. It is not obvious that an overall tendency for men to be more turned on by short-term sex and sexual variety than women would necessarily have imposed a net loss in reproductive fitness. The key is that humans (both men and women) have evolved flexible mating goals and strategies, and that such strategies have evolved in a complemen-tary fashion across genders.

A handsome man, reeking of status and resources, can have his cake and eat it too. That is, he can maintain a primary long-term relationship with a loving wife, but also have discrete extra-pair mating episodes. Alternately, he can switch tactics when it suits him, sowing his wild oats when he is young, and then settling down in later life. The Hollywood actor Warren Beatty, who reputedly had sex with hundreds of women and had affairs with a galaxy of Hollywood film stars, finally discovered the joys of intimacy, faithfulness, and children at 55 years of age, and married Annette Benning.

The tendency of men to desire – if not always to achieve – sexual variety may have also served women well over the millennia (in reproductive terms) by enabling them to easily dip into a (superior) gene pool when the prevailing circumstances suited them. For example, when fertile women outnumbered suitable men, then a woman could make do with a homely and unattractive man who was happy to invest time and commitment, and with some judicious extra-pair mating pick up some good genes elsewhere. On the other hand, if the women were outnumbered by the available men, a woman could obtain a handsome and athletic mate, but also afford to hold out for, and insist on, high levels of commitment and investment.

Evolutionary approaches to mate selection proceed by borrowing theories developed from within sexual selection theory, such as parental investment theory, and using data from other species (from birds to primates) for illustrative purposes or as supporting arguments. Nothing wrong, per se, with doing this – such an approach is extremely powerful. However, this work often falls into the trap of treating mate selection as a one-shot process in which men and women weigh up the mating criteria and choose a specific partner, specifically in relation to whether they are pursuing a short-term or a long-term sexual relationship.[51] This focus, in isolation, misrepresents the nature of the human intimate relationship mind. What is needed is supplementation from a social psychological analysis.

The Multiple Functions of Mate Ideal Standards

Mate selection cannot be properly understood apart from mate deselection. In both cases the critical proximal-level forces that drive the development of the relationship comprise, first, each individual's relationship evaluations, and second, the nature of the behavioral interaction between the two individuals. As documented previously, these two factors are the best predictors of relationship dissolution. However, as argued strongly by David Buss,[52] ideal standards are not put to sleep after a mate is chosen, and continue to be pressed into action

(often unconsciously) throughout the course of the relationship, helping drive both the behavioral interaction and the relationship evaluations of relationship participants.

From a social cognitive standpoint (see chapter 2), ideal standards
comprise a set of expectations and beliefs that operate in that part of the
intimate relationship mind that (potentially) predate local relationships.
They should be constantly accessible mentally, and be readily triggered
off by any event or stimulus related to sexual relationships. However,
such ideal standards continue to be used after mates have been chosen
and commitments forged by being rapidly (and often automatically)
compared to relevant perceptions of the partner or relationship. The
gap between mate ideal expectations and perceptions of reality can then
be used to accomplish four pivotal major goals in intimate relationships
– evaluation, explanation, prediction, and control.[53]

Take Fiona, who places huge importance on passion and sex in relationships and, thus, places a premium on vitality and attractiveness in
evaluating a mate. Fiona was very attracted to Charles initially, mainly
because he was athletic and attractive. Two years into the relationship,
Charles has gained a lot of weight, and he has lost interest in going to
the gym. Fiona's evaluations of Charles are, as a result, on the slide, and
she is having doubts about the long-term future of the relationship (the
evaluation function). Fiona can use the gap between her ideals and
perceptions to help provide her with an explanation of why she is dissatisfied with her relationship – Charles is letting himself go (the *explanation* function). Fiona can also use the gap between her ideals and
perceptions to predict the future of the relationship – unless Charles
takes himself in hand, the relationship is doomed (the *prediction* function). Finally, on the basis of her evaluation, explanation, and prediction, Fiona may actively attempt to change her partner's behavior; for
example, by buying Charles a year's subscription to a health club for his
birthday (the *control* function).

Jeffry Simpson and I (along with other collaborators) have been carrying out a program of research, using the scales already described, to
measure the three main categories of ideal standards. This research has
substantiated my theorizing about Charles and Fiona, along with a few
twists. We have found that mate-ideal standards not only operate to
screen out inappropriate partners who fail to meet minimum standards,
but are also used to drive evaluative judgments of ongoing relationships. Thus, the smaller the gap between the perceptions of the partner

and the importance attached to ideal standards, the more positively people will evaluate their relationships (the associated correlations vary from .30 to .60).[54]

In one study we tracked 100 individuals across the first three to four months of their new dating relationships.[55] As the reader may imagine, it was devilishly difficult to get hold of participants in such a narrow window. We canvassed almost the entire student population of the University of Canterbury for two years running. The closer the gap between individuals' perceptions of their partners and their ideal standards, the less likely the relationships were to break up one month later (not surprisingly, the breakup rate was high in the early stages of dating relationships – over a three-month period, 46% of the relationships broke up). However, more fine-grained statistical analyses suggested that the way this process worked was that bigger gaps between individuals' ideal standards and perceptions first caused relationship evaluations to deteriorate, which, in turn, actually produced the higher probability of relationship breakup.

In a study by Lorne Campbell and others it was found that the higher that individuals set their ideal standards, the more demanding they were in terms of how closely they expected their partners to match those ideal standards.[56] Although this may seem paradoxical, it is understandable given that individuals with more positive judgments of their self-perceived mating value (e.g., on the vitality-attractiveness dimension) possess both higher ideal standards and less flexible ideal standards. For example, if Mary perceives herself as very fit and highly attractive, she can set high expectations for obtaining a partner who is also highly fit and attractive. Moreover, if the chosen partner subsequently turns into a "couch potato" and gains weight, then she is in a strong position to demand her partner changes or she will look for – and probably find – an alternative partner who meets her exacting standards.

We have found that ideal standard ratings, on all three ideal categories are stable over time (with correlations ranging from .76 to .88 over one-month periods).[57] However, to emphasize again the power of ongoing relationships, when we track dating individuals over time, we find that individuals with more positive perceptions of the partner/relationship at earlier points in time tend to bend their ideals a month or two later to fit into those perceptions.[58] For example, if Mary thought Brian was very warm and loyal, this would have led Mary to later inflate the importance of this specific ideal category.

To what Extent Do we Really Select our Relationships and Mates?

Not everyone agrees with the account presented in this chapter. An alternative (although minority) view is that people exercise little choice in mate selection, and that people do not possess the kind of strategies posited in evolutionary accounts of mate selection.[59] On this "random-mating" account, the mate one ends up with is largely a result of who happens to be available in the mating pool (proximity). Provided a potential mate passes some bare minimal standards, the main factor that decides who Mary or John end up with is simply a matter of who makes a play for Mary or John. The point that bonding and love often naturally and automatically unfold as a function of physical intimacy and time spent together is also emphasized.

No one can doubt that proximity and chance play a huge role in mating and relationship development. Nevertheless, this approach has serious flaws. First, there is good evidence (cited previously) that ideal standards play a more fine-grained and powerful role than would be predicted by a random-mating account. Second, arguing that the main determinant of whether X is attracted to Y is that Y is attracted to X, begs the question as to why Y is attracted to X in the first place. Third, like standard evolutionary models, this random-mating theory fails to deal adequately with the developmental course of intimate relationships.

A commonly cited study in support of a random model of mate selection, by David Lykken and Auke Tellegen, had 738 middle-aged twins, along with their partners, provide information about themselves on personality, attitudinal, religious, and a few other scales.[60] Lykken and Tellegen argued that if the twins chose their partners in a lawful fashion, then not only would the spouses be similar on these factors, but the married partners of the twins (especially the identical twins) should also have been similar on the same variables. The findings showed that the married partners of the twins were not more similar than would be expected to occur by chance. Thus, Lykken and Tellegen concluded that romantic infatuation determines mate choice, and that human mate selection is random in the same way that chickens randomly imprint on whatever animal is in close proximity during the critical period after hatching. Strong claims, wrong claims.

191

Lykken and Tellegen's interpretation of their results is dubious, be-cause it assumes that they successfully measured the specific criteria that people actually do use in selecting their mates. This they failed to do, not assessing what we now know to be the pivotal factors that people pay most attention to in mate selection – Warmth/Loyalty, Vitality/Attractiveness, and Status/Resources. The closest they came was to ask a subsample of the twins' partners to what extent they were (initially) attracted to their spouses' twin. But this is a hopelessly loaded way of asking the question – given that individuals were being asked to what extent they fancied their wives' sisters. The research moral is that com-ing up with the right answers depends on asking the right questions.

Conclusions

The human mating world would be straightforward if humans displayed their mating values on a 1–10 scale on their foreheads, as is done in the classroom exercise I described at the beginning of the chapter. The real psychological processes are much more convoluted.

I have argued that human mate selection does not start and stop after initial mate selection occurs. It is a continuous process, with essentially the same psychological processes at work throughout the course of the relationship. No other animal species (including primates) exhibits the same degree of flexibility, fluidity, and conscious control revealed in the development of human sexual relationships.

One brand of mate-selection model is based around the idea that the process works like a filter, with people first determining the potential partner's status resources and physical attractiveness, then moving on to developing an understanding of their partner's personalities and atti-tudes. However, I do not think this model is correct. From the word go, people advance tentative personality attributions. An individual can *look* successful, arrogant, conceited, interesting, or sad across a crowded room. Women, for example, prefer a rugged and dominant stereotypi-cal masculine exterior to be leavened by a baby-face overlay that be-speaks an underlying softness and sensitivity. Moreover, judgments of sexiness, vitality, or physical appearance are not set in stone at first sight, but seem to be about as stable as provisional personality and attitudinal attributions.[61]

Of course, intimate relationships develop along familiar trajectories, with substantial changes taking place in the nature and complexity of the associated local relationship theories. Nevertheless, the full-blooded resources of the intimate relationship mind are pressed into action from the time boy meets girl (or girl talks to boy in a Web chat room). To return to the title of this chapter, humans select both mates and relationships, and they never cease so doing.

Part III

Sex and Violence

Chapter 9

Sex and Passion

*and then I asked him with my eyes to ask again yes and then he
asked me would I yes to say yes my mountain flower and first I put
my arms around him yes and drew him down to me so he could feel
my breasts all perfume yes and his heart was going like mad and
yes I said yes I will Yes.*
James Joyce, Ulysses

In the field of intimate relationships, common-sense truisms often come
into conflict with science. One such item of conventional wisdom is
that men have a stronger sex drive than women. Yet, contemporary
psychology textbooks specifically dealing with human sexuality, along
with a good number of feminist authors, deny this.[1] Indeed, one recent
textbook suggested that women may even have a stronger sex drive
than do men.[2] The views of the man (and perhaps the woman) in the
street are characterized as simply false, or sometimes, in stronger terms,
as male fantasies, based on patriarchal cultural practices and beliefs that
have infantilized and oppressed women.

Evolutionary psychology is on the side of the conventional wisdom
when it comes to this question, with Trivers' ubiquitous parental investment theory (yet again) being drafted into action. To wit, women
have faced higher investment in offspring than men; thus, women should
have evolved patterns of mate selection that are more selective and less
promiscuous than men. Thus, so the argument goes, women have
evolved generally less urgent sexual desires than men – a theory dis-
missed as "rank nonsense" in Natalie Angier's recent bestselling feminist treatment of women's biology.[3]

Feminists have commonly (and correctly) noted that male scientists
(including psychologists) tend to produce observations and theories
that reflect male "chauvinist" beliefs. It is perhaps more difficult to

control the influence of one's personal biases and experiences with respect to the study of sexuality than other aspects of intimate relationships. For my own part, I confess that a description of my personal
inherent sexual nature as hasty, fickle, and promiscuous sounds rather
less prepossessing than if it were described in more refined terms as coy
and selective. Still, I will do my best to squarely face the biological and
psychological reality, however unpleasant (or pleasant) it might be for
men or for women.

This chapter deals with sex and passion, not just sex. Human love, I
have argued, is composed of three quasi-independent modules – intimacy, commitment, and passion. In this chapter, I will deal with passion as an independent functioning system, with sexuality taking center
stage. I will give equal attention to male and female sexuality and discuss their differences in detail. However, it is important not to lose
sight of the inevitable large within-gender differences, and to pay attention to the similarities between men and women, as well as their differences. The strategy I will use to thread my way through the minefield
of conflicting views and arguments will be to distinguish (as far as possible) between the facts of male and female sexuality and those theories
that might explain the facts. First, I will deal with the basic biological
features associated with male and female sexuality, and associated arguments about their evolutionary origins. Second, I will examine the evidence concerning gender differences in sex drive, and evaluate the causal
roles of culture and genes. Third, I will analyze the nature and causes of
sexual jealousy. Finally, I will evaluate the origins of homosexuality in
both men and women.

The Facts of Life

Humans come furnished with some strange sexual equipment. Human
males have a huge penis compared to other primates, such as gorillas
and chimpanzees. The average length of an erect human penis is a shade
under 6 inches (15.23 cm) and a bit under 5 inches (12.69 cm) in
circumference, although one suspects that such figures are inflated, so
to speak, because the relevant research is based on self-reports.[4] There
is considerable individual variability, however, with self-reported measurements ranging from about 4 (10.15 cm) to 9 inches (22.84 cm) in
length.

198

Men can become anxious about the size of their penis, but they always have available some downward comparisons with other primates like the mighty gorilla, who has a penis that is 2 to 3 inches long in the erect state. The human penis also has an unusual method of remaining erect; after becoming engorged with blood in special spongelike tissues, muscles in the shaft of the penis compress the veins with the result that the blood stays put. As young men know, and old men fondly recall, given enough sexual stimulation (mental or physical), such states of erection can last – admittedly uncomfortably – for several hours. Memories of such youthful virility have doubtless helped propel the sale of viagra to middle-aged and older men to monumental levels since its introduction.

The seat of the woman's sexual enjoyment is the clitoris, which is similar in structure to the man's penis, possessing a shaft and glans, and with a similar amount of variability across individuals as for men. It is much smaller than the penis, typically about .63 of an inch (1.6 cm) in length at rest, but swelling to about twice that length when engorged with blood. It remains rather springy in the erect state, compared to the erect penis, because it does not have the same muscular mechanism for remaining hard as does the man's penis.[5] When men climax with an orgasm, their ardor is normally over, at least for an hour or two, during which time they often fall asleep. Women, in contrast, have the renowned capacity for experiencing multiple orgasms, as they may point out to their male partners (if they are heterosexual) when they wake up.

However, the greater capacity for sexual enjoyment that women have, compared to men, comes at the cost of lower reliability. Most men experience orgasms from adolescence on – via masturbation – and usually have no difficulty in reaching orgasm during sexual intercourse (provided they can sustain an erection). Male human sexuality is stereotypically simple and direct. Heterosexual men have little difficulty in empathizing with another heterosexual man's sexuality, because they are likely to be boringly similar. Women, in contrast, are considerably more variable, in terms of both their sexual experiences and their sexual proclivities.

Take orgasms. Women are capable of experiencing more orgasms in a shorter period of time than are men during sexual intercourse, but they are also more likely to report not having one at all. Women also report more difficulty with achieving orgasms generally than do men. In the University of Chicago's 1994 sex survey of USA adults, 29% of married women and 30% of single women reported that they always had orgasms during sexual intercourse, whereas 6% of married women and 14% of single women reported that they rarely or never had an orgasm during sexual intercourse. In contrast, 74 to 75% of men reported they always had orgasms during intercourse, and only 1 to 2% said they never had orgasms during sexual intercourse.[6] Women are also more likely to seek help for, or be diagnosed as suffering from, problems of low sexual desire than are men.[7] Moreover, in surveys of heterosexual couples, a general lack of sexual interest and desire is more commonly reported by women than by men.[8]

When it comes to sex surveys, everyone has heard of Kinsey's pioneering attempts carried out from the 1930s to the 1950s. Kinsey used intensive face-to-face interviews and ended up with a whopping sample of 18,000. However, the data are old, and the sample was not representative of the population because the majority of the participants were volunteers. A rash of sex surveys were published in the 1970s, including the *Hite Report*, the *Redbook Report*, and the *Playboy Report*, all purporting to reveal the sexual practices and preferences of the American people. These surveys were uniformly unscientific and poorly designed. Hite, for example, sent out surveys to specific groups in the community, such as abortion rights groups, and a mere 3% of the sample returned the questionnaires. The question immediately arises as to how the sample who completed the surveys differed from the vast number who did not volunteer (it is not the size of the sample that matters so much – there were 3,000 in the Hite report – as the percentage who actually respond).

Social scientists have known for many years how to conduct good scientific surveys, but politicians (especially conservative ones) are typically leery about any government funding being used for anything as nefarious as a sex survey. Science and politics make uneasy bedfellows. The AIDS epidemic in the 1980s initially spawned plans to conduct a good scientific survey on sexual behavior, but the US Senate passed an amendment to a funding bill for the National Institutes of Health in 1991, specifically prohibiting the government from financially supporting a wide-ranging sex survey. Fortunately, the researchers found private funding and were able to complete the research, which was published by the University of Chicago group in 1994.

The 1994 sex survey tracked down a representative (random) sample across the USA of 4,369 households, which contained at least one adult between the ages of 18 and 59. Of these individuals, the well-trained interviewers managed to persuade an astonishing 79% of the initial sample to complete intensive face-to-face interviews. The resultant sample of 3,432 individuals represented a good match for the demographic profile of the USA population in terms of age, gender, race, education level, and marital status. Because of its scientific quality and recent vintage, and the consistency of its results with other recent sound surveys on related topics, in this chapter I will frequently cite the results from this particular sex survey.

Returning to orgasms, one reason for the relative capriciousness of achieving orgasm for women during sexual intercourse may be the odd location of the clitoris, several centimeters away from where the action takes place between the vagina and the penis. The other critical gender difference is that men must normally have orgasms to inseminate women and pass their genes on. Women can happily reproduce without experiencing much in the way of sexual pleasure at all, let alone a full-blooded orgasm. These differences have persuaded a few evolutionary theorists, notably Steven Gould and Donald Symons, to argue that the clitoris is not an adaptation at all, but constitutes a biological homologue (or byproduct) of the human penis.[9]

If such an idea strikes you as ludicrous, then consider the case of nipples. Nipples have important and obvious functions in women (both sexual and for feeding milk to babies). They have no obvious functions in men. What are they doing there? The human fetus is biologically unisex up to the sixth week. At that point, if it is a chromosomal male (with an X and a Y pair of chromosomes), a potent form of testosterone (dihydrotestosterone) will duly be produced and the fetus will develop as a male. If it is a chromosomal female (with a pair of X chromosomes), no surge of testosterone is produced, and the fetus will develop into a female. Thus, both sexes are built initially from the same body plan and parts, and all the fully developed organs specific to one gender are present in the other in rudimentary form (such as nipples in the male). Both male and female genitalia develop from exactly the same genital ridge of the developing fetus, with either a clitoris or a penis duly appearing.

In short, male nipples are biological byproducts of the fact that women need them. Nipples have no function in men. However, the case for female orgasms being akin to male nipples is anything but clear-cut. First, there is good evidence that in other primates closely related to

201

humans, such as chimpanzees, females have orgasms during copulation.[10] Second, the human female clitoris contains about 8,000 nerve fibers – twice as many as the penis, and quite different to the insensitive blob of flesh that constitutes the man's nipple. It also becomes engorged with blood in concert with a whole series of physiological changes, including an infusion of blood into the vagina, vulva, and uterus, the release of lubricating fluids into the vagina, and the production of related hormones such as testosterone and oxytocin. In short, we have all the signs of complex adaptive design here, involving an orchestrated biological system, clearly designed to encourage the occurrence and desire for sexual intercourse when sexual arousal reaches a peak. Any plausible evolutionary story is surely obliged to assign adaptive value to women having the capacity to gain pleasure from sexual intercourse or sexual play.

Admittedly, whether the woman's suite of physiological arrangements is specifically designed to have orgasms as such remains moot. Orgasms could just be coming along for the occasional ride. However, Robin Baker and Mark Bellis have suggested that women's orgasms can increase the chances of fertilization.[11] Currently, the evidence for this hypothesis is sparse but the biological mechanism is plausible. When a woman has an orgasm, her cervix pulses rhythmically and dips into the pool of semen left by the man, which has the effect of paddling the semen closer to the cervix. Several TV documentaries have shown this process as it occurs by attaching a small camera to the end of the man's penis and filming what happens during intercourse – a remarkable sight. Moreover, several studies have found that women tend to have more orgasms with partners who are more symmetrical and more physically attractive.[12] If orgasm is (in part) an adaptation designed to selectively enhance fertilization in our evolutionary past, then this is exactly the pattern of findings one would expect.[13]

The unusual length and width of the human penis (compared to other primates) has typically been explained via sexual selection, but in two different ways. The first is in terms of women's preferences, and the second is in terms of sperm competition. I will examine each in turn.

The former hypothesis comes down to answering with a resounding yes the age-old question does size matter? In brief, so the argument goes, women obtained more sexual enjoyment in the past with the better-endowed men of our species, and, thus, tended to select them as mates over their penis-challenged compatriots. This process, in turn, seems likely to have been driven by the evolution of longer and wider vaginas in women as a function of the increasing size of the human brain, and thus the human head, over the last million years or so of evolution. Even so, giving birth for women continues to be a difficult and risky business. Unfortunately, there is no decent research (that I could find) that has investigated the preferences of women in terms of penis length or width. However, anecdotally, it is not uncommon for women to claim that penis width matters more than length, when it comes to sexual satisfaction during intercourse.

The explanation in terms of sperm competition runs as follows. In our evolutionary history men competed for sexual access to females, and females typically had multiple sexual partners – the sort of group sex arrangements that one finds in chimpanzees, for example. Thus, males have evolved a variety of adaptations designed to combat the semen coming from the opposition. Robin Baker and Mark Bellis have argued that this may have occurred in two ways in humans.[14] First, men developed a large penis, and a set of copulatory behaviors involving a lot of thrusting, designed to pump out the semen left in the vagina a few minutes or hours previously by other men. Second, human semen, they have claimed, contains not just sperm designed to inseminate the female egg, but other kinds of sperm with different functions, to which they have assigned colorful names. *Killer sperm* were designed to destroy the sperm from other men, and *blocker sperm* had coiled tails designed to impede the progress of other men's sperm.

These latter claims of killer sperm, and the like, caught the public imagination in the 1990s, were featured in popular TV documentaries, and have been widely cited by evolutionary psychologists. Unfortunately, these empirical claims are almost certainly wrong. More sophisticated studies, mixing sperm from different men, have found no evidence for any sperm warfare.[15] And, tellingly, no evidence has been found for such sperm competition among other species in which the males are massively more promiscuous and virile than are human males. Human sperm does come in different shapes and sizes, but they do not appear to have the different functions ascribed to them by Baker and Bellis. Tim Birkhead, in his wonderful recent book *Promiscuity*, champions the concept of sperm competition, and the battle of the sexes over control of reproduction across species, but concludes that the Baker and Bellis view of human sperm competition is "little more than a sexual fantasy – phallus in wonderland."[16]

Almost every species, monogamous or otherwise, has been found to sexually stray, but comparing humans with other mammals suggests that humans are located on the low end of the promiscuity scale over recent evolutionary history.[17] Human males have testes that are modestly sized compared to most other primates, somewhere between gorillas and chimpanzees (adjusting for body size). Comparative data across species have shown that the main factor that correlates with male testicle size is the promiscuity of the female.[18] Female chimpanzees, for example, are highly promiscuous, copulating up to 1,000 times for each pregnancy, and with many different males per each pregnancy. Thus, male chimpanzees, who will at times line up in a good-natured fashion to take their turn, have evolved to produce large amounts of semen, so they can compete effectively with other male chimpanzees. In such a group-sex setting, having the biggest gonads really counts.

Other comparisons tell the same story. Both the rate and quality of human sperm production is low compared to other mammals and primates. Approximately 25% of the sperm in normally healthy men are biologically defective, compared to only 5% in chimpanzees, for example. The ram can ejaculate from 30 to 40 times a day, and each ejaculate contains eight times the number of sperm that men produce. Male chimpanzees can ejaculate once an hour for five hours and use less than half of their stored sperm. After six ejaculations in 24 hours (if that can be managed) a man has nothing left in the sperm tank.[19]

On balance, the most plausible explanation for the oddities of the human penis is in terms of the preferences of women over long periods of time. However, comparisons between humans and other species should be made with caution. The evolutionary biologist Steve Jones in his recent book *Darwin's Ghost* ridicules the sexual selection argument for the human male's large penis on the (accurate) grounds that, in almost every known culture on earth, human genitals are hidden by clothing. Thus women do not get to view the size of their partner's penis (flaccid or erect) before choosing them.[20] Quite so. But Jones falls into the fallacy, I discussed in the last chapter, of assuming that mate selection occurs in humans only at the beginning of a sexual relationship (like virtually all other species), whereas we know that mate selection in *Homo sapiens* is a continuous process that operates throughout the long (or short) history of a relationship. Eventually, couples disrobe and have sex, and the moment of truth arrives. The size and shape of one's partner's genitals (in sexually aroused or in other states) becomes apparent, along with his or her sexual skills, proclivities, and appetites. Both performance and appearance will eventually be judged and found wanting or otherwise.

Hormones

Many different hormones are involved in sexual activity and desire, as they are in most human behavior. However, research consistently shows that testosterone plays the dominant role in adult sexual activity.[21] Even though testosterone is often viewed as a "male" hormone, this proposition is true for both men and women. The levels of testosterone produced vary from person to person, but most people have an average level that varies to some extent according to a diverse range of factors, such as the time of the day, sexual arousal, and so forth. Men, on average, produce about 5 milligrams a day, which is a tiny amount not visible with the naked eye. Moreover, only about 2% of this amount actually exerts any real metabolic effects, the remainder being metabolized in the liver and excreted in urine. Still, such small amounts of testosterone contain billions of molecules, enough to produce powerful effects on human behavior and biology.

Men produce about ten times more testosterone than do women on an average daily basis. For both genders, testosterone production is controlled by the brain, but produced by glands in the body. The hypothalamus (at the base of the brain) operates like a thermostat. It constantly monitors the level of testosterone in the blood, and increases production when needed by sending signals to the pituitary gland (also in the brain). This gland, in turn, produces hormones that tell the testes in men (or ovaries in women) to produce testosterone, along with the adrenal glands (next to the kidneys). Just as with genes, people are mistakenly prone to think of humans as helplessly locked in the remorseless grip of their hormones. In reality, we control testosterone as much as it controls us. If people decide to indulge in dangerous and competitive pursuits, or choose to sexually arouse themselves with an orgy of sexual fantasies and related bouts of sexual activity, their testosterone levels (along with other hormones) will tend to increase.[22] When it comes to sex, the brain and body operate in tandem.

The production of hormones for women is considerably more variable than for men, being cyclically tied to the menstrual cycle. Levels of testosterone peak just prior to ovulation. The production of estrogen also varies considerably with the menstrual period, but this hormone does not appear to be connected to sexual drive or libido. Its main sexual function concerns the lubrication and elasticity of the vagina. In contrast, higher levels of testosterone right across the menstrual cycle are related to increased sexual desire. One study charted the levels of testosterone and sexual activity in 43 couples, and reported that higher testosterone levels in the women were substantially related to more frequent initiation of sexual activity and to the overall frequency of sexual intercourse.[23]

Other research has found that testosterone therapy is effective for re-establishing sexual desire in women who have low sexual desire. For example, in one well-controlled double-blind study a group of women who had had their ovaries removed were supplied with a testosterone patch, or a placebo patch, after establishing a base line of their sexual activities (being a double-blind study means that neither the participants nor the researchers knew, in advance, which patches were the testosterone ones). Twelve percent of the women reported sexual fantasies at least once a week at base line, 10% during placebo treatment, and 24% during the testosterone treatment. Three percent of the women reported masturbating at least once a week at base line, 5% during placebo treatment, and 10% with the help of the testosterone. Finally, the percentage of women who engaged in sexual intercourse at least once a week was 23% at base line, 35% with the placebo, and 41% with the testosterone patch.[24] Research with men tells the same story, with men who suffer from low sex drive as a result of medical procedures or steroid treatment reporting substantial increases in sexual desire after the administration of testosterone.[25]

To avoid readers of this book stampeding to their doctors and demanding huge doses of testosterone, some caveats are in order. First, many researchers have concluded that once average levels of testosterone are reached, there is not a lot that can be gained by increasing levels much further for either men or women.

Second, as pointed out previously, testosterone may help produce sexual desire and activity, but sexual desire and activity also increases testosterone; thus, positive correlations between levels of testosterone and sexual activity can be misleading (what is causing what?). A middle-aged man who falls in love with a beautiful younger woman may be amazed at his youthful sexual ardor and virility, which he thought was long gone – his levels of testosterone will probably be pushed around as much as they are doing the pushing in this context.

Third, there is a whole cocktail of hormones – not just testosterone – involved in sexual activity, whose roles scientists are struggling to understand, particularly in terms of the direct effects they might have on the brain. Oxytocin (the bonding hormone) is one such hormone that I have already mentioned. Another set of hormones energizes and helps charge up the sexual system, including adrenalin and dopamine. Yet another set of hormones are produced by sexual activity, but are designed to dampen sexual activity rather than heighten it (what goes up must come down). These include serotonin and prolactin.[26] Finally, hormones almost always have multiple functions; thus, testosterone is not just related to sexual functioning. It is also elevated in situations of competition or challenge, and it signals cells to build muscle, make red blood cells, or to grow hair.

Gender Differences in Sexuality

As noted in the introduction to this chapter, the proposition that men have higher sex drives than women has sharply divided scientists and academics. Roy Baumeister (a methodical and cautious scientist not given to hyperbole) and colleagues have exhaustively reviewed the evidence in a recent article, and concluded that "the combined quantity, quality, diversity, and convergence of the evidence render the conclusion indisputable"; namely, that men, indeed, have a higher sex drive than women.[27] Baumeister and his colleagues (reasonably) define *sex drive* in terms of the craving or desire for sexual activity and sexual pleasure. They are careful to distinguish sex drive from concepts like *sexual capacity*. For example, as previously mentioned, women have higher sexual capacity than men, in the sense that they are capable of experiencing multiple orgasms. What is the evidence regarding sex drive that Baumeister finds so compelling?

First, daydreaming about sex is a good measure of sex drive because it is relatively unconstrained by social pressures or external factors. One can have sexy daydreams sitting in a church or in a bus, watching TV, or sitting in a university lecture. Numerous studies have shown that men report thinking and fantasizing about sex a lot more than do women; for example, the University of Chicago's 1994 sex survey found (in a national sample) that 54% of the men reported thinking about sex every day, whereas only 19% of the women reported thinking about sex that often.

Second, research consistently finds that men report experiencing spontaneous sexual desire more often than do women, usually about twice as often or more. One caveat here is that physiological symptoms of sexual arousal are more salient and obvious for a man – having a penile erection is not an easy thing to miss. In contrast, the physiological set of indicators for sexual arousal in women is more subtle, and may be less noticeable.

Third, men report initiating and desiring sex more often than women, in heterosexual relationships (about twice as often). This gender difference is illustrated in Woody Allen's movie *Annie Hall*, in which a psychiatrist asks Alvy how often he has sex. Woody replies "hardly ever, maybe three times a week." When Annie (Alvy's wife) is posed the same question by her psychiatrist, she answers "constantly, I'd say three times a week." This gender difference is evident in the early dating stages of relationships, and at every stage of marriage, right on through to old age. The one exception to this pattern is when romance is at full flood in relationships, and the happy couple is in the obsessive, can't-get-enough-of-each-other, phase. Gender differences may well disappear during this phase, which may last for a year or so.

An obvious artifact that may dampen sexual desire for women is the fear of pregnancy, which is likely to be stronger than for men. One way to address this factor is to examine sexual desires in same-gender sexual relationships, in which pregnancy is not possible. This analysis also takes account of the possibility that men and women in heterosexual relationships characteristically influence each other in ways that may produce gender differences in sexual desire. For example, if men generally make lousier and more selfish lovers than do women, this could turn women off sex, but lead men to desire sex more frequently than their partners.

The research reveals clear-cut tendencies for gay men to have more frequent sexual activity than lesbians, and this is true in both committed relationships and in short-term casual sex outside committed relationships. Philip Blumstein and Pepper Schwartz reported that two-thirds of their sample of gay men were having sex three or more times a week, whereas only one third of the lesbians were having sex at this frequency. After ten years in a relationship, 11% of the gay men were maintaining this high frequency of sex, whereas only one percent of the lesbian women remained at this level.[28] In summary, neither fear of pregnancy, nor the interaction between heterosexual men and women, appears to be responsible for causing gender differences in sex drive.

Fourth, all the research shows that men masturbate more than women. This gender difference is large, and it is consistent across age groups and countries. Again, this is a good measure of straight sex drive, as masturbation can normally be carried out in a clandestine fashion, and it is not confounded with the influence of the partner. The figures from the University of Chicago's 1994 sex survey revealed that 60% of men and 40% of women reported masturbating at least once in the past year, and 40% of men and 10% of women masturbated at least once a week. Contrary to stereotypes, men and women who were married were more likely to masturbate than those who were single, and this was true across all age groups.

Fifth, women report a higher frequency of problems of low libido or sexual desire in relationships than do men. In one study of over 900 clients who were being seen for a variety of sexual dysfunctions, about four times as many women as men were diagnosed as suffering from low sexual desire.[29] In relationships and marriages more generally, arguments about the desirable frequency of sex predict higher levels of dissatisfaction. More often than not, as reflected in the Woody Allen movie example given earlier, the man is upset about his partner withholding or showing little interest in sex, whereas the woman is concerned about her husband pressuring her for more sex.[30]

Finally, men commonly pay money or present gifts in return for sexual favors, but women almost never do. Men also spend considerably more money than do women on pornography, and spend much more money than do women on magazines, like *Playboy*, that specialize in publishing titillating pictures of nude or semi-nude individuals in provocative poses. Women, in contrast, spend much more money on romance novels than do men. True, magazines similar to *Playboy*, but designed for women and featuring nude pictures of men, have been floated on the marketplace (such as *Playgirl* and *Viva*). However, such magazines have either folded or shifted their emphasis away from blatant sexual titillation because this approach has proved not to be commercially viable.

One final set of evidence cited by Baumeister and colleagues concerns the hypothesis that men have a stronger desire for sexual variety than women; thus, men are naturally more promiscuous than women.

At the outset, however, I do not think this issue is relevant to the question of sex drive. Take a man who desires to have, and succeeds in having, sexual intercourse once each with ten women over a period of five weeks. Why should his rate of sexual intercourse constitute a higher sex drive than a woman desiring to have, and having, sexual intercourse with the same man ten times over the same period? On the other hand, as noted in the last chapter, this particular hypothesis is at the heart of at least one major brand of evolutionary psychological theory, and so merits attention.

Several studies have asked men and women how many individuals they would ideally like to have sex with in the future. The results consistently show that men cite higher numbers, on average, than do women. One study found that young men ideally desired a mean of eight partners over the next two years, whereas women wanted an average of about one.[31] Another study reported that men ideally would have liked to have an average of 64 partners for their entire lives (if not constrained by the law or the prospect of catching diseases); the women, in contrast, aspired to an average of 2.7 partners.[32] These data are a trifle misleading, however, because such mean differences are mostly driven by a minority of men who give incredibly large numbers of potential mates. When the median scores (those in the middle of each distribution) are examined, men and women usually look the same. For example, in the study just described, the median number of desired partners throughout life was one for both men and women.

Other studies have asked heterosexual individuals to report the numbers of sexual partners (of the opposite gender but not including prostitutes) they have actually had throughout their lives, and the results uniformly reveal that men report having had about double the number of sex partners (on average) than women report.[33] This result is a logical impossibility. Each man must have sex with one woman; thus, the mean number of sex partners must be the same for each gender. One explanation might be the way men and women define sex. Everyone agrees that vaginal and anal intercourse constitute sex, but that kissing does not. When President Clinton wagged his finger at the American people and told them he did not have sex with "that" woman, he later explained himself by claiming that he did not view fellatio as having "sex" proper. Research has shown that Clinton is unusual among American men; that is, men tend to count activities such as heavy petting and fellatio as constituting sex, but women are less likely to do so.[34]

Other research has suggested that gender differences in estimating the number of sexual partners is caused by men and women using different recall techniques.[35] Men tend to estimate a number; then round up (e.g., "It is somewhere between 25 and 30 – let's say 30"). Women think about intimate relationships more than men and possess more elaborate memories of such relationships, even the short-lived ones. Thus, women are more likely to actually recall each one in turn, and count as they go (e.g., "Let's see, my first one was Frank – a lovely boy – then there was Larry, who was absolutely hopeless and didn't last long, and then there was John – huge ego"). This method tends to produce an underestimate as the individual totals mount and sexual encounters may be forgotten. The timeworn stereotype that men who have many sexual partners are swashbucklers, whereas women who do the same thing are sluts, probably still has some currency. Thus, these biases in recall of sexual encounters (men overestimate, women underestimate) may have a motivational element driving them along.

In summary, folk wisdom has it about right and the standard textbooks in the area are woefully mistaken. Men do generally have a stronger desire for sex, and associated sexual pleasure, than do women. Note that I am claiming that women's sex drive is lower than men's sex drive (on average) – not that women have a weak or low sex drive. If women possessed weak sex drives, it is not obvious why cultures would bother trying to control and curtail the sexual behavior and desires of women. Yet, virtually every known culture makes strenuous attempts to control female sexual expression.

Perhaps the most extreme example of controlling women's sexuality is the practice of female genital mutilation, which can range from removing part or all of the clitoris, right up to slicing away the clitoris and inner labia, and then stitching the outer labia together leaving a small opening for the passing of urine and menstrual blood. This horrendous procedure is usually performed when young girls are eight or nine years old, with no anesthetic, and under unsterile conditions. Female genital mutilation remains popular in many African and Asian countries (about 28) with estimates of about two million girls every year currently being added to the list.[36] In these cultures, it is (presumably correctly) believed that this operation improves the chances of the girl remaining a virgin until marriage, and decreases the chances of sexual infidelity in adulthood.

Finally, to repeat a now familiar caveat, it is vital to keep in mind that

211

men and women differ more substantially within gender, on almost any measure of sex drive one cares to examine, than between gender. Accordingly, in many intimate relationships, the woman will have a similar or even a higher sex drive than the man. Moreover, men and women develop sexually along different trajectories. The peak of women's interest in and desire for sex is typically in their 30s, whereas men are on a slow downward slide in terms of sex drive from about 18 years of age.[37] Thus, gender differences in sex drive should be at their maximum when individuals are under 20 years of age and at their minimum around 30 to 40 years of age (although, to my knowledge, this specific hypothesis has not been empirically examined).

Nature versus Nurture

The facts on sex drive are in, but how should they be explained? An evolutionary explanation proposes that gender differences in sexuality are produced by gender-linked genes, which produce biological differences in sex drive. But, cultural explanations remain popular and have been provided for every gender difference I have described. The cultural explanation for gender differences in sexual desires and behavior in Western cultures typically posits that societal attitudes, norms, and socialization repress sexuality among women, whereas they tend to approve of, and encourage, sexual activity and prowess among men. Thus, young men are encouraged to sow their wild oats, but women are condemned if they are sexually active. Men are expected, as part of their social role, to initiate sexual activity, whereas women are obliged to adopt a more passive and ladylike posture or be tagged with distressing labels like "slut" or "whore." Sexual ardor in men is virile and manly, whereas sexual desire in women is vaguely disreputable or suspect. These attitudes may strike one as Victorian, but are arguably still floating around the cultural zeitgeist. These culturally derived beliefs and attitudes potentially exert a double whammy – they could influence both people's interpretations and memories, and thus self-reports of their behavior, and exert a direct influence on their actual behavior.

It would be bizarre to argue that culture plays no role in producing gender differences. However, the view that culture is alone responsible for the gender differences I have described is equally inane. For example, consider the fact that men masturbate much more than do women.

Masturbation in Western cultures has never exactly been in favor, but in the last three centuries a concerted campaign has been waged against the practice. Standard medical opinion in the 1700s viewed masturbation as causing a medley of nasty complaints, including neurosis, poor eyesight, epilepsy, memory loss, and tuberculosis. In America, by the middle of the nineteenth century, doctors and self-appointed health experts had jumped on the bandwagon and written bestselling books describing the nasty consequences of masturbation and advising people on how to recognize and prevent it.[38]

In Will Kellogg's bestseller, published in 1888, he described 39 signs of masturbation to watch for, including rounded shoulders, weak backs, paleness, acne, heart palpitations, epilepsy, bashfulness, boldness (and timidity), mock piety, confusion, smoking, nail-biting, and bed-wetting.[39] Sylvester Graham (the inventor of the Graham cracker) wrote in his 1834 book *A Lecture to Young Men* that masturbation (or what he terms self-pollution) would transform a young boy into "a confirmed and degraded idiot, whose deeply sunken and vacant, glossy eye, and livid, shriveled countenance, and ulcerous, toothless gums, and foetid breath, and feeble, broken voice, and emaciated and dwarfish and crooked body, and almost hairless head – covered perhaps with suppurating blisters and running sores – denote a mature old age! a blighted body – and a ruined soul!"[40]

To curb masturbation, Kellogg recommended a range of solutions including eating his newfangled cornflakes, bandaging the child's genitals, covering the genitals with a cage, tying the hands together, circumcision without an anesthetic, or (for girls) applying carbolic acid to the clitoris, and strongly advised against anyone consulting a "quack" (apparently not including himself in this category). Graham advised men to eat grain, avoid meat, and sleep on hard wooden beds. Other entrepreneurs developed devices (some patented) including a genital cage that used springs to hold a boy's penis and scrotum in place, or a device that sounded an alarm if the boy had an erection.

By the middle of the twentieth century, medical doctors and psychiatrists had backed away from the ludicrous claims of charlatans like Kellogg, and jettisoned the proposition that masturbation caused blindness or other physical maladies. However, it was still widely believed the practice could cause mental disorders and produce sexual dysfunctions, such as impotence and premature ejaculation. Given the cultural history attached to masturbation, and the continuing belief in religions like Catholicism that the practice is sinful, it is not surprising that a certain unease remains about the activity and that some people feel guilty about it.

In summary, a reading of Western cultural history related to masturbation makes it clear that the bulk of the social pressure and dire warnings were directed against men, not women. In line with this interpretation, a study in 1974 reported that men felt guiltier than women after masturbating, and also considered the practice to be more perverse than did women.[41] The upshot is that if culture were all-pervasive, then men should masturbate less than women. The alternative explanation for Western cultural history is that the norms and social pressures were mainly focussed on men, because it was (correctly) ascertained that men were more likely to masturbate than women, if left to their own devices.

If we consider interpersonal sexual activity, then research on the Catholic Christian clergy suggests that men find celibacy a harder row to hoe than do women. In her questionnaire study Sheila Murphy found that more priests (62%) than nuns (49%) reported having been sexually active since taking their vows of celibacy. Moreover, 24% of the men, but only 3% of the women reported having had more than five partners since talking a vow of celibacy.[42] Biology will out, even when pitted against the powerful subculture of the Catholic Church.

Thus far I have examined gender differences in sex drive. However, although sexuality and the desire for sexual activity comprise the basis for passion in a sexual relationship, it is not equivalent to full-blooded passion. It is quite possible to have sexual intercourse with another, and even have an orgasm, without enjoying it very much and with little passion. Prostitutes do it regularly, and it is not all that uncommon in consensual sexual relationships even where no money changes hands. As anyone who has been in love knows (man or woman), sexual activity can be elevated to a more intense and exalted realm when integrated with high levels of commitment and intimacy. The act of giving sexual pleasure, for example, can become as important as receiving it. Again, however, gender differences emerge; namely, women have a less gonadal focus to sexuality, and a more relational orientation, than do men. In a study by Pamela Regan and Ellen Berscheid, young heterosexual men and women were asked to define sexual desire. Women more often stressed the relationship context (e.g., it was "a longing to be emotionally intimate and to express love to another person"), whereas men more often stressed the sexual activity per se (e.g., "wanting someone else in a physical manner. No strings attached. Just uninhibited sexual intercourse").[43]

The upshot is that men are prone to, or capable of, keeping the sexual component separated from commitment and intimacy to a greater extent than are women. Sexuality comprises a more biologically encapsulated system for men than for women, and is less permeable to other beliefs and cultural influences. In evolutionary parlance, sexuality is more modular for men than for women. Popular wisdom has it that men have less control over their sexual urges than do women. In one sense this is true. Male priests masturbate and have sex with women, even though these are mortal sins in the Catholic Church. American presidents have casual sex with young women in the White House, including sexual play with cigars, even though they are painfully aware of the disastrous and humiliating consequences if they are found out.

In a complementary fashion, sexuality for women is more open-ended and permeable, more responsive to social conditioning, circumstances or context, and the influence of culture than is true for men. In short, women's sexual desires and behavior are less biologically determined than are men's. Some support for this thesis has already been documented, but I will provide abundant additional evidence as I proceed.

The sexual careers of individual women show more swings across time than is true for men. It is common for women to have lots of sex for some months or years, followed by a lengthy sexual drought, then back to regular sexual activity.[44] If men experience relationship breakup, or become physically separated from their partners, they almost always resort to masturbation – women are less likely to do so.

Education and religious experiences exert more influence on the sexual practices of women than those of men. Results from the 1994 Chicago sex survey showed that well-educated women, and less-religious women, were more likely to have oral sex and anal sex. For example, 79% of women with a university degree reported they had performed oral sex, compared to 41% for women who did not complete high school. The liberalizing effect of education was also true for the men, but was less marked (80.5% versus 59%). College (university) education – versus high-school education only – increased the probability for women to report they were gay or bisexual by a staggering nine times. In comparison, for men, the chances of becoming a homosexual merely doubled if they attended university.

215

The increased sexual malleability (or "erotic plasticity", as Roy Baumeister has labeled it) of women over men extends to sexual orientation. About 80% of lesbians report they have had sexual intercourse with men, compared to about 50% of male homosexuals who report having had sex with women. Women are more likely to report being bisexual than are men.[45] It is not uncommon for women to claim that they became a lesbian for political reasons associated with the feminist struggle (in which sleeping with men is sometimes held to be tantamount to sleeping with the enemy). Men never report becoming gay for political reasons. Accounts of mate-swapping and mate-swinging illustrate the same point. In such settings it is quite common for heterosexual women to have sex with other women, usually after being encouraged to do so by the men who like to watch. But, the women often come to enjoy the experience. The heterosexual men, in contrast, while enjoying such bacchanalian pursuits, typically remain resolutely heterosexual.[46]

Finally, cross-cultural accounts reveal the same story – more variability in sexuality for women than for men.[47] In some cultures women are not believed to experience orgasms. Descriptions of sexual intercourse as something that men want, but women endure, appear depressingly frequently across cultures in the anthropological literature.[48] In other societies, however, women expect to have orgasms, and apparently do so with some regularity. In a similar vein, some cultures view sexual behavior and intercourse as ugly and shameful, whereas others view it as erotic and beautiful. For the Gusii of southwest Kenya, coitus is seen as inherently hostile and with disgust by the women. Sexual intercourse in this culture has been described by anthropologists as resembling a form of ritualized rape – it is a battleground, in which men physically overcome the women, in the process causing them pain and humiliation. The hostile nature of sexual activity for the Gusii is exemplified in a bizarre ritual during adolescence. Adolescent boys are secluded following circumcision, whereupon adolescent girls are encouraged to perform nude erotic dances, while making disparaging remarks about the boys' mutilated genitals (the purpose being to produce excruciatingly painful erections).[49]

In contrast, pre-European Pacific cultures, such as that of Hawaii, were famous for their open and positive attitudes to sexuality. In the Mangais, one of the Cook Islands in the South Pacific, young men were given extensive education in lovemaking techniques by other men,

216

and also given practical exercises in sexual intercourse by older women. Sexual intercourse was supposed to be enjoyable for both men and women, and a man's reputation could be ruined if he was not a good lover and his partner did not regularly experience orgasms.[50]

Caveat time again. I am making claims about gender differences. I am not for a minute arguing that men's sexuality is impervious to manipulation by circumstance or cultural forces. Just to give one example, a man's sexual orientation will bend alarmingly (albeit temporarily) under sufficient social or culture pressures. About 30 to 45% of men are estimated to engage in consensual homosexual acts in prison situations. Consistent with the prior argument that women have more malleable sexuality than men, the rates of lesbian activity are higher for women in jails than men (about 50%).[51] However, the comparison I draw attention to here is between the frequency of homosexual male behavior in settings where women are not available, and the rates in normal cultural settings (which are considerably lower).

Cultures, too, can exert enormous influence on the sexual behavior of men. In some Melanesian cultures, such as in the Sambia in Papua New Guinea, the young adolescent boys are required to carry out fellatio with older adult bachelors as part of initiation into manhood. Such practices are based on the belief that swallowing the semen of older men helps in the development of bravery and other masculine traits in adulthood. Gilbert Herdt, in his classic treatise on the Sambia, describes how young adolescent males were persuaded (even coerced) into such behavior. To begin with, the youngsters react with revulsion and fear when they discover what is in store for them. But, most are persuaded to take part, getting used to the idea with practice sessions using a bamboo flute. Interestingly, Herdt claims that the incidence of homosexuality (as a lifestyle choice in later life) was no higher in Sambian culture than Western culture, and that the majority of men married and lived "normal" heterosexual lives (marrying signals the end of homosexual behavior for the Sambia).[52]

Finally, there is one apparent exception to the rule that men evince less malleability in their sexuality than do women. That is, men are much more likely than women to suffer from paraphilias (odd or perverted patterns of sexual behavior). Such behaviors range from the innocuous to the criminal and the disgusting. Paraphilias include fetishes (such as an obsession with female undergarments or rubber clothing), cross-dressing, flashing, peeping Tom behavior, pedophilia, sexual sadism, sadomasochism, frotteurism (rubbing against strangers in public), necrophilia (having sex with corpses), bestiality, formicophilia (becoming aroused by having small creatures like ants or snails crawl over your genitalia), and urophilia (colloquially known as the golden shower), which involves being urinated upon, to name but a few.[53]

Relatively little is known about the causes of odd and sometimes criminal sexual behaviors, but it is unlikely that there are genes for specific paraphilias, given the absence of rubber clothing or female sheep in the ancestral plains of Africa. It is clear that such obsessional behaviors typically originate during childhood and adolescence, and show all the hallmarks of a basic conditioning process, which hooks budding sexual arousal onto peculiar stimuli or behavior. Once human males are past puberty, however, they become more or less fixed in their sexual behavior and urges. Thus, paraphilias are strongly resistant to treatment, even when individuals are highly motivated and receive expert professional help.

Human behavior for both men and women is exquisitely sensitive to social and cultural contexts, and sexual behavior is no exception. To what extent the social environment can alter one's basic sexual orientation laid down in the genes and the womb is another matter, which I will consider later.

The green-eyed monster

I previously argued that men have a more gonadal-centered attitude to intimate sexuality, whereas women have a more relationship-focussed approach. This gender difference is reflected in how men and women experience jealousy. The pioneering work in this area was completed by David Buss and his colleagues, but in study after study in Western and Asian cultures, the same gender difference has been replicated using simple pencil-and-paper tasks that pose (usually heterosexual) men and women questions about how they would feel in response to their partner's infidelity.[54] Women tend to report they would experience more jealousy in response to the possibility that their partner is in love with another than in response to the illicit sexual activity per se. Compared to women, men report more fierce jealousy in reacting to the idea that their partner is having sex with another person than in terms of a possible emotional entanglement.

In a (not very politically correct) cartoon a blonde woman is pictured holding a newborn baby and exclaiming, "Is it mine?" The reason this is a joke is obvious – women know that they are the genetic mother of their children, whereas men can never be completely sure they are the genetic father of their children. In most mammals sexual activity takes place in narrow windows of time, with females signaling their fertility and sexual availability in one way or another. Baboons, for example, signal their ovulation with a pronounced reddening and swelling of their backsides. However, the process of ovulation is hidden from view in women (as it is in some other primates). In addition, women are, more or less, constantly sexually receptive. This all adds up to a severe problem for men; namely, how to ensure that the prolonged investment lavished on their mates and their children will help send their own genes, and not those of other men, into future generations? Sexual jealousy encourages men to guard their mates assiduously, to punish their errant partners, or to fight off potential competitors – all, so it is claimed, in the service of increasing paternity certainty. This, in a nutshell, is the standard evolutionary argument for counting sexual jealousy as a bona fide evolved emotional adaptation.

The evolutionary thesis concerning the origins of sexual jealousy has not gone unchallenged. Some social psychologists, including David DeSteno and Peter Salovey, have argued that, when thinking about hypothetical mate infidelities, men and women base their reports of sexual jealousy on stereotypes about gender differences; stereotypes like "men have sex without love, but for women they tend to go together."[55] When women are told their partners are having sex, they will not blandly assume their partners are in love; thus, their relationships will not necessarily be threatened. In contrast, when men are informed their partners are having sex, they will tend to assume their partners are likely to be in love, and so they will experience high levels of threat. Thus, when men and women are asked to imagine their partners having sex with other people, men will naturally report being more upset and jealous than will women. To support this hypothesis DeSteno and Salovey, and others, have carried out several studies, using the standard paper-and-pencil research paradigm, and have reported that when such stereotypical beliefs held by men and women are statistically controlled for, the gender differences in sexual jealousy disappear.

Let us grant, for the moment, that the critics are correct, and that the gender differences in relation to what causes sexual jealousy are produced as a function of stereotypical beliefs about gender differences in sexual behavior (i.e., "men, but not women, have sex without love"). What impact would this have on the evolutionary thesis? None at all! Consider where such stereotypical beliefs come from. The most likely hypothesis is that the stereotypical beliefs in question are derived from lay, everyday observations of people's sexual attitudes and behavior. Such behavioral gender differences, in turn, may very well be rooted in human biology and genes.

Thus, the causal chain might work as follows. Genes cause men and women to behave differently, which in turn generate the development of (correct) related stereotypical beliefs, which in turn initiates sexual jealousy in different doses for men and women, depending on the information they have on hand. This causal model is perfectly consistent with contemporary evolutionary theory. Moreover, if it is correct, the empirical results of the studies carried out by the critics are exactly what one would expect; that is, the effects of gender on sexual jealousy should disappear when the beliefs are statistically controlled for (if x causes y through a mediating variable m, then the relation between x and y should disappear when m is statistically controlled for). The arguments of the critics implicitly assume that stereotypical beliefs about male and female sexuality are simply produced by the culture, rather than (also) being linked to gender differences in sexuality rooted in genes and biology. Such an assumption is, frankly, implausible.

In addition, the standard evolutionary thesis would predict that sexual jealousy exists in all cultures, that it should occur in specific circumstances, and that it should especially motivate men to guard or punish their partners if their partners are caught indulging in extra-pair mating or are suspected of harboring sexual desires for others. The cross-cultural and anthropological evidence is broadly consistent with these propositions. The treatment across cultures of women who commit adultery is uniformly worse than the punishment meted out to men for the same crime. Moreover, reports of sexual jealousy as a motive for wife-beating (or worse) are common across societies, including hunter-gatherer cultures.[56]

One apparent exception to the general rule that men are driven (in evolutionary terms) by the need to establish paternity and, thus, become jealous when their partners have sex with other men, are a group of traditional cultures in the Amazonian reaches of South America, including the Ache, the Barí, and the Canela. In these cultures, it is (or was) believed that babies inherit characteristics from all men that have had sexual intercourse with a woman during the course of her pregnancy. Moreover, both the primary father (the husband) and the secondary fathers in these cultures are expected to provide food, and to help in raising the subsequent offspring. Accordingly, women who discover they are pregnant attempt to seduce men who are good hunters, or have high status. Stephen Beckerman's analysis of the Barí showed that children with secondary fathers had the best survival rates at 15 years of age (80%), whereas of those who had one father only, just 60% survived to 15 years of age.[57] Thus, the woman's motivation in these cultures to attract secondary fathers is not misplaced.

Do men in these Amazonian cultures experience sexual jealousy? Men from the Ache deny they are jealous, but they often beat their wives for having sex with other men.[58] For the Canela, both men and women are expected to have sex freely, including group sex, from adolescence onward. Men are obliged to have sex with any woman that requests it, as a matter of duty. The obligation for women is not as strong, but repeated requests that are denied result in the charge of "sexual stinginess" and subsequent retribution. William and Jean Crocker describe a case where a "stingy" married woman was raped by six men, while she was held down by other women. If a woman (or a man) continues to behave in a "stingy" fashion, he or she will essentially be sent to Coventry, probably have a spell directed in his or her direction, and will face a bleak and uncertain future.[59]

However, Canela husbands can experience jealousy, and the Canela go to great lengths to "teach" them how to repress and control such feelings. The Crockers describe a case where a husband, consumed by jealousy, confined his new wife to his house and stood at his door with his machete to prevent access by a group of men. Several days later, the same men abducted his wife, while her husband was absent, and had sex with her in turn in the woods. Her mother followed, with machete in hand, but could not keep up.[60] William Crocker also describes how, 12 years after his original ethnographic work, increasing contact with modern Brazilian society had produced the most marked cultural changes in the rules governing extramarital sex. Young husbands had rapidly become likely to express their sexual jealousy and to assert ownership of their wives.[61] In short, elaborate cultural arrangements designed to squash men's tendency to exert proprietorial control over the sexuality of their women partners are fragile and difficult to maintain.

In conclusion, there seems little doubt that the green-eyed monster is rooted in basic biological processes, and that this is true for both men and women. However, evolutionary logic suggests that the threat is likely to be different for men and women. For women, the principal threat is losing the relationship and, thus, the support of their mate. The cuckolded man, in contrast, faces the prospect of investing huge resources over time in children to whom he is not genetically related. The subtle differences for men and women in the contexts that promote sexual jealousy represent another variation on the theme that women (on average) possess a stronger relationship-orientation to sexuality than do men.

Sexual Orientation: A Riddle, Wrapped in a Mystery, inside an Enigma[62]

The existence of gays and lesbians is sometimes triumphantly produced as the ace in the pack for critics of Darwinian evolutionary theory or evolutionary psychology. And, certainly, if there is a genetic basis to homosexual preferences, this fact poses problems for evolutionary theory. Without reproduction, genes for homosexuality cannot be passed on to the next generation. Thus, homosexual genes should have long since been stamped out, because such genes, on the face of it, should reduce reproductive success. It is true that homosexuals can, and do, have children. Indeed, in the 1994 Chicago survey, about the same number of women who identified themselves as lesbians had children as compared to heterosexual women (67% versus 72%). However, in the same survey, only 27% of gay men reported they were fathers compared to 60% of the heterosexual men. Yet, the evidence indicates that the genetic influences on homosexuality in men are considerably stronger than for women.

If no genetic predispositions are involved in determining sexual orientation, this implicates the causal role of the culture, childhood experiences, and the environment. As already noted, there is good evidence that the social environment can bend people's sexual behaviors and inclinations around quite strongly, so this possibility cannot be ruled out.

The question of what causes sexual orientation often arouses vitriolic debate in everyday culture, partly because it is intertwined with religious and normative beliefs about the morality and appropriateness of homosexual inclinations. The Catholic Church, for example, still officially holds that homosexual acts are against natural law, and are intrinsically disordered.[63] In this chapter, as always, I seek to describe the facts and to explain them. I will leave any moral issues involved to one side. It seems obvious to me, however, that our ethical, moral, or legal systems can benefit from being informed by a sound knowledge and understanding of human nature and behavior.

How many gays and lesbians are there in Western countries? You (the reader) might guess around 10%, given that this is the figure endlessly recycled in the media. This figure is often, wrongly, attributed to Kinsey and his research. Kinsey emphasized that answering the question depends on how one defines sexual orientation. Figures from the 1994 Chicago sex survey (which are similar to other recent surveys) revealed that 1.4% of the women labeled themselves as lesbians or bisexuals, and 2.8% of the men identified themselves as gay. However, about 6% of the men and 4% of the women also said they were sometimes sexually attracted to others of the same sex. These figures may seem low, given the visibility and political clout of lesbians and gays in big cities like San Francisco, New York, and Sydney. However, homosexuals overwhelmingly choose to live in cities rather than in rural areas. In the Chicago sex survey, if only the 12 biggest cities in the USA are counted, 9% of men identified themselves as gay, and 6% of women said they were lesbians.

Homosexuals are not merely products of feminism, gay parades in Sydney and San Francisco, or the supposed destruction of family values in contemporary Western culture. Homosexuality has been around at least as long as recorded history, same-sex sexual relationships being alluded to in early Greek writings, for example. The existence of male homosexuals, or gay sexual activity, is also common in non-Western cultures.[64] When the cultural conditions have allowed it, lesbian relationships also crop up across cultures. In nineteenth-century China marriages were arranged and were typically oppressive institutions for women. In the 1800s the establishment of silk factories permitted young women to avoid marriage and gather independent wealth, and thousands joined sisterhoods and lived in co-operative housing. Long-term sexual relationships were apparently not uncommon (the Communist Party banned such sisterhoods after 1949). Intimate and loving relationships between women, which often include sexual activity, have also been reported in cultures such as the Lesotho and the Azande in Africa, and the Suriname in South America.[65]

What causes some men and women to become homosexuals in adulthood? Anne Peplau has argued (along with others) that the answer is complicated because the causal story for men and women seems to be different.[66] In a nutshell, and consistent with my previous arguments, the evidence suggests that genes and biology play a more substantive role for men than for women in causing sexual orientation.

Several empirical findings suggest a genetic basis for male homosexuality. First, there is a tendency for male homosexuality to run in families, with gays having about 15% more homosexual brothers than do heterosexuals.[67] Second, gay adults are much more likely to have expressed feminine traits and behaviors in childhood, such as playing with dolls or choosing to be the mom in pretend-family games, than is the case for heterosexual adults. This generalization is largely based on studies that have asked adults, and sometimes their parents, to recall childhood behavior. However, a few studies have also identified and then tracked young boys exhibiting strong cross-gender behavior in childhood through into adulthood. The results vary depending on which source of evidence is consulted, but, according to Michael Bailey, the more conservative figures from the research relying on retrospective reports reveal that feminine young boys have a 51% chance of becoming gay men (compared with a base rate of about 3% of gays in the wider community).[68]

With women, the data tell a similar story but in a much weaker form. About 10% of gay women have gay sisters.[69] And, about 6% of girls who insist on behaving like boys in childhood become gay women (compared to a population rate of about 2%).[70] As Peplau points out, vast numbers of women report they were tomboys in their youth in the USA (about 50%), yet very few grow up to be lesbians.[71]

When gays and lesbian adults are examined in terms of their psychological profiles, the findings reveal that gays are more different from heterosexual men than lesbians are different from heterosexual women. The popular stereotype of a gay man is a person who dresses and behaves in a somewhat effeminate fashion, is more sensitive and empathic than the average man, and is likely to be a hairdresser, a dancer, an interior decorator, or maybe a nurse. My own hairdresser guessed that about 30% of the male hairdressers in the trade in Christchurch were homosexuals. The equivalent stereotype for a lesbian is probably an assertive, no-nonsense individual who wears trousers, is athletic and chunky, and is a policewoman, a firefighter, or has joined the armed services.

Remembering that all stereotypes are probabilistic generalizations that describe some but not all people in a given category, how accurate are they? Although both stereotypes contain germs of truth, the gay stereotype has turned out to be more accurate than the lesbian stereotype. My hairdresser was correct. Gays tend to have more feminine personalities, possess a greater interest in stereotypical feminine pursuits, and prefer to take up stereotypical female occupations compared to heterosexual men. Lesbians, on the other hand, are essentially indistinguishable from heterosexual women in terms of personality, physical appearance, and behavior,[72] although one study by Richard Lippa reported that lesbians are more interested in male-stereotypical hobbies and jobs than are heterosexual women.[73] Of course, some lesbians are quite masculine in appearance and behavior (the so-called "butch" lesbians), but then so are some heterosexual women.

In terms of sexual behavior and proclivities, however, a crucial point is that, apart from their sexual preferences, gays and lesbians do not look massively different from their heterosexual counterparts. Researchers have repeatedly found that many of the same gender differences between heterosexual men and women occur when comparing lesbians with gays. Heterosexual men have higher sex drives than heterosexual women; gays have higher sex drives than lesbians. The average levels of testosterone are the same when comparing heterosexual men with gays, and comparing lesbians with heterosexual women. Heterosexual men have a more gonadal approach to sexuality compared to the relationship-focus of heterosexual women; the same is true when comparing gays with lesbians; and the list could go on and on.

A study by Michael Bailey and colleagues compared homosexual and heterosexual men and women on seven aspects of mating psychology, including an interest in uncommitted sex, frequency of casual sex, and the importance of physical attractiveness, youth, and status. Gender differences were found for all seven measures, along the traditional lines, whereas on most measures gays and lesbians were indistinguishable from their heterosexual counterparts.[74] In short, many central patterns of sexual attitudes and behavior are more closely linked to gender than to sexual orientation. If one wants to understand gays and lesbians, a good place to start is by looking at heterosexual men and women respectively.

The most influential biological theory of sexual orientation proposes that gay men have feminized brains, and lesbian women have masculinized brains (at least to some extent). This theory proposes that this process occurs during critical periods in the womb, under the influence of hormones like testosterone, that masculinize or feminize the brain in terms of sexual preferences and behavior.[75] The evidence points to a key role played by the hypothalamus, a small organ located at the seat of the brain. This is an ancient organ that helps regulate sex hormones, and related sexual behavior, in both humans and mammals. If a male rat fetus is deprived of testosterone during the critical period, critical regions of its hypothalamus remain small, and it turns into a homosexual male adult (trying to have sex with other male rats and ignoring female rats). If a female rat fetus has its testosterone boosted, it exhibits strong lesbian tendencies as an adult rat, and the same critical bits of the hypothalamus increase in size.[76]

Humans are not rats, of course, and experiments involving the manipulation of testosterone in the womb cannot be conducted for obvious ethical reasons. However, a genetic condition termed congenital adrenal hyperplasia (CAH), which afflicts women, has created a natural experiment. CAH leads to the production of excessive quantities of testosterone in the womb for chromosomal women, leading to the masculinization of the genitals. Some women with CAH have even been wrongly identified and raised as males. However, the majority of such women are now correctly classified as chromosomal girls at birth, and receive early surgery and ongoing hormonal therapy to prevent excessive development of male physical characteristics, such as body hair growth. Follow-up research on these women has shown that they do tend to prefer stereotypical male activities during childhood and adulthood, and are also somewhat more likely to report being lesbians or bisexual as adults. Nevertheless, the bulk of adult women suffering from CAH report being heterosexual, not homosexual.[77]

If exposure to hormones in the fetus (in part) causes brains to become more or less masculine (or feminine), then the brains of homosexuals should be different from heterosexuals, especially the hypothalamus. Indeed, they are different. In 1990 Simon LeVay carried out brain autopsies of 18 homosexual men and compared them to 16 men and 6 women (whom he assumed were heterosexual). He paid particular attention to specific areas of the hypothalamus (termed INAH2 and INAH3) that prior research has shown were much larger in men than in women. His findings showed that the INAH3 area was two to three times larger in the heterosexual men than in the gay men, whereas there was not much difference in size for the same brain region comparing gays with heterosexual women.[78] The critics were quick to point out that LeVay's findings were not conclusive, given that it is possible that these specific regions of the hypothalamus may develop prodigiously in heterosexual men during adulthood as a function of their sexual experiences or, conversely, that they might shrink after puberty in homosexual men.[79]

Twin studies are also relevant to the origins of homosexuality, although in chapter 6 I argued that behavioral genetic studies with twins tend to produce inflated estimates of genetic heritability contributions. Research by Bailey and his colleagues has reported substantial estimates of the heritability of sexual orientation, for both men and women, based on comparisons between monozygotic (identical) and dizygotic (nonidentical) twins. However, in the most rigorous and largest study to date (4,901 twins in Australia) Bailey and others found heritability estimates of 45% for men but close to zero for women.[80]

Which brings us round to the awkward question first posed – if homosexuality (for men anyway) has a genetic base, how does this square with an evolutionary stance? The example often used in relation to this question is the gene for sickle cell anemia, quite common in Africa and among African Americans. It turns out that carrying one copy of the gene, although mildly harmful, just happens to confer resistance to malaria. If one is unlucky enough to inherit two copies of the gene (one from each parent) it is frequently fatal. The net outcome is that in malaria-infested regions (where the gene is most common) most people are more likely to survive if they carry the sickle-cell gene and will, thus, be more likely to successfully reproduce. In an analogous fashion, if, over eons of time, women have preferred mates who are sensitive, kind, and empathic as long-term mates and fathers, then this process should have selected for genes that conferred such qualities onto their offspring. If the genes involved (there is almost certainly no sole homosexual gene) occasionally produce men with a homosexual orientation, this does not harm an evolutionary explanation, as long as the net outcome (in terms of reproductive success) has been positive for most men and women.

In one of the more sensational announcements Dean Hamer reported in 1993 that he had found a candidate region of "homosexual" genes on the tip of an X chromosome, the only set of genes inherited exclusively from mothers.[81] The media immediately (and inaccurately) termed it the "gay" gene. Hamer was alerted to this possibility after interviewing 110 families with gay members, and discovering that homosexuality ran along the female line – if a man was gay, it was more likely that his mother's brother was gay, but not his father or his father's brother. However, other researchers have failed to replicate his findings,[82] and the relevant genes have not, as yet, been identified.

Another striking discovery in the last decade has suggested a different genetic possibility; namely, men who have older male siblings have an increased probability of becoming a homosexual. Each additional male brother increases the odds from 30 to 40%. These findings have been replicated for white and black men, across different countries, and have even been found in samples of male pedophiles (with the presence of older brothers increasing the odds that young boys will be preferred over young girls).[83] These increased probabilities are working on low base rates, it should be noted, so that a 30% increase lifts a 3% probability of being a homosexual into a 3.9% probability of becoming a homosexual. The presence of older girls as siblings has no effect on rates of male homosexuality, and the probability of a woman becoming a lesbian is not altered, regardless of how many older brothers or sisters she has.

One plausible explanation for these puzzling facts is connected to a set of three genes on the Y chromosome (possessed by males only). These H-Y genes produce antigens in the fetus, which provoke an immune response from the mother. Ray Blanchard argues that the main function of the H-Y genes is to masculinize portions of the brain (certainly the case in mice). Thus, the immune response of the mother effectively curtails the extent to which the fetus becomes psychologically male, which can occasionally tip the balance of sexual orientation toward the homosexual end.[84] One appeal of this theory is that it explains why adult male homosexuals have strong sex drives, and fully developed male genitalia. This is because the flow of testosterone that occurs after the six-week point for the fetus, and triggers the masculinization of the genitals, is known not to be related to the actions of the H-Y genes.

Thus, homosexuality in men (but not women) may be a function of an ancient genetic battle of the sexes, with the genes of the women pushing male biology toward the kind of mate that helps their own reproductive fitness – virile, but warm and loyal. Such a tug of war has produced a genetic compromise that occasionally seems to produce homosexual men.[85]

228

Considering all the available evidence, there is a strong case that sexual orientation has a biological and genetic basis, with the caveat (now familiar) that this seems to be the case for men but not for women. However, scientists are a long way short of understanding the complex dance between hormones, gender, sexual orientation, and brain development for either men or women.

Conclusion

There is no such thing as a free lunch when it comes to human nature. The genetic programs that have designed us to fall in love, to bond, and to enjoy sexual excitement and orgasms also set us up to experience profound grief when our loved ones leave us, to suffer the torments of the green-eyed monster when our partners become interested in others, to experience anger, and at times to act aggressively or violently toward our partners. The next chapter in the book deals with this last-mentioned dark side of intimate relationships – violence and aggression.

Chapter 10

The Strange Case of Aggression in Intimate Relationships

And most of all would I flee from the cruel madness of love, the honey of poison-flowers and all the measureless ills.
Alfred, Lord Tennyson, *Maud*

The day before I started to write this chapter I went to a performance of the opera *Carmen* (by Georges Bizet) at the Sydney Opera House. This famous and beloved opera contains the traditional themes of classical opera – a doomed love affair, jealousy, passion, and heated arguments, leading inevitably to the murder of Carmen by her former lover Don Jose at the end of the final act. Such stories of human intimacy are not confined to the opera. The association between love and passion on the one hand, and jealousy and violence on the other, is a common and longstanding theme in religion, art, music, and literature.

We know much about the prevalence and nature of intimate aggression. Disagreement among competing views in any science, including psychology, is par for the course. However, the vitriolic levels of argument in this arena are legendary, and consensus has been hard to reach. The reasons have to do with the serious implications this debate has for public policy, and the associated fiercely held and contrasting ideological positions. Putting it bluntly, political correctness is alive, well, and kicking in this domain. When one of the leading researchers in the field, Murray Straus, first presented data at a conference in 1979 that suggested women were as violent as men in relationships, he was howled down by the audience and forced to abandon his talk. In subsequent years he has been subjected to numerous threats, including death threats – presumably those making the threats did not appreciate the irony involved! Some researchers have also apparently suppressed data from

230

large-scale studies that would have supported the contention that women in intimate relationships are frequently violent toward men.[1]

The same kind of political correctness is evident in the public media. For example, every time I have heard an "expert" being interviewed on TV or the radio, the interviewer asks a question concerning the prevalence of wife-beating across socioeconomic classes. The answer is inevitably to the effect that wife-beaters come from all socioeconomic strata, and that wealth and privilege do not protect women from the violent behavior of their partners. But such a reply does not answer the question (a point interviewers never seem to pick up).

As everyone who is even vaguely familiar with the research literature (or has anecdotal personal experience from working in the casualty ward of a hospital or in a women's refuge) knows, there exists a strong link between serious partner-abuse and socioeconomic status. Men who have lower incomes, lower-status jobs, or are unemployed are considerably more likely to use physical aggression against their partners.[2] My guess is that "experts" are loath to admit such a fact in public because (1) it sounds too much like the confirmation of a negative stereotype (and as everyone knows stereotypes are bad), and/or (2) admitting that many men do not brutalize women may not easily be handled within a feminist perspective, which holds that violence by men against women is part and parcel of a pervasive patriarchal system.

The regular eruptions of polemic in this domain, the competing interpretations of data, and the counterintuitive nature of some of the findings made this a challenging chapter to write. I felt like a detective facing a complex patchwork quilt of conflicting evidence and clues that one knew must fit together, but was not quite sure how – thus, the title of the chapter. Hopefully, my efforts to unravel the mystery are closer to Sherlock Holmes than Inspector Clouseau!

Consider the following question. In intimate heterosexual relationships, who are more violent and physically aggressive – men or women? My guess is you answered "men." Everyone knows that men are generally more aggressive and violent than women. Moreover, a substantial campaign over the last three decades has been directed at raising public awareness of the problems of wife-battering and abuse that were previously condoned or hidden. In the process, laws have been changed, police practices have been substantially altered when dealing with domestic abuse, and networks of women's refuges or safe houses have been established.

Numerous campaigns, media interviews, books, and magazine articles in Western countries, including New Zealand, have painted the same picture of the prototypical violent episode of a marital couple – male partner (probably drunk) comes home, complains about the dinner not being ready, and physically lashes out at his wife in an unprovoked assault. Conversely, the couple has a heated verbal argument, leading to the man attacking the women brutally with his fists. Male violence is always portrayed as an attempt to control the wife or punish her for some imagined or real unwifely behavior, and the woman is cast as the helpless and bullied victim.

When researchers began to measure rates of violence in intimate relationships from the 1970s on, the results created a storm of controversy. Most of this research has used a measuring instrument termed the Conflict Tactics Scale, developed by Murray Straus.[3] This scale has borne the brunt of the subsequent criticism of the related body of research.[4] The scale asks individuals to report how often they have experienced a range of events (19 in all) in the past year of their relationship. These events range from behaviors like sulking or crying, to throwing or slapping, to beating the partner up, to using a knife or gun. Most studies ask people to report both how often they have initiated each "violent" activity, and how often they have been the recipient of such behavior from their partner. This scale (or slight variants) has been used in over 70 studies, involving more than 60,000 participants.[5] They have been carried out in different countries, including the USA, Canada, New Zealand, Korea, Israel, and the United Kingdom, with both married and dating couples and, more recently, with lesbian and gay couples.

The results have consistently revealed surprisingly high frequencies of aggressive behavior in the previous year.[6] For married couples, about 16% of couples report at least one act of physical aggression in the previous year.[7] For dating and cohabiting couples (who are, of course, younger than samples of married couples) the rate of dating violence is about double the married rate, the estimates being closer to 30%.[8] As might be expected, the reported rates for minor physical violence are considerably higher (in the 15 to 30% range) than for severe physical violence (in the 5 to 15% range).[9]

Several factors predict who will be more violent in intimate relationships. More violent individuals in relationships are younger,[10] more likely to be dating and cohabiting than married,[11] less well-educated,[12] more likely to be unemployed,[13] more likely to abuse alcohol and other drugs,[14] are less satisfied with the relationship,[15] and more depressed and anxious.[16] Moreover, associations between these variables and the incidence of reported violence are substantial, usually attaining correlations in the .20 to .40 range. However, the bombshell from this body of research is the gender differences obtained, which are in stark contrast to the sex-role stereotype described above of the violent male and the victimized woman. The rates of violent acts (both minor and major) reported by men and women in intimate relationships are roughly equivalent; however, there is a slight tendency for both men and women to report that women are more likely to be initiators of violence than men.[17] Moreover, the prevalence and correlates of violence in lesbian and gay relationships is similar to those found in heterosexual relationships, and lesbian relationships are no less violent than gay relationships.[18]

These findings of a symmetry in intimate violence across gender have been obtained in both dating and married samples, across several countries, and using a variety of sampling and interviewing techniques (e.g., telephone and face-to-face interviewing). Most of this research has been reported in peer-review journals, has used exemplary methodologies, and has included large samples (some in the thousands). In short, these research results are remarkably robust and well replicated. They have also resulted in claims that the incidence of violence of women against men in intimate relationships has been ignored or trivialized, and even that there exists a well-hidden "battered husband syndrome."[19] It is not difficult to see why these findings have provoked a storm of controversy.

Can our intuitions and popular stereotypes really be that wrong? Have we all been dupes of a well-orchestrated feminist plot? My answers are (more or less) no and no; but this is not because the data from the Conflict Tactics Scale are wrong or uninformative. To begin to unravel the mystery I will examine some of the most common criticisms leveled at the body of research using the Conflict Tactics Scale, including those related to:

- the reliability and validity of the scale,
- research that has examined the contexts and motives of partners involved in violent episodes in intimate relationships,
- research that has examined how couples in violent relationships interact when discussing problems, and
- the consequences of aggressive acts, including the most severe consequence imaginable – death.

Finally, I will consider how we might explain the amount and nature of intimate violence.

Is the Conflict Tactics Scale Reliable and Valid?

In response to the counterintuitive results produced by the Conflict Tactics Scale strong criticisms have been leveled at both its reliability and validity. The reliability of a scale is concerned with its consistency. Consistency can be measured in at least two major ways. One method is in terms of the internal consistency of a scale. If a scale purportedly measures one construct (such as the tendency to be aggressive in a specific relationship), then people who complete the scale should be consistent in their responses across the items; that is, if respondents say they sometimes choke their partner, they should also be likely to report that they sometimes push their partner. The second method used is to get the same group of people to complete the same scale at two different points of time, leaving enough time (normally at least three weeks) between the two administrations to remove the possibility that people are simply remembering their prior responses and repeating them. The Conflict Tactics Scale has performed well using either measure of consistency, with good internal reliability being reported[20] and also good reliability found over time using overall indices of violent aggression.[21]

Evidence of reliable measurement merely shows that the measuring instrument is assessing something other than random noise (e.g., mistakes made by the respondents) or some construct that is inherently wildly variable (such as daily mood). Such evidence does not tell us what construct is actually being measured. The issue of whether a test or scale measures what it is intended to measure is termed its validity. Can we trust the Conflict Tactics Scale to accurately reveal levels of violence and aggression in intimate relationships? There are several standard ways of testing the validity of any scale or test. However, they all come down to the same thing – does the test predict people's affect, behavior, or cognition in a fashion that is consistent with the underlying theory specifying what the test or scale supposedly measures?

How accurate are the self-reports from the Conflict Tactics Scale? It is certainly plausible that people might underreport levels of violence in their own relationships, given the possible shame or discomfort engendered in admitting such behavior to a total stranger. Surveys have shown that there exists general disapproval of intimate violence in Western countries, and this attitude has strengthened to some extent over the last three decades. One analysis of a series of large surveys from 1968 to 1994 in the USA, by Murray Straus and others,[22] showed that approval by respondents of slapping a wife's face by a husband (under some circumstances) dropped from 20% in 1968 to under 10% in 1994. In the same time span, the percentage of respondents approving a wife slapping a husband's face (under some circumstances) increased slightly from 22% to 23%.

This kind of asymmetry in approval of violence depending on the gender of the assailant (at least the less severe variety) may be a function of strength and size differences between men and women. A man hitting a woman is never funny because it resembles bullying, whereas a woman hitting a man can be amusing (witness TV sitcoms where a woman hitting or pushing a man, or pouring beer over his head, is often designed to get a laugh).

Consistent with the unsavory nature of intimate violence, there is evidence that both men and women tend to underreport their own levels of violence on the Conflict Tactics Scale, although in samples of couples seeking counseling, men seem more loath to admit their own severe violence than do women. Richard Heyman and Karin Schlee estimated that people underreport their own aggression by about 40%.[23] Such estimates are actually guesswork, not being based on comparisons of self-reports with actual behavior, but on comparisons with how often men report being a perpetrator of violent behavior with their partners' reports of being victims of the same behavior (and vice versa).

However, it is unlikely that the lack of gender differences in reported intimate violence could be an artifact of underreporting. The reason is that most research has asked men and women to report their violence in terms of being both victims and assailants. Regardless of whether the self-reports of the men or women are used, the results are generally the same – women commit more or less the same number of violent acts in a relationship as men. Underreporting by either gender or both genders could not produce such a consistent pattern of results.

In the course of a vigorous attack on the validity of the Conflict Tactics Scale, Russell Dobash and his colleagues argued that research showing poor agreement between partners of couples who have completed the Conflict Tactics Scale decisively invalidates the scale.[24] Actually, the percentages of agreement across partners for each item are high (around 90%), but this is mainly produced by couples agreeing that no violence occurred in the last year. When the data are examined for couples in which at least one individual reported a violent act, the results show relatively weak levels of agreement, considering each item on the Conflict Tactics Scale separately.[25] However, given the vicissitudes of memory, response biases, and general noise, this is exactly what one should expect, especially given the inherent difficulty of accurately recalling who did what to whom concerning specific relationship events that occurred up to a year before.

Notice, however, that there is weak evidence of agreement between partners when taking each item on the Conflict Tactics Scale separately. When faced with this situation, good psychometric practice is to sum the different measures of the same construct and then recalculate the relation between the two measures. Aggregating data in this way has the effect of substantially increasing the reliability of the measure, which in turn produces a far more accurate estimate of how this measure relates to other factors. To explain why, imagine assessing the relationship between the ability of a group of baseball batters and some measure of physical hand–eye co-ordination obtained in the laboratory. If one used the number of safe hits in a single game as a measure of batting ability, one would find that the two variables (safe hits and hand–eye co-ordination) would be related weakly at best. This is simply because there is so much luck and random noise involved in how successful a baseball batter is in a single game that performance in one game constitutes an exceptionally unreliable measure of batting ability.

To obtain a more accurate measure of batting performance one needs to sum batting performance across many games, say a whole season. If we then correlated this expanded measure of batting ability with hand–eye co-ordination, we would come much closer to accurately assessing the real strength of the link between the two variables. If the relationship between batting ability and test performance was high as a matter of empirical reality, our test would now reveal this (assuming that our measure of hand–eye co-ordination is also reliable and valid).

What goes for baseball goes for violence in relationships. Thus, the solution is to combine the individual indices of violence in relationships – from the Conflict Tactics Scale – and recalculate the amount of agreement across partners. When this has been done, the agreement between partners is quite high (rather than nonexistent or weak) with correlations of up to .70.[26] These correlations represent more accurate estimates of the extent to which partners agree, and are not simply the inflated results of statistical tricks. Moreover, in a study by Lynn Magdol and colleagues of a large sample of couples,[27] it was found that the same factors (educational attainment, employment status, and so forth) successfully predicted the incidence of violence – as assessed by the Conflict Tactics Scale – in exactly the same way regardless of whether the rates of violence used came from the individuals' reports of self as protagonist or the reports of their partners as victims. These particular results provide powerful evidence for the validity of the Conflict Tactics Scale.

Finally, there is solid evidence that responses to the Conflict Tactics Scale predict what is often thought of as the gold standard in psychology – behavior. For example, several studies have found that couples who report high levels of severe violence, when matched against couples who are equal in terms of perceived marital quality but low in reported violence, are observed to be more caustic and critical with one another when discussing marital problems.[28] The scale also predicts divorce with spectacular success. Erika Lawrence and Thomas Bradbury followed 56 recently wed couples over a four-year period, and found that couples who reported any aggression (48% of the sample) sustained a 137% higher risk of separation or divorce than the nonaggressive couples.[29] Couples who reported severe levels of violence (kicking, beating, and so forth) were especially likely to separate – 96% of this group failed to last the four years out.

In summary, in spite of claims to the contrary, a dispassionate analysis of the evidence shows that the Conflict Tactics Scale provides reasonable ballpark estimates of the frequency of violence in intimate relationships. However, the critics are a long way short of being done.

What Do the Results from the Conflict Tactics Scale Really Mean?

As critics never tire of pointing out, a problem with the Conflict Tactics Scale is that it is not informative about the context and motives in which intimate violence occurs. It is possible, for example, that women are violent or aggressive mainly in defending themselves or in protecting their children. Evidence from interviews with battered women describes the popular account, already alluded to, of almost anything triggering the man's violence (from wearing the wrong clothes, to being late, to making a critical comment). The explosion of violence from the men is subsequently followed by abject apologies and empty promises that it will not happen again. The antecedent is typically reported by the women as a challenge to the authority of the partner, and the women claim that they rarely hit first.[30] The main difficulty with this body of research is that it only asks women about male-to-female violent episodes, and uses self-selected samples of women who were battered by their husbands. It is folly to draw substantive conclusions about the natural ecology and nature of violence in intimate relationships from such work.

One clue about the nature of relationship violence is that one of the most powerful predictors of whether either men or women report being a victim of violence is simply the extent to which they also report being perpetrators of violence. A recent study by Lynn Magdol and her colleagues, with a sample of 861 young adults from New Zealand, found that women who were victims of severe violence from their partners were 10 times more likely to be perpetrators of severe violence, while victimized men were 19 times more likely to be perpetrators.[31] This evidence suggests that violence and aggression is a two-way street rather than simply consisting of one individual (man or woman) beating up a hapless victim. Moreover, several studies have found that women report striking the first blow in an argument as often as men.[32]

Various studies have also examined the attributions of the participants, using either general samples or couples seeking marital therapy. Again, these studies show a largely symmetrical pattern of reported explanations for the violence (of self or partner) across gender for both moderate and severe violent episodes, although there is some evidence that women attribute their own violence to self-defense somewhat more than men.[33] There is little evidence from such research, however, that women are most commonly violent or aggressive in relationships simply in response to the threatened or actual physical violence of their partners.

It is certainly the case that the incidence of violence is asymmetrical in some relationships. However, this asymmetry is not always from the male to the female. A study by Dina Vivian and Jennifer Langhinrichsen-Rohling of couples seeking marital therapy found (to the authors' surprise) that a subgroup of verbally and physically abused husbands emerged,[34] in addition to a somewhat larger group of abused wives. The largest group, consistent with what I have already outlined, was composed of couples who were equally abusive (albeit at relatively low levels).

Individuals and Relationships Differ

One way of resolving the inconsistent findings of the battered wife (feminist-grounded literature) with the more general research examining relationship violence (using the Conflict Tactics Scale) is that they are both right, but are examining different kinds of sample. Women who escape to refuges, or end up in hospital with injuries, might be partnered with violent men who use physical aggression to intimidate and control their partners. For this kind of sample, severe violence might also be largely asymmetrical with most directed against women by men. When surveying or studying more general community-based samples, however, this kind of couple, and associated relationship violence, might fade into a 5% tail in one of the distributions, and become less statistically visible.

The numbers of women ending up in hospital as a result of assaults from their husbands, in women's refuges, or even killed by their husbands, can make it appear as if such male violence is an epidemic. In fact even a superficial analysis makes it obvious that quite small numbers of men could be responsible for such violence. Take the apparently horrendously high figure of close to 5,000 women per year ending up in women's refuges in New Zealand, which has a population of 3.8 million.[35]

Assuming that each woman is assaulted by one man, this 5,000 figure entails that fewer than 1% of the adult men in New Zealand, who are involved in cohabiting or marital relationships, are forcing their partners to seek help from a women's refuge (using New Zealand census data). Relatively small numbers of people can and do wreak havoc in society. The same victims (who may also be offenders) also tend to be counted again and again in crime statistics. As an illustration, in a recent survey of criminal offending with a large randomly selected sample of adults in New Zealand, a mere .05% of the sample (both men and women) accounted for a whopping 68% of the total number of times that people reported being physically or sexually assaulted. In short, a very small number of people are apparently repeatedly being criminally assaulted, whereas most people are never or seldom assaulted.[36]

239

There are also massive differences across couples and individuals in the propensity toward violence. Perhaps because they are so busy explaining (and being aghast at) violence in relationships, psychologists and others sometimes forget that in 50% or more of intimate relationships, at least in Western countries, recourse to any sort of physical violence is nonexistent or extremely rare. Michael Johnson has suggested that there are basically two different kinds of intimate relationship violence: *normal couple violence* and *patriarchal terrorism*.[37] Normal couple violence consists of less severe violence, with both genders being victims and perpetrators. This kind of violence is common and is largely a function of normal dyadic social psychological processes. Patriarchal terrorism, in contrast, is carried out by men who systematically use severe forms of violence to intimidate and control their partners – these are the classic wife-beaters whose partners escape to refuges, or end up in hospital, or dead.

Others have focussed on individual differences in men. An analysis by Amy Holtzworth-Munroe and Gregory Stuart suggests that at one end of the intimate violence spectrum are men who might occasionally use the less serious forms of violence in their relationships.[38] These men are not especially violent outside the family, have not suffered excessive violence in their childhood, are not particularly impulsive, have secure attachment styles, have reasonable social skills, do not have hostile attitudes toward women, and do not approve of violence generally. At the other end of the spectrum is every married woman's nightmare – the prototypical wife-beater. This individual regularly uses severe forms of violence in his relationships, is generally violent outside the family, has suffered from excessive violence in his childhood, is impulsive, has insecure attachment styles, poor social skills, has hostile attitudes toward women, and generally approves of violence.

Approaches to intimate violence that take a dyadic social psychological approach are not common. I suspect this is partly because such research does not conform with the politically correct (feminist) canons, which specify that the victims (women) should be the focus of research, not the aggressors (men), and that implicating women in relationship violence is tantamount to blaming the victim and justifying men's behavior. Accordingly, such research can be difficult to get funding for and to get published. However, some scientific work has thrown up several features of the relationship that predict levels of male violence. Higher levels of male violence in intimate relationships are associated

240

with higher levels of female violence,[39] lower levels of perceived marital quality,[40] higher levels of conflict,[41] more caustic and critical verbal arguments,[42] and, finally, an imbalance in status in the relationship with higher levels of socioeconomic status or decision-making power residing with the female partner.[43]

In spite of everything I have said, there exists an important and severe asymmetry between male and female intimate violence, which may account for the persistent intuition that men are more violent than women in intimate relationships. Simply put, men are bigger, stronger, and more skilled at inflicting violence than women; hence, acts of violence by men against women are bound to usually cause more severe injuries and physical damage than the same acts carried out by women against men.

Severity and Consequences of Physical Violence

Surveys based on self-reports and large community-based samples have found that the likelihood of intimate assaults by men causing injury are approximately six times higher than the same kind of assaults perpetrated by women against men.[44] Studies of more restricted samples, such as military couples, or couples seeking marital therapy, have also found that when violent incidents occur (even when both partners are violent) women report being afraid, whereas men do not.[45] Studies from emergency rooms in hospitals reveal that women are much more likely to report being injured by their partners than are men. For example, a national sample of 1.4 million people admitted to hospital departments in 1994 in the USA found that 50% of the women and 8% of the men reported being injured by their partners – a remarkably close gender disparity to that found in self-report studies of couples.[46]

The sheer difference in physical strength and size between most men and women is also apparent in Jocelynne Scutt's descriptions of typical violent episodes in a study of 127 married couples in Australia. Husbands were:

> slapped with an open hand or hit with hands; beaten with fists; kicked, scratched and bitten; had hair pulled; were hit with objects, including a frypan, saucepans, skillet, brooms, mugs, an ashtray and a squeegee mop. Three were threatened with a kitchen knife; two had crockery thrown at

them; one was poked with a peeling knife. One was pushed down stairs and one had a pannikin of hot, soapy water from the washing machine thrown over him.[47]

It is perhaps hard to imagine much nastier violence. However, it is informative to read (on the same page) Scutt's list of behaviors that violent men performed that women did not:

> No husband victim was punched about the head and shoulders, or in the stomach. Punches were aimed at the chest. No husband was attacked in the groin. No wife directed punches so injuries would not show; nor did wives say this is what they would do. . . . No husband was threatened with a gun or chased with guns, knives, axes, broken bottles or by car. Husbands were not kicked or stamped on with steel-capped boots or heavy work boots; no husband was "driven furiously" in a family car, nor was any tossed out at the traffic lights. None was pushed against a wall or flung across the room; they were not held down in threatening positions, or against the wall unable to move. Strangling and choking were not used. No wife attempted suffocation with a pillow. Husbands were not locked out, confined to particular areas of the house, or isolated from friends, nor were any given ultimatums about time spent away from home shopping. . . . No husband had arms twisted and fingers bent; none was frogmarched out to the garden to hose, dig or mow the lawn. None was ordered to weed the garden whilst being kicked from the rear. Nor was any husband dragged out of bed at midnight to change the washer on the kitchen tap.

Many men, because of their strength and size advantage, can use physical aggression or the threats of physical aggression to coerce, humiliate, and control their partners in a fashion that women are generally unable to emulate (even if they wanted to). This does not mean that women do not also attempt to control, coerce, and humiliate their male partners, but they will generally not have access to the broad menu of physically violent activities, available to men, in the pursuance of such goals.

Till Death us Do Part: Homicide in Intimate Relationships

The gender asymmetry in the consequences of intimate violence extends to homicide rates in intimate relationships. In virtually all countries from which data are available, men kill their partners more often than women. Margo Wilson and Martin Daly have collated data that showed that for every 100 such homicides perpetrated by men,[48] women kill zero men in India, 6 in several African cultures, 17 in Denmark, 23 in England/Wales, 31 in Australia and Canada, and 40 in Scotland. The same pattern is true in New Zealand, with 15 men killed for every 100 women.[49] The record for the relative number of homicides by women against men is held by the USA. An analysis from 1976 to 1996 (published by the USA Bureau of Justice) reveals that for every 100 homicides committed in America in intimate relationships (including marital, de facto, dating, and ex-partners from dissolved relationships), 65 were perpetrated by men against women.[50] In big cities, such as Chicago, the intimate gender ratio approaches parity, with women killing men in intimate relationships about as often as the other way around.[51]

Before attempting to explain the USA data, a few background facts are useful to know. Intimates (including ex-partners) kill one another much more frequently in the USA than in all other Western countries. Homicide in intimate settings in the USA, for example, is between three to four times higher than the rate in Canada and Australia. However, in all Western countries, including the USA, men kill one another much more frequently outside intimate relationships than do women. In the USA over the last three decades close to 30% of all women homicide victims were killed by a partner or ex-partner, whereas only 6% of men were killed by an intimate.[52]

More fine-grained analyses of data sets from Chicago by Carolyn Block, and Margo Wilson and Martin Daly, along with a 1998 report by the USA Bureau of Statistics,[53] have produced a consistent set of findings that help to explain these data, but also create some new puzzles. I outline these below (all refer to the USA):

- Homicide rates are different for black and white Americans. The intimate homicide rates for African-Americans are much higher than for whites (running at about four times the white rate across the USA). In addition, African-American women kill their partners at an even higher rate than African-American men kill their partners. In contrast, the white rate is actually quite close to that of other Western countries, running at around 30 men killed for every 100 women killed.

- The weapon of choice for a woman is a knife. Men are more likely to use an automatic firearm or a handgun,[54] or to batter the victim to death.
- Men in all racial groups are much more likely to kill a woman after the couple has separated than are women. Most murders by women occur when couples are still together.
- Men quite frequently commit suicide after killing their wife. Women hardly ever do. For example, in Carolyn Block's analysis of Chicago intimate homicides from 1965 to 1990, 25.2% of white men committed suicide after killing their partner, but not a single white female did so.
- Men are more likely than women to kill others along with their wife (such as children or other kin), whereas women are more likely to use an accomplice in killing their partners.
- Women are particularly at risk of being killed when their partner has an arrest record, or is suicidal.
- Use of a gun is common in intimate homicides (about 60%), but the unusual gender ratio of intimate homicides relating to African-Americans is not related to the availability of guns. African-American women tend to use knives more often than African-American men, whereas the latter prefer to kill their partners with guns.
- The murder rate and gender ratio of killing in intimate relationships for Latinos is similar to that of whites, even though Latinos largely live in urban areas, have similar socioeconomic status to African-Americans, and have similar crime and homicide statistics to African-Americans (other than intimate relationship settings).

I will return to these facts later. Up to now I have concentrated on establishing the broad empirical realities, amid the din and battle of competing views and interpretations. I now turn to some explanations for the distressing reality of violence in intimate relationships. I deal with three: an evolutionary approach, a feminist perspective, and a social psychological view.

An Evolutionary Perspective

At first blush, intimate violence or homicide seems like a tough nut for an evolutionary account to handle, given that such activities seem likely to decrease (not increase) the chances of insemination occurring or of children surviving until adulthood. All the evidence points toward dyadic violence constituting a largely maladaptive way of dealing with conflict. Asymmetric violence, such as wife-beating, is likely to be even more corrosive. The prototypical script for developing hatred in relationships is the suffering of unjustified pain and humiliation at the hands of one's partner that one is powerless to prevent – a good description of wife-beating. Wife-beating in Western societies is associated with increased chances of separation, spousal homicide (by both men and women) and male suicide. In short, as a strategy for controlling one's spouse, it looks downright dysfunctional, viewed either in contemporary terms or in terms of long-term adaptive advantages in our evolutionary past.

However, the way in which biological evolution can influence behavior is subtle and convoluted. I draw mainly from the work of Margo Wilson and Martin Daly in the following discussion.[55] Their emphasis is on explaining the propensity of men to be violent toward women, leading in its most extreme form to homicide. They do not dismiss the fact that women are sometimes violent and even kill their husbands, but they argue that female intimate violence is usually a reaction to, or a defense against, male violence (I will return to this point later). In the hands of Wilson and Daly, an evolutionary approach to intimate violence is intellectually subtle and sinuous – so I will take some time to expound it.

The argument is a familiar one. It is based on the observations that human males have a problem with establishing paternity, and that female humans are sexually receptive almost constantly. Sexual competition, and the costs of being cuckolded by other men, are assumed to be strong selection pressures that have influenced the evolution of psychological processes and structures. The need for men to establish paternity, and the associated long-term effort involved in helping raise one's children to maturity, so the argument goes, have evolved tendencies in men to take a proprietary view of women's sexuality and reproductive capacity – to be "motivated to lay claim to particular women as songbirds lay claim to territories, as lions lay claim to a kill, or as people of both sexes lay claim to valuables."[56]

The cross-cultural evidence supports the postulation of an evolved male sexual proprietorial tendency, with a set of features that are virtually ubiquitous across cultures; namely, institutions of marriage with rights and obligations, the valuation of female faithfulness, the "protection" of women from outside sexual contacts, the conception of adultery of women as a property violation, and the special case of a wife's unfaithfulness as a "justifiable" provocation for male violence.[57] The claims of one school of anthropologists that in some cultures sexual activity is a free and easy affair with no sexual jealousy or possessiveness involved should be placed in the fantasy category.

Women are also possessive of their male mates, and should be powerfully motivated to hold on to their male partners to help raise the children. The difference between the genders is that men are more focussed on the sexual aspects than are women – thus, as described in the previous chapter, men suffer from sexual jealousy primarily as a response to their partners having sex with another person, whereas women are more psychologically attuned to losing the relationship.

The final step in the argument is that because men have greater physical strength and aggressive prowess than women they will be tempted to use this resource to exercise control over their partners and to express their sexual jealousy. Hence, there is no suggestion that men have evolved psychological mechanisms to attack and kill their partners and their own children. Rather, the tendency for men to be violent toward women is essentially a byproduct of men's greater physical size and aggression, combined with a syndrome of evolved psychological tendencies to view sexual access to their mates as a valuable personal possession to be guarded and protected. On this account, excessive intimate violence by men represents extreme dysfunctional manifestations of generally functional adaptations. The tendency of a minority of men to behave in such a dysfunctional fashion does not endanger the evolutionary thesis, provided that the average advantages to fitness have been sustained over evolutionary time by the evolved mechanisms. Evolutionary adaptations often carry costs that are outweighed by the advantages in terms of reproductive fitness.

Such an evolutionary account is theoretically plausible, and is consistent with the evidence from several studies across different countries that sexual jealousy and threats of women leaving (or actually leaving) are the most common reasons for men murdering their partners or ex-partners. Homicide by women, in contrast, is more often motivated by defending themselves or their children against their partner's physical abuse.[58] The partners in question will often be boyfriends or stepfathers rather than the genetic father.

A principal challenge for any evolutionary approach is to explain the wide variability, both within and between cultures, in intimate violence. The existence of such differences in intimate violence is typically explained by evolutionary psychologists in terms of the way in which cultural and environmental factors interact with, and either suppress or exaggerate, universal biologically inherited dispositions. For example, the tendency for men (but rarely women) to stalk and murder their ex-partners – often accompanied with the chilling vow of "if I can't have her no one will" – is an extreme manifestation of a distinct male pattern of possessiveness.

The ability to anonymously stalk one's ex-partner in Western cultures has been ominously enhanced with the fast growing availability of e-mail and the Internet – to the point that some states in the USA have passed cyberstalking laws. The first person to be prosecuted in California under this law, in January 1999, was Gary Dellapenta, who posted messages under his ex-partner's name (with attached phone number and address) in online chat rooms describing her supposed desire to be raped by a stranger. She subsequently received dozens of obscene phone calls and terrifying house calls by men in the early hours of the morning. It took some determined computer sleuthing to catch the villain.[59]

However, certain kinds of men are considerably more likely to murder their partners in Western countries; namely, men who are highly depressed, suffer psychiatric problems, are of low socioeconomic status, and have drug-related problems.[60] For such men, the loss of their partners and children may be the final nail in the coffin of their perceived worth and social status. The common tendency of men to commit suicide after such murders is consistent with this account – they have nothing left to live for, and their wives (so they believe) deserve to die along with them. Severe violence, threats of such violence, or death threats, represent final throws of the dice by desperate men, impelled by an evolved psychological cocktail of sexual jealousy and the desire not to lose their last precious "possession" – their wives and children.

Another factor that should influence intimate violence is the intensity of intrasexual competition. If there are lots of spare men floating around, this should increase the tendency for men in sexual relationships to more vigilantly guard their mates, be more likely to suffer from sexual jealousy, and hence, to fall back on violence to control their partners. Consistent with this proposal, wife-beating is more common in polygamous societies (that have more spare men hanging around) than in monogamous societies.[61]

Whether marriage is arranged or based on choice is also related to differences in violence across societies. This in no way implies that in cultures that practice arranged marriage that romantic love and extra-marital affairs are unheard of, or that the normal processes of bonding, love, and intimacy do not develop in arranged marriages. However, when arranged marriage is combined with both a dowry arrangement and with the woman going to live with the husband and his immediate family, this combination of factors seems to place women in a more dangerous position. A prime example is the well-publicized cases of bride-burning in India. There is also evidence that in India the female in-laws often combine with or encourage the husband in the physical abuse of young wives.[62]

Overall levels of aggression and crime in a society perhaps also produce a climate in which violence and aggression are regarded as legitimate forms of behavior in the exercise of power, and this may spill over into intimate relationships. An analysis by Wilfred Masumura of 86 traditional cultures found that higher levels of wife-beating were associated with relatively high rates of personal crime, theft, aggression, homicide, and feuding.[63] However, one should be wary of taking this generalization too far, given that cultures often have disparate social norms that apply to separate domains, and also differ in terms of specific social norms and sanctions against male violence against women either inside or outside marriage. For example, the much lower rate of intimate homicide in the USA among Latinos as opposed to among African-Americans, even though the two groups have similar socioeconomic and crime profiles, can be explained by the strong prohibition of violence against women in Latino culture.[64] This strong prohibition in Latino culture may be linked to the fact that Latinos are predominantly Catholic, and Catholicism assigns a special status to wives and mothers (exemplified in the deification of the mother of Jesus – the Virgin Mary).

Another factor that operates within cultures comprises the set of variables indicating women are prime candidates to be poached by other men. If a wife is good-looking and young, for example, then her mate may be more vigilant and more prone to sexual jealousy. Admittedly, such factors are also likely to precipitate positive ways of ensuring fidelity, such as buying gifts, arranging romantic dinners, providing sexual satisfaction, and so forth. Moreover, attractive women are more likely to find another mate who might help protect them. Still, we might expect that men will be particularly prone to sexual jealousy in such situations, especially if they are uncertain of their wives' love and commitment, or their wives display interest in other men.

One difficulty with developing explanations for differences in intimate violence across cultures is that cultures are so complex that many of the features interact in ways that will not be detected by simply correlating two variables across cultures (say, levels of violence with polygamous versus monogamous marriages).

For example, consider the puzzling anomaly previously noted that the rate of intimate homicide among African-American is roughly equivalent across genders. How can this be explained? The stereotypical picture (represented, for example, in the burgeoning of "African-American" films by directors like Spike Lee) suggests that there is a lot of banter and mock insults in the interaction of African-American couples, with the women being especially verbally assertive with their male mates. This makes life zesty and volatile, but also seems likely to provoke confrontation and conflict. A study by Joseph Veroff and his colleagues, which followed large groups of black and white couples over the first four years of marriage in the Detroit area, confirmed this stereotype.[65] African-American marriages not only had more conflict and more tension than white families, but arguments were more often about issues of power and commitment to the relationship – precisely those areas that seem to be at the heart of many male intimate homicides.

In addition, women of the African-American underclass maintain strong and accessible links to their families, which might allow and encourage women to take strong action against their partner's violence.[66] African-American families (especially underclass African-Americans) also probably have a relatively high number of de facto stepfathers, or male boyfriends, although there are no exact data available (that I know of). The reason this seems likely is that African-American women are more likely to report being single parents than white women (according to the latest USA census report 49% of African-American women are single parents, as against 16% of white women).[67] And, stepfathers are 70 to 100 times (yes, 100 times!) more likely to kill or abuse their stepchildren than are genetic fathers.[68] Accordingly, African-American women may be particularly likely to be violent against their partners in order to

249

protect their children. Add to these specific features the ready availability of guns in the USA, and a culture in which violence is glorified or accepted, and we have a plausible explanation for the unusually high rate at which African-American women kill their partners and ex-partners.

The strength of an evolutionary account (indeed its main aim) is that it provides causal explanations for human dispositions and proclivities that are widespread across cultures. Thus, the evolutionary argument presented here postulates the existence of evolved tendencies in men to take a proprietary attitude toward their women partners. Excessive violence such as homicide, in turn, is treated as an occasional dysfunctional outcome, as an evolutionary trade-off associated with this evolved male proprietorial attitude to women. This kind of explanation predicts the existence of systematic gender differences in intimate violence across cultures. From the evidence I have reviewed here, extreme forms of violence – leading to injury and death – are indeed mainly perpetrated by men against women across cultures.

Daly and Wilson's evolutionary approach also impressively deals with some of the puzzling findings concerning the factors associated with male homicide, and the profound differences in the contexts in which homicides are perpetrated by men and women; for example, men often kill their ex-partners, whereas women hardly ever do, and men often commit suicide after intimate homicides whereas women hardly ever do.

I conclude that an evolutionary approach nicely explains what Michael Johnson has termed "patriarchal terrorism." However, it does not explain, or even deal with, what he has termed "normal couple violence." The use of minor to moderate forms of violence is equally prevalent in men and women in Western countries, and, hence, requires a different sort of analysis. Moreover, the fact that many intimate relationships in Western countries (as high as 50%) are virtually free of any physical aggression should be kept in mind. Theories that explain the presence of intimate violence also need to explain its absence. Evolutionary approaches tend to repeat the error of a feminist approach in that they typically treat all interpersonal violence as something men do to women, rather than in terms of dyadic interchanges that often involve women initiating a physically violent interchange.

Finally, evolutionary explanations for the massive variation in intimate violence, both within and between cultures, can exploit the manifold ways in which environmental and cultural factors interact with basic inherited characteristics. Such interactions can combine to produce cultural groups in which women are as lethal as men in intimate relationships (e.g., African-Americans in the United States), or cultural groups in which the incidence of severe male violence is extremely rare (e.g., upper-class men living in Scandinavia). Such cultural differences point to the power of the culture in shaping human psychology, and provide evidence of the malleability of biological imperatives in the human species. However, cultures may have to work hard to combat incipient tendencies deriving from our biological inheritance. Almost certainly, no culture in the history of humankind has worked harder than Western cultures over the last 50 years (impelled, in part, by the women's movement) to develop laws and institutions that give women and men a just and level playing field in marriage and intimate relationships, in addition to the wider society. Yet, serious intimate violence by men against women continues to be a major problem in Western cultures.

A Feminist Perspective

Not all those who argue that violence in intimate relationships is something that men do to women adopt a feminist approach, but feminist approaches do advocate such views. According to this approach, gender is a pivotal social and political structure or principle that pervades and structures society. Thus, the use of violence by men against women in intimate relationships is part of a general societal pattern in which men maintain their power through the subjugation and mistreatment of women. Intimate violence is placed in the same category as rape, sexual harassment, and incest, in which men are inevitably the perpetrators and women are the victims. Intimate violence in relationships is thus caused by men, and is linked to their dominant role in society.[69]

Even a superficial knowledge of the history of Western society makes it obvious that women have been discriminated against and repressed, especially in marital and sexual relationships. Until relatively recently, Anglo-American women were regarded in law as the property of their husbands, with husbands being legally entitled to confine wives against their will and to use force to enjoy their conjugal rights. Adultery by the wife was regarded as a basis for seeking financial compensation through the law, and often also as a reasonable defense for killing one's

251

wife. Related laws and legislation have only slowly been dismantled over the last hundred years, and this process continues today. In Texas, for example, if a man killed his wife because she had been unfaithful to him, this constituted a legal defense until 1976.

Feminist approaches to intimate violence lean toward a postmodernist orientation. Thus, they stress political and practical aims rather than standard scientific goals. Such political aims deal with policy, law, the provision of women's refuges, police practices dealing with rape and intimate violence, and so forth. It is not difficult to see why those adopting a feminist approach to intimate violence have reacted against the work of Murray Straus and others using the Conflict Tactics Scale, which has suggested intimate violence in heterosexual relationships is a two-way street.[70] Not all postmodernists are feminists, however. For example, Paul Heelas, adopting a strong relativist position, argues that Yanamamö wife-beating should not be considered aggression because inflicting physical injuries is how a husband shows that he cares for his wife in this culture.[71] The fact that wife-beating among the Yanamamö often causes serious injuries, and even death, and that Yanamamö women try hard to avoid such treatment, are points that seem to have escaped Heelas.[72]

The feminist approach has strengths. First, it reasonably stresses the link between societal norms and values and what happens within intimate relationships. Second, it correctly identifies the differences in power that men and women have traditionally had in relation to sex, intimate relationships, marriage, and so forth, as central to understanding violence in intimate relationships. However, it has two weaknesses. First, it has nothing to say about the origins of such societal patterns. Second, it has no explanatory resources to deal with the huge differences across heterosexual relationships. Why are many relationships in Western society devoid of violence, and why does the incidence and extent of violence vary so much within and between cultures? Feminist approaches, as a matter of principle, stick to a broad sociological level of analysis and, hence, have relatively little to offer in this regard.

A Social Psychological Approach

A straight personality account seeks to explain the tendency for intimate violence in both men and women in terms of stored personality characteristics, beliefs, attitudes, and the like. A full-blooded social psychologi-

252

cal account (which includes personality) of interpersonal violence goes further, and describes the way in which such stored dispositions interact with cognitive and affective processes, both within individuals and also in terms of interpersonal interchanges. The evidence I have marshaled in this chapter suggests that relationship violence can profitably be interpreted and explained with the focus on the relationship, rather than simply on one individual using physical violence against a helpless victim. Asymmetric violence happens in relationships to be sure; however, physical aggression also frequently occurs in the context of dyadic conflict and argument. At low levels of couple violence, the evidence indicates that women are equally likely to initiate physical aggression. As the intensity and lethality of violence rises, however, the dangers for women increase more sharply than for men. Even when the violence in a relationship is one-way traffic, the nature of the relationship, and of the participants' relationship cognition and affect, remain an important component of a social psychological explanation for the violent behavior.

The major strength of a social psychological account is that it offers a fine-grained explanation of the proximal-level processes involved in the dyadic interchanges that lead to physical violence. Thus, it deals well with the wide individual and couple differences one finds within cultures. However, it has two major lacunae. First, it does not address the ultimate causes of dispositional proclivities to violence in men or women, which also means that the causes for fundamental gender differences are not dealt with. Second, it fails to consider the wider cultural contexts that clearly play a role in the explanation of violence in intimate relationships.

Conclusion

Although I obviously have my favorites, none of the theoretical approaches are flat-out wrong, unless they are presented as stand-alone grand theories that attempt to exclude other approaches – which unfortunately is sometimes the case. They offer partial views of the incidence and nature of intimate relationship violence. I will postpone a systematic integration of such approaches until the final chapter. However, it is already clear why the script of the opera *Carmen* remains such a familiar story of human attachment, and why jealousy and violence can be such a short psychological journey from love and passion.

Part IV

Conclusion

Chapter 11

Assembling the Intimate Relationship Mind

Several blind men were presented different parts of the elephant to feel. When asked what sort of a beast it was, the person who felt the tusk said it was like a spear, the individual who felt the trunk said it was like a plough, the one who felt the tail thought it was like a pestle, the man who felt the foot felt it was like a pillar, and so forth. They proceeded to disagree and to quarrel, each insisting that he had the correct model of the elephant, and eventually came to blows.
Indian parable from the Buddhist canon

The parable of the blind men and the elephant illustrates some key themes in this book. Just like the elephant, intimate relationship phenomena maintain an independent reality outside of the theories in laypeople's (or scientist's) heads. However, because of the complexity of relationship phenomena, different scientific disciplines and theories deal with separate components or operate at disparate levels of analysis and, thus, can be misleading about the nature of the overall beast. Like the blind men, scientists (or laypeople) often come to (verbal) blows about the nature of relationship reality. However, simply adopting an ecumenical approach, and declaring everyone a winner, is unhelpful and vacuous. The vastly more tedious, disciplined, and difficult project is to figure out how the different components and approaches should be integrated and understood in terms of the causal processes involved. Playing the game this way does produce winners and losers, but it also allows for the possibility that different theories and approaches may be complementary rather than contradictory.

I start with a simple model, which reflects a few of the ideas I have presented (see figure 11.1). This model proposes that culture and local environment (which can include family, friends, schooling, specific

257

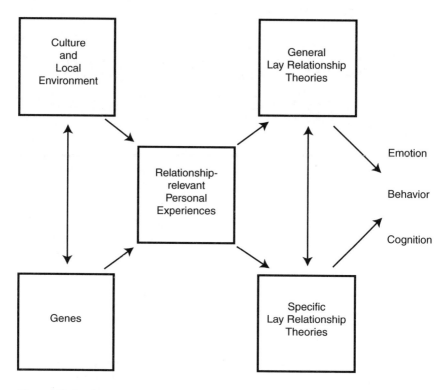

Figure 11.1 An overarching model of the causes and effects of the intimate relationship mind

relationships, and so forth) and genetic inheritance work together to produce the relationship-relevant personal experiences of the individual. These, in turn, influence the development of two pivotal components of the intimate relationship mind – general lay relationship theories and specific lay relationship theories. Finally emotion, behavior, and cognition are churned out at the end. For the sake of simplicity I have omitted the paths that show how emotion, cognition, and behavior have feedback loops to antecedent components. The hidden complexities, and how this model relates to intimate relationships in the real world, will unfold as I proceed.

Interactions are pivotal in intimate relationships. The effects that genes and the cultural and local environment exert on the individual typically come packaged in interactions, not simply in terms of straight additive effects. The correct formula is typically "genes × environment" not "genes + environment". Thus, many of the gender differences I have described come and go in magnitude depending on the culture and local environments. Men tend to kill their partners more than the other way around across the world, except for African-Americans living in the USA, where a set of local cultural conditions have conspired to produce a statistical rarity. Of all the relationship modules, sexuality is the most obvious case for the powerful roles of biology, genes, and our evolutionary heritage. But, even here, the evidence reveals that the relative roles of genes and environment interact with gender, the genetic leashes being tighter for men than for women.

Explaining how children develop into adults requires an understanding of how the genetic templates become intertwined with the social environment, switching individuals onto different developmental tracks as they advance into adulthood. Thus, ambivalent or cold parental care of a girl, combined with the child encountering extended contact with genetically unrelated males, such as boyfriends of her mother, will tend to push her toward an insecure attachment style and an opportunistic mating strategy geared toward early reproduction and lower parental investment. In contrast, a warm and loving relationship with both parents during childhood will tend to produce an adolescent girl with a secure attachment style and a penchant for long-term relationships, along with a desire for a partner replete with warmth and loyalty.

Some psychologists (most famously Freud) assumed that the learning process stops during childhood, and that we are stuck fast with our psychological legacy once we reach early adulthood. Nothing is further from the truth. The learning process never stops, and humans remain exquisitely attuned to the power of intimate relationship experiences and the forces of the wider culture throughout their lives. Attachment working models, for example, are stable, but can and do change considerably from relationship to relationship and over time.

The power of interactions in the workings of the adult intimate relationship mind can also be seen at the everyday level of the relationship. Consider the following question: Is honesty, or clear communication, or expressing anger, or dealing with problems head on, or reading one's partner's mind with unerring accuracy good for relationships? Such queries extract the infuriating answer from the relationship scientist – it depends. In some contexts, and for some relationships, the answer is yes, and for others the answer is no. For example, if John expresses

PARTNER 1   PARTNER 2

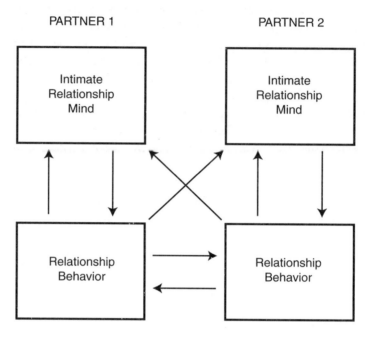

Figure 11.2 A simple model of relationship interaction

anger within the context of a problem-solving discussion with his partner, this will probably turn out to be neutral or even beneficial for John's
relationship. In contrast, if John expresses anger when his partner has
crashed the car (through no fault of his partner) this is likely to be
corrosive for the relationship.

Giving this kind of "it depends" advice sounds wishy-washy and complicated, and would probably not sell relationship self-help books. This
may account for why relationship self-help books often contain unhelpful or even pernicious advice.

Finally, there exists a key interaction; namely, that between the partners themselves (see figure 11.2). Individuals' intimate relationship minds
influence their own behavior in myriad ways. One core process, I have
argued, involves the links between individuals' expectations and ideals
(that can predate specific relationships) and their judgments of the partner and relationship. If key expectations and desires match perceptions
of relationship reality, then happiness and commitment result; if not,
happiness and commitment slide, and the demise of the relationship

may be imminent. However, individuals are not simply free to build golden relationship theories while ignoring reality. One person's intimate relationship mind is (partly) locked into the intimate relationship mind of the other, through the conduit of behavior. If Joan's theory of the relationship becomes divorced from reality (which includes the relationship theories in her partner's head), her partner is likely to deliver a painful correction to Joan's theory at some point.

Humans possess wonderfully sophisticated intimate relationship theories, for the same reasons that scientists have theories – to explain, evaluate, predict, and control their relationships. But such aims, and the way they are fulfilled, will vary depending on the circumstances. If Mary's partner does something negative and unexpected (like forgetting her birthday), Mary will be kicked into conscious attributional overdrive, and will attempt to explain and perhaps control her partner's behavior. On the other hand, if Mary's partner repeats a much-rehearsed and expected negative behavior, such as squeezing the wrong end of the toothpaste tube, Mary will probably do nothing cognitively or behaviorally, except perhaps unconsciously attribute the event to her well-founded belief that her partner is a slob.

Social Psychology and Evolutionary Psychology

How do the two approaches I have devoted most attention to – social psychology and evolutionary psychology – stack up, and how do they fit together? Obviously, they offer complementary theories and models, with standard social psychological theories focussing on the proximal-level cognitive machinery and behavior, and evolutionary theories concerned with origin accounts, and associated evolutionary adaptations, of the intimate relationship mind.

Humans are animals that have evolved in the recent past (in evolutionary terms) from other animals. Thus, it is hardly surprising that footprints from our evolutionary past can be seen all over the intimate relationship mind. I have given many examples throughout the book, but let's take the example of gender differences. Evidence concerning gender differences in relationships has been scattered throughout the book. In table 11.1 I have systematically grouped those gender differences in intimate relationships that have been extensively documented in both Western and non-Western cultures.

261

Table 11.1 Well-documented gender differences in intimate relationships

- Women are more motivated and expert lay psychologists than men in intimate relationships

  Women are more likely than men to:
  - decide to leave intimate relationships
  - approach conflict and communicate about relationship problems
  - talk openly to their friends about their intimate relationships
  - monitor and think extensively about their intimate relationships
  - be more accurate at mind-reading
  - produce complex explanations for the demise of relationships
  - possess detailed and vivid memories of local relationships

- Men adopt a more proprietorial attitude toward women's sexuality and reproductive behavior, than vice versa

  Men are more likely than women to:
  - become sexually jealous at possible or actual sexual infidelities and react violently
  - kill or seriously injure their partners

- Men possess a stronger and less malleable sex drive, and a stronger orientation towards short-term sexual liaisons, than do women

  Men are more likely than women to:
  - fantasise about sex
  - seek out short-term sexual liaisons
  - masturbate
  - initiate sexual activity
  - maintain one sexual orientation throughout adult life
  - report strong and frequent sexual desires.

- Women are more focussed on level of investment in intimate relation-ships than are men

  Women are more likely than men to:
  - perceive physical attractiveness as relatively unimportant in mate selection
  - perceive mate status and resources as important in mate selection

As can be seen, the established gender differences fall into four co-herent patterns: (1) women are more motivated and expert lay psy-chologists than men in intimate relationships, (2) men adopt a more proprietorial attitude toward women's sexuality and reproductive behavior than vice versa, (3) men possess a stronger and less malleable sex drive, and a stronger orientation toward short-term sexual liaisons, than do women, and (4) women are more focussed on the level of investment in intimate relationships than men.

I have argued that the most plausible explanation for these system-atic gender differences is in terms of the existence of sex-linked evolu-tionary adaptations. Culture assuredly plays a role in either minimizing or accentuating these basic gender differences, as is abundantly obvious from the anthropological and cross-cultural record, but these particular gender differences are remarkably resistant to being extinguished.

Which brings me to the final purported "knockdown" argument I will consider. This argument posits that David Buss and others use data to establish universal gender differences derived mostly from agrarian or postindustrial cultures.[1] These cultures, it is pointed out, have only existed in full-blown form since the last ice age, a period of about 12,000 years. In agrarian, non-nomadic cultures it is possible to build up re-sources and food reserves, expand populations, build cities, develop powerful armies and technology, institutionalize norms and rules, and develop complex and hierarchical political systems.

Thus, so the knockdown argument continues, small biological dif-ferences between men and women have become transformed, because of cultural changes over the last 12,000 years, into huge gender differ-ences; namely, men have taken control of the resources and political power and confined women to second-class citizen status. In other words, it is not fundamentally biology but culture that has produced the consistent gender differences displayed in table 11.1. From an evo-lutionary perspective, so the case continues, one should closely exam-ine gender differences in hunter-gatherer cultures, which represent the kind of social environment in which *Homo* evolution has taken place for 99% of the last million years. And, in hunter-gatherer cultures such as the !Kung in Africa we find relatively egalitarian social systems with monogamous marriages and assertive women who have considerable power and freedom.

How should this argument be evaluated? I do not quibble with the point that culture can exert massive influences on gender differences.

However, as a knockdown argument this one is fatally flawed. One problem is that there is huge variability among hunter-gatherer cultures in relation to gender differences and the status of women.[2] Australian aboriginal cultures like the Tiwi, for example, look very different to African hunter-gatherer cultures. Second, ethnographies of relatively egalitarian hunter-gatherer cultures reveal that the most obvious gender differences occur precisely in accordance with the four generalizations in table 11.1.[3] For example, !Kung women have much older husbands assigned to them at a young age. It is true that if they protest long and loud enough, they are usually able to separate from their assigned husbands, most ending up with the husband of their choice. However, young brides are required to protest – such rights are not granted to them as a matter of course. In addition, men physically attack their partners much more than vice versa, especially in cases of sexual infidelity.

In short, even in the most liberal and egalitarian of hunter-gatherer cultures, men adopt a more proprietorial attitude toward women's sexuality and reproductive behavior than vice versa. Finally, there is good evidence that all four general gender differences are alive and well in what almost certainly comprises the most egalitarian and emancipated group of cultures that has ever existed, in terms of the economic and political power wielded by women; namely, Western cultures like those of New Zealand, the USA, England, Australia, and so forth (which is not to say that such Western cultures are perfect in this regard). The fact that the worst excesses of gender-linked prejudice and inequality were defeated in Western cultures only after a prolonged and determined political battle over many years illustrates the power wielded by both culture and our evolutionary heritage.

I have criticized radical versions of feminism at times, so it is worth pointing out that evolutionary theory and feminism are at one in postulating the widespread tendency of men to attempt to control the sexuality of women (although feminism and evolutionary psychology disagree about the origins of such tendencies). One naïve response to a feminist viewpoint is that women often adopt the dominant role in educating their sons and daughters into the mores and norms of their culture. Female genital mutilation, for example, is usually carried out by women, who wholeheartedly believe in the practice and who persuade their daughters of its value. I say "naïve" because this is the way cultures work – people are socialized from childhood into accepting the values and beliefs of the wider culture. The fact that women can be socialized into accepting a set of beliefs and practices that repress and restrict women, more than men, is a testament to the power of the culture, and to the gullibility of humans.

One of the remarkable features of evolutionary answers to the origin of gender differences is their ability to explain the extreme forms of human behavior that appear to pose an intractable problem for evolutionary theories because they wreck the individual's chances of achieving reproductive success. Examples discussed previously include men killing their wives and children, then committing suicide, or the prevalence of homosexuality. The key to solving this conundrum is that such consequences are rare and affect relatively few individuals. The genes that produce the normal range of human behavior have been selected for because they have generated more successful reproductive strategies in the past for the vast majority.

Thus, in our ancestral past women probably selected men who possessed feminine personality qualities like sensitivity and kindness for long-term mates. In the same vein, men who adopted a proprietorial approach to their female partners tended to prevent sexual infidelities and, thus, to send their own genes into the future more effectively than men who were completely relaxed about their female partner's extracurricular sexual activities. The fact that such evolved tendencies can pull in starkly different directions (kindness versus jealousy and aggression) fits human nature perfectly.

As I have repeatedly stressed, the existence of gender differences should be juxtaposed with the wide variability operating within each gender. This brings interactions back into the picture, along with the need to explore the proximal-level structures and processes occurring in the intimate relationship mind. However, evolutionary approaches continue to play an important role. Asking the right questions is one of the main tricks in doing good science, and evolutionary psychology encourages psychological scientists to ask a key question – what are the functions of ordinary human cognition and emotion? Social psychology has sometimes failed to ask this question effectively, for example, by proposing that people have an built-in drive to be happy, or to attain high self-esteem, as ends in themselves. The aims of being happy or having sky-high self-esteem are not, on their own, sensible functions. The psychological reality is considerably more complex.

Evolutionary psychology and social psychology need each other.

Perhaps because they have been the new kids on the psychology block, evolutionary psychologists have concentrated on persuading other psychologists, with evangelical fervor, that they should pay close attention to evolutionary psychology.[4] As evolutionary psychology steadily infiltrates mainstream psychology, and the missionary zeal softens, evolutionary psychologists should consider taking on board the proposition that they pay close attention to the work of social psychologists (and others), which details how the intimate relationship mind (and behavior) works at the proximal level. One example is the social cognitive research on mate selection, which reveals the ways in which mate standards and expectations help drive relationship judgments and processes throughout the history of specific relationships, up to and including decisions to leave.

How does a central assumption of evolutionary psychology – that the human mind is fundamentally modular – stand up? Ripping apart complex relationship phenomena, and analyzing them in terms of independent modules, is a valuable strategy. For example, it is clear that adult human love is composed of three components (commitment, intimacy, and passion) that are represented separately in lay cognition, are underpinned by different neurophysiological and hormonal systems, and are capable of acting independently. On the other hand, this kind of modularity is variable, with different units sometimes acting in concert and profoundly influencing one another. Moreover, humans have the ability to cognitively join together what biology and genes have originally kept apart as modular, unconscious, and instinctual processes.

What, if any, are the unique features of human mating and the intimate relationship mind? A lengthy list of purportedly unique characteristics of human mating has been proposed over the years, but many of these have turned out not to be unique at all. For example, it has been suggested that humans are special in that ovulation is hidden in human females, who are constantly sexually receptive. But female chimpanzees have sex regularly, even when not in estrous. Moreover, echoes of the ancient cycle of sexual receptivity tied to ovulation remain present in women's menstrual cycle, with fluctuating hormonal levels producing a peak of sexual interest around the time of ovulation. Women are certainly at the extreme flexible end of the biological continuum when it comes to sexual receptivity, but it is a continuum rather than a yawning chasm that separates humans from other species in this regard.

Flexibility in mating is a hallmark of the human species, with mating selection and deselection processes operating throughout the course of relationships. Human males are unique among primates in the amount of care, support, and provisioning they supply their mates (although this kind of behavior is found in monogamous birds). Human males will also help care for the children of the women with whom they form sexual relationships, even though they know they are not the genetic father of the children (although they do not typically offer the quality of care that genetic fathers provide). This kind of behavior is in stark contrast to almost every other mammal, who at worst kill the offspring of new mates they take up with that they did not father (like lions) or, at best, ignore them.

I say almost every other mammal, because there exists one remarkable exception to the general rule – the gibbon. Observations of gibbons in the wild by Ryne Palombit have revealed a pattern of mating and care-giving that is eerily similar to humans.[5] Gibbons are monogamous, but both male and female gibbons will leave their mates if their relationships become problematic, especially if other available single gibbons of the opposite sex appear on the scene. Moreover, the new male in the gibbon nuclear family will adopt any unrelated infants and help care for them (e.g., by carrying and defending them). However, there are hints that (like humans) stepfather gibbons are not as solicitous as genetic fathers. To complete the analogy with humans, Palombit suggests that gibbons continuously monitor the quality of their mates, while taking into account the availability of alternative mates.[6]

One feature of human mating, which I have not mentioned thus far, concerns the fact that women can live for decades after menopause, a feature unique among primates. The evolutionary reason for not living much past menopause is obvious – why bother extending life for decades, when the ability to reproduce is gone? The consensus view has been shifting toward the proposition that this characteristic feature of women is an evolved adaptation, based on the evidence that grandmothers play an important role in many cultures (including hunter-gatherer cultures) in helping to help raise their own grandchildren.[7] Thus, the concept of inclusive fitness is drafted into action – helping one's close genetic relatives to survive and reproduce is the next best thing, genetically speaking, to successfully rearing one's own offspring.

To sum up, human mating behavior, desires, and goals are clearly at the flexible end of the reproductive spectrum compared to other species. However, comparisons with other species show that continuities are ubiquitous, and reveal our mammalian and primate evolutionary heritage. I return, then, to what is truly unique and most remarkable about the human species; namely, the development of the human cerebral frontal cortex, in conjunction with the ability to use language, and the ability to learn and to plan ahead. These capacities have generated the development of culture and technology, which have enabled humans to take a step that no other animal has managed – to figure out how sexual reproduction works. This step potentially short-circuits the evolutionary feedback mechanism of reproductive success as the lever of biological evolution.

Understanding the causes of reproduction does not turn off the sexual desires, goals, and emotions that evolution has programmed into humans. However, it does mean that humans can fall in love and have sex, but prevent having offspring if they so choose. The choice not to reproduce is open to humans – and is being taken up in droves in countries with high standards of living – but closed to other species. This is the basic reason why many commentators have claimed that biological evolution in humans has effectively ceased.

Science and Intimate Relationships

This book (I hope) shows that science is alive and well in the study of intimate relationships, and that relationship science does not work very differently to other domains in psychology, or any other scientific discipline for that matter. I have heard it said that what are termed the soft sciences (psychology, sociology, economics, and so forth) should really be called the hard sciences because they are so hard to do. Well, they are hard, but they are not impossible. Supposedly ineffable things like love are readily and reliably measurable, and are on the way to being well understood. Relationship scientists can also predict relationship phenomena, such as marital separation, with quite high levels of accuracy. The evidence regarding these points belies the common belief that human behavior (especially in intimate relationships) is far too complicated and random to be predictable.

I have also tried to give a decent burial to the proposition that evolutionary psychology is not testable. Testability is a complex concept and does not simply reduce to confirming or disconfirming empirical claims. Of course, empirical tests and evidence are central to the scientific process, but so are argument, plausibility, and consistency with other accepted knowledge. Theories, along with postulated causal mechanisms and entities, operating at the cutting edge of science will always be in dispute, with a good chance of being revised or eventually abandoned. For example, in evolutionary psychology, making judgments about what are, and what are not, adaptations is often a work in progress.

The standard thesis offered by evolutionary psychologists for judging claims about adaptations is derived from George Williams, who posited that adaptations should be marked by criteria like efficiency, precision, and reliability.[8] But when adaptations are examined closely in humans, or in other species for that matter, those produced by sexual selection are frequently imprecise, overelaborate, unreliable, complex, costly, and poorly engineered. Consider, for example, the peacock's tail, or the tendency of human males to become caught between the desire to commit to their partners and the desire for sexual variety. Such adaptations work well enough, in terms of reproductive success, to have survived. But this puts evolutionary psychology back into the frightful position that almost anything now qualifies as an adaptation.

The standard psychological evolutionary approach derived from Williams is too weak to capture the way in which scientists make decisions about evolutionary adaptations, especially in humans for whom the genetic leash on behavior is often long. I think a better approach is for psychologists to make judgments about adaptations in the wider context of theory evaluation, using every sensible criterion available and taking into account *all* the available evidence.

The links between the science of intimate relationships and conventional wisdom are complex. Sometimes I have suggested that standard psychology textbooks are wrong and that common sense is correct (e.g, men actually do have stronger sex drives than women). More often I have argued that common-sense beliefs are overly simplistic, problematic, or even flat-out wrong. Even if folk psychology is a complete crock, however, this does not mean the relationship scientist can afford to ignore it – folk theories, regardless of their validity, influence people's behavior.

I have attempted throughout to focus on the science of intimate relationships, and not to sail into moral, legal, or political waters. But, I do not mean to downplay the importance of the latter issues, nor imply that a good scientific understanding of intimate relationships is not relevant to this domain. Sometimes people (including scientists, alas) are motivated to either suppress knowledge, or advise against finding out how the world works, on the grounds that prejudice and discrimination might be encouraged. However, the connections between scientific knowledge and the wider society are seldom straightforward or obvious.

To take an example, there has been a shift in public opinion toward the belief that homosexuality has a genetic origin. Moreover, there is a link between such beliefs and prejudice toward lesbians and gays. Several polls in the USA have shown that those who believe that individuals choose homosexuality as a lifestyle rather than being born as a homosexual (about 40% of the USA population) are more negative toward gays and are less likely to favor nondiscrimination statutes based on sexual orientation.[9]

In a program related to homophobia, talk-show host Jerry Springer opined that

> hardly a month goes by where we don't read of some new study suggesting or confirming that being gay, or at least being disposed to being gay, is a genetic circumstance determined at birth, not something someone chooses . . . arguing that gays are doing something deviant or sinful loses some of its steam if it's determined that some people are simply born that way through no choice of their own. It'd be like hating people because they're short, or tall, or blonde, or blind.[10]

Although apparently laudable, Jerry Springer's argument does not survive scrutiny. There is good evidence that men have a genetic predisposition to act aggressively and to attempt to control the sexuality of women. Does this mean we should not hold men responsible for rape or for assaulting their partners when they become jealous? Should we punish women for having sex with other women, but not men who have sex with men, on the grounds that sexual orientation is more biologically based for men than for women? When science discovers the exact genetic wellsprings of sexual orientation, this could encourage the pathologizing of homosexuality, and result in brain surgery or genetic engineering being used to "cure" people against their wishes. Conversely, discovering the exact nature of the social and cultural environment that produces homosexuality could encourage social engineering on a grand scale, and the pruning of civil liberties, in order to achieve the same aim.

In short, scientific knowledge can be used for good or ill, and can be exploited to justify contradictory moral and political stances. This does not imply, of course, that ignorance is bliss. Ignorance and closed minds are fertile grounds for prejudice, discrimination, and human folly. Used wisely, psychological science, and scientific methods and attitudes, can help us understand our own intimate relationships, and also allow professionals to develop more effective relationship therapies to help those in relationship distress.

Conclusion

Intimate relationships are a marvelous domain for apprehending the complexity and wonder, the sublime and the terrible, of human nature. In truth, the positives and the negatives of the intimate relationship mind are two sides of the same coin. The needs for intimacy and love come as a package deal along with the fear of rejection and the pain of loss. This is part of the human condition, which we humans are unique among species in grasping and understanding.

Notes

Chapter 1

1 As quoted in Sayre, 1995, p. 106.
2 See Baumeister & Leary, 1995, for a review of research confirming the point that the desire to form intimate interpersonal bonds is a central and pervasive human motivation.
3 The International Society for the Study of Personal Relationships (ISSPR) has over 600 members, of whom 68% see themselves as belonging to the discipline of psychology (as against communication, sociology, clinical psychology, etc.).
4 For a review of the research see Berscheid, 1985.
5 See Gottman, 1994.
6 Rubin, 1973.
7 See, e.g., a special issue on love: *Personal Relationships*, vol. 3, 1996.
8 Kelley et al., 1983.
9 See Sternberg & Beall, 1991, who specifically argue this point in connection with work on love.
10 See Tooby & Cosmides, 1992.
11 For a contemporary version of such a traditional empiricist approach in psychology see Kimble, 1989.
12 For a presentation and defense of postmodernism applied to psychology see Gergen, 1995. For general critiques of postmodernism see Fletcher, 1996; and Bunge, 1991; 1992.
13 See Siegel, 1987, for an excellent analysis of the problems with relativism.
14 Karl Popper's model is termed a "falsificationist" approach, because he argued that scientific theories can be falsified but never proved true. This general brand of scientific model is also known as the hypothetico-deductive model (see Fletcher, 1996).
15 This is a modified version of a model I originally presented in Fletcher, 1996.

16 See Burchfield, 1975.
17 For some case studies of science confirming the arguments here see Laudan, 1996.
18 For my more extended views on the connections between folk psychology and the psychological sciences see Fletcher, 1995.
19 For an extensive discussion of this issue see Fletcher, 1996.
20 Harris, 1978, p. viii.

Chapter 2

1   Dennett, 1995.
2   For more detailed accounts of this model see Fletcher & Thomas, 1996. For general treatments of the role of cognition in intimate relationship contexts see Baldwin, 1994; and two edited collections: Fletcher & Fincham, 1991a; and Fletcher & Fitness, 1996.
3   Dunbar & Duncan, 1997, found that women talked about personal relationships for between 37% and 46% of the time across three separate samples, whereas men talked from 15% to 50% of the time about personal relationships.
4   Shostock, 1981; Haviland, 1977.
5   See Fletcher & Fincham, 1991b; and Fletcher & Kininmonth, 1991.
6   Fletcher & Ward, 1988.
7   See Fletcher & Fincham, 1991b; and Fincham, 2001, for reviews.
8   Heider, 1958.
9   The device was invented originally by Francis Galton, in 1889, in an attempt to precisely measure the relationship between the height of children in relation to their parents. The formula was developed in its modern form by Carl Pearson among others in the 1930s.
10 Rosenthal & Rubin, 1982.
11 The way the technique works is simple: (1) Remove the decimal point from the correlation (.50 becomes 50); (2) Divide the resultant figure in half ($50/2 = 25$); (3) Set up the four-cell table initially as if the correlation is zero, in which case there will be the same probability in each cell; (4) Add 25 (from step 2) to the 50 in the top-right cell, then go round the four cells counterclockwise keeping the rows and columns adding up to 100%.
12 Karney & Bradbury, 1995.
13 See Fincham, 2001, for a review.
14 See Fincham, 2001, for a review.
15 Fehr, 1999.
16 Fitness, 1996.

17 Fletcher & Kininmonth, 1992.
18 Fletcher et al., 1999.
19 Aron, Aron & Norman, 2001.
20 This scale was developed by Spanier in 1976.
21 Gottman, 1990, p. 78.
22 Fletcher, Simpson & Thomas, 2000a.
23 Fletcher & Kininmonth, 1992.
24 Fletcher & Thomas, 1996.
25 Wegner & Bargh, 1998.
26 Baldwin et al., 1990.
27 Fletcher et al., 1994.
28 Smith, 1998.
29 Chaiken & Trope, 1999.
30 One critical defining element in general connectionist models consists of the postulate that knowledge or information is not localized but is distributed throughout the cognitive system. Whether this is true or not remains a contentious issue (Page, 2000). However, this issue is not germane to the validity of the model at the level at which I have presented it.

Chapter 3

1 Desmond & Moore, 1991.
2 See *New York Review of Books*, June 26, 1997; October 9, 1997; see http://cogweb.english.ucsb.edu/Debate/CEP_Gould.html for Gould's articles, and for a response by Tooby and Cosmides. For a concise and lucid analysis of the arguments between Dawkins and Gould see Sterelny, 2001.
3 Dennett, 1995.
4 Desmond & Moore, 1991, p. 492.
5 Petrie & Halliday, 1994; Petrie, 1994.
6 Darwin probably knew of Mendel's research and work (Mendel sent Darwin his scientific papers) but ignored it in favor of his own (wrong) theory of inheritance, termed pangenesis, which never gained many adherents.
7 See Dennett, 1995; Frank-Kamenetskii, 1997; Ridley, 1999.
8 Dawkins, 1986.
9 Darwin's solution was in terms of the sterile ants or bees assisting the reproductive success of the entire nest or hive (termed group selection). The concept of group selection was regarded as passé after the success of the gene's-eye view but continues to have its proponents today (see Dennett, 1995).
10 Hamilton, 1964.
11 Cronin, 1991.

12   G. F. Miller, 1998; 2000.

13   Trivers, 1972.

14   G. F. Miller, 1998; 2000.

15   Fisher, 1930.

16   Andersson, 1994.

17   Darwin, 1859.

18   Stringer & McKie, 1996.

19   Stringer & McKie, 1996.

20   Stringer & McKie, 1996.

21   For an excellent summary of evolutionary psychology see Durrant & Ellis, in press.

22   Gould, 1980.

23   Gould, 1997, p. 52.

24   See Ketelaar & Ellis, 2000, and responses.

25   See Pinker, 1997.

26   Pinker, 1994; Haig & Durrant, 2000.

27   See Dennett, 1995; Blackmore, 1999.

28   Brown, 1991.

29   One popular account proposes that selection pressures for increased social intelligence provided the fuel for the increase in brain size for the ancestors of *Homo sapiens*: see Corballis & Lea, 1999.

30   The general principle revealed by these examples is not confined to humans. Species regularly produce changes in their social and physical environment that may subsequently influence their own genetic constitution and associated reproductive success. Elephants, for example, while eating trees and shrubs, help create the open woodlands in which they thrive, and beavers create small lakes with their dam building in which they are well adapted to survive. See Dawkins, 1992.

31   See Ridley, 1999.

32   See, e.g., Eagly & Wood, 1999.

33   Wilson, 1998.

34   See Hrdy, 1999.

35   For an excellent discussion of this point see Dawkins, 1999.

36   Dawkins, 1986, p. 215.

37   Fodor, 1983.

38   For a broad-based discussion that illustrates the complexity and subtlety of the arguments and disagreements concerning modularity see Hirschfeld & Gelman, 1994.

39   See, e.g., Stanovich & West, in press.

Chapter 4

1   See Fitness, 1996; and Fehr & Baldwin, 1996.

2   There is a minority view that people can introspectively access their own feelings and beliefs in a direct and perceptually immediate way, much as we might identify a chair or a tree (see, e.g., Goldman, 1993). However, the most widely endorsed approach is that introspective reports are mediated by functional lay theories, in which the raw experience is interpreted within a complex network of other events and processes (see Gopnik, 1993).

3   See Clark et al., 1996.

4   Schachter & Singer, 1962.

5   Hatfield & Rapson, 1987.

6   Dutton & Aron, 1974.

7   See Hatfield & Rapson, 1993, for a review.

8   Insel, 2000.

9   Fisher, 1998; Regan, 1999.

10 Darwin initially proposed (with some evidential support) that the principal emotions were expressed in the same way across different aboriginal populations. However, it took until the 1960s for Paul Ekman to provide the telling evidence for Darwin's thesis (Ekman, 1982).

11 See Shaver et al., 1996.

12 Oatley & Johnson-Laird, 1987.

13 Roseman, 1994.

14 Damasio, 1994.

15 Darwin, 1872.

16 Damasio, 1994.

17 MacLean, 1990.

18 Pinker, 1997.

19 Shaver et al., 1996.

20 de Rougemont, 1940/1983.

21 Young & Uenukukopako, 1995.

22 Jankowiak & Fischer, 1992.

23 Buss, 1989.

24 Shaver, Collins, & Clark, 1996.

25 Shaver et al., 1996, p. 93.

26 Aron & Westbay, 1996.

27 See Baumeister & Bratslavsky, 1999.

28 Shostak, 1981, p. 268.

29 Caplan, 1984, pp. 46–8.

30 I have drawn heavily from Helen Fisher's (1992) analysis here, especially her ch. 2.

31 See Wolf (1995) for an analysis of Westermarck's thesis, and subsequent controversy including Freud's alternative.
32 Shepher, 1971.
33 Wilson, 1998, ch. 8.
34 de Munck, 1998.
35 Rockman, 1994.
36 Gupta & Singh, 1982.
37 Fisher, 1992, p. 74.
38 Fisher, 1992.
39 Fisher, 1992.
40 Goode, 1993.
41 Fisher, 1992.
42 Goode, 1993; Fisher, 1992.
43 See Acitelli & Young, 1996.
44 All the marriage and divorce statistics in this chapter concerning New Zealand were taken from a Statistics New Zealand Report (1999).
45 Goode, 1993; Fisher, 1992.
46 See Buss (1999) for a review.
47 Buss, 1999; Fisher, 1992.
48 Shostak, 1981, p. 271.

Chapter 5

1 Taylor & Brown, 1988.
2 Taylor & Brown, 1988.
3 Fletcher, 1995.
4 Colvin et al., 1995.
5 Paulhus, 1998.
6 Baumeister et al., 1996.
7 Gerrard et al., 2000.
8 Heine et al., 1999.
9 Huxley, 1884, p. 244.
10 Murray & Holmes, 1996; Murray, 2001.
11 Murray & Holmes, 1993, p. 712.
12 MacDonald & Ross, 1999.
13 Murray et al., 2001.
14 Correlations across partners usually range from .40 to .60 for both dating and married samples. See, e.g., Campbell et al., 2001; and Fletcher & Thomas, 2000.
15 Fletcher & Thomas, 2000.
16 Rogge & Bradbury, 1999.

17 Planalp & Rivers, 1996.
18 Taylor & Gollwitzer, 1995.
19 Gagné & Lydon, in press.
20 Kenny, 1994; Funder, 1995.
21 Ambady et al., 1995; Levesque & Kenny, 1993.
22 Funder & Dobroth, 1987.
23 Funder, 1995.
24 See, e.g., Kenny, 1994.
25 See a meta-analysis by Davis & Kraus, 1997.
26 Ickes, 1993.
27 This technique was based on one developed by William Ickes.
28 Thomas et al., 1997; Thomas, 1998.
29 Davis & Kraus, 1997.
30 Fletcher et al., 1986.
31 See Fletcher et al., 1992; Fletcher et al., 1990.
32 Fletcher et al., 1992; Thomas, 1998.
33 Noller & Ruzzene, 1991.
34 Simpson et. al, 1995.

Chapter 6

1   Navran, 1967.
2   Locke & Wallace, 1959; see Fincham & Bradbury, 1987.
3   See Fincham & Bradbury, 1987; Fletcher et al., 2000a.
4   Spanier, 1976.
5   Noller et al., 1994.
6   Gottman & Krokoff, 1989; Karney & Bradbury, 1995.
7   See Gottman, 1998.
8   Given that lower relationship happiness is quite strongly related to more negative behavior being expressed, it was necessary to statistically control for each partner's overall level of negative behavior produced before calculating the link between relationship happiness and the extent to which negative thoughts and feelings were expressed. This was easily done as I already possessed measures of how negative each person's behavior was (produced by observer raters).
9   Fletcher et al., 1999.
10 Rusbult et al., 2000.
11 Bradbury et al., 1995.
12 Fletcher et al., 1999.
13 Fletcher et al., 1999; Gottman et al., 1998.
14 Christensen & Heavey, 1990.

15   Gottman, 1994.
16   Fitzpatrick, 1988.
17   Pasch & Bradbury, 1998.
18   See Karney & Bradbury, 1995, for a recent review of the marital litera-ture. No one has to date reviewed the dating literature, but my impres-sion from the studies I have read is that the findings are similar to those obtained with married samples.
19   The original figures from this meta-analysis were reported in terms of correlations. To make the results easier to follow, I have translated them into percentages using the method described by Ozer, 1985, for situa-tions where continuous-level variables predict a dichotomous variable (in this case intact relationship versus separated).
20   Some researchers have used the technique of calculating differences be-tween numerical measures on traits between partners to index the degree of similarity. However, this is a problematic procedure. Consider, for ex-ample, if one used this method to assess the similarity of couples in terms of neuroticism. Big difference scores (meaning low similarity) would be produced if one of the partners was very neurotic. But, we already know that higher levels of within-individual neuroticism predict increased rela-tionship dissolution. Thus, this kind of analysis confounds the within-individual variance with the level of couple similarity. Fortunately, there are methods available that avoid this problem.
21   See, e.g., Acitelli et al., in press; Robins et al., 2000.
22   Acitelli et al., 1993; Hammond & Fletcher, 1991; White, 1985.
23   Fletcher & Thomas, 2000.
24   For a review see Rogge & Bradbury, 1999.
25   Carrère et al., 2000.
26   Rogge & Bradbury, 1999.
27   Rogge & Bradbury, 1999
28   Jacobson & Chistensen, 1997.
29   Gottman et al., 1998.
30   For a critical analysis (and an associated reply by Gottman) of this particu-lar study see Stanley et al., 2000.
31   Wile, 1995, p. 2.
32   Fletcher & Thomas, 2000.
33   See Gottman, 1998.
34   See Gottman, 1998.
35   See Gottman, 1998.
36   Gottman, 1998; Jacobson & Addis, 1993.
37   Turkheimer, 2000.
38   McGue & Lykken, 1992; Jockin et al., 1996.
39   Collins et al., 2000; Stoolmiller, 1999.

40 Behavioral geneticists have statistical procedures for nonadditive models that take account of situations where specific genes inherited from one parent influence the genes at the same locations on the chromosome, which are inherited from the other parent (termed "interactions at the same allele"). However, interactions across genes (termed "apostasies") are potentially much more likely to cause the kind of bias I have discussed, and modeling this situation is considered an intractable problem except in breeding experiments with rats, fruit flies, and the like.

41 Stoolmiller, 1999.

42 For reviews documenting these generalizations, see Acitelli & Young, 1996; Cross & Madson, 1997.

Chapter 7

1 Gopnik et al., 1999.

2 The exact role played by oxytocin in human–infant attachment is unclear. This is mainly because of ethical problems in doing the appropriate research with humans. This ethical problem is created because oxytocin (unlike other hormones like testosterone) is rapidly metabolized in the bloodstream, and so has to be injected centrally in the brain to have any effect. Injecting hormones into the brain can be done with rats and voles but is not ethically feasible with humans. However, there is good experimental and observational evidence in other mammalian species (such as rats and voles) showing that oxytocin is a key hormone in generating a range of maternal and attachment behaviors (see Insel, 2000, for a review).

3 Russell et al., 1983.

4 Gopnik et al., 1999.

5 Bowlby, 1969; 1973; 1980.

6 Ainsworth et al., 1978.

7 The latter two styles are sometimes termed anxious-avoidant and anxious-ambivalent when applied to infants. As applied to adults, relationship researchers sometimes use the terms "avoidant" and "anxious-ambivalent." Others, following Mary Main, use the terms "secure," "dismissive" and "preoccupied" to apply to adults. To avoid terminological confusion, I will use the same terms throughout to apply to both children and adults: "secure," "avoidant," and "ambivalent."

8 See Simpson, 1999.

9 Bowlby, 1979, p. 129.

10 Hazan & Shaver, 1987.

11 Web of Science search engine. This figure does not include citations in

book chapters and books, of which there have been many.

12 Shaver et al., 1988.

13 See Shaver et al., 1996; Cassidy & Shaver, 1999.

14 Hamilton, 2000; Lewis et al., 2000; Waters et al., 2000; Weinfield et al., 2000. These studies did not use the Hazan and Shaver adult attachment scales, but an alternative method developed by Mary Main that uses complex and lengthy adult interviews.

15 These percentages need to be treated with caution, as the sample sizes are low when the sample is cut up like this.

16 Baldwin & Fehr, 1995.

17 Kirkpatrick & Hazan, 1994.

18 Grossmann et al., 1981.

19 Hrdy, 1999.

20 Hrdy, 1999.

21 Hrdy, 1999, p. 316.

22 Hinde, 1982, pp. 70–2.

23 Trivers, 1974.

24 Belsky et al., 1991.

25 I say girls rather than boys deliberately, because the model, and related research data, are articulated most clearly with respect to girls. The picture is not as clear with boys.

26 Hetherington, 1972.

27 Hetherington, 1972, p. 322.

28 Brennan & Shaver, 1995.

29 Simpson, 1999.

30 Ellis et al., 1999.

31 As anyone who has mixed with seventh- or eighth-grade children knows, there is wide variation in pubertal development. The average age for menarche (the first menstrual period) is 12 years, 9 months in the USA, but can vary from 11 to 17 years. Boys mature, on average, 2 years later than girls and first ejaculate semen with live sperm at 14.5 years on average.

32 Ellis et al., 1999; Ellis & Garber, 2000.

33 Sanders & Reinisch, 1990.

34 Baldwin et al., 1996.

35 Morgan & Shaver, 1999.

36 Hammond & Fletcher, 1991.

37 Collins & Allard, 2001.

38 Morgan & Shaver, 1999.

39 Simpson et al., 1992.

40 Mikulincer et al., 2001.

Chapter 8

1 Ellis & Kelley, 1999.
2 Buss, 1989.
3 E.g., Fletcher et al., 1999.
4 The items used in the cross-cultural research by David Buss were based on a factor analytic study of a large set of items initially produced by Harrison Gough (see Buss & Barnes, 1986).
5 Fletcher et al., 1999.
6 Church & Lonner, 1998.
7 Hawkes, 1991; Smith & Bird, 2000.
8 Gurven et al., 2000.
9 G. F. Miller, 2000.
10 Direct evidence for Miller's thesis is scanty, but it is plausible.
11 For an excellent analysis and review on physical attractiveness and its role in human mating see Berry, 2000.
12 Cunningham et al., 1995.
13 Cunningham et al., 1997.
14 Cunningham, 1986.
15 Cunningham et al., 1990.
16 Rhodes et al., 2000.
17 Slater et al., 1998.
18 For a balanced recent review and analysis of the facial attractiveness literature see Zebrowitz & Rhodes, 2001.
19 Langlois et al., 2000; Singh & Luis, 1995.
20 Singh & Luis, 1995.
21 Singh, 1994.
22 Singh, 1993.
23 Pennebaker et al., 1979.
24 See Gladue & Delaney, 1990; Madey et al., 1996. For a failure to replicate see Sprecher et al., 1984.
25 Gangestad & Simpson, 2000. Also see a lively debate concerning this article in the same issue.
26 Langlois et al., 2000.
27 Kalick et al., 1998.
28 Singh & Luis, 1995; Zaadstra et al., 1993.
29 Personal communication from Jeffry Simpson.
30 Rhodes et al., 1998.
31 Gangestad & Simpson, 2000.
32 Gangestad & Simpson, 2000. Fluctuating asymmetry is not the only factor involved in making faces look attractive. A well-replicated finding is

that the more average a face is (derived from averaging the dimensions of large samples of faces) the more attractive it appears to be. Moreover, Rhodes et al., 1999, have reported that both fluctuating asymmetry and averageness independently contribute to perceptions of attractiveness. No research to date has investigated to what extent averageness is related to superior health or fertility. It is possible (perhaps plausible) that averageness in appearance is an honest advertisement of superior fertility. Conversely, averageness might be unrelated to fertility, and has simply evolved on the back of fluctuating asymmetry as a correlated feature.

33 Simpson et al., 1999.
34 Fletcher et al., 2001.
35 See Gangestad & Simpson, 2000.
36 Penton-Voak et al., 1999.
37 The most influential psychologist in this domain is David Buss, and I have borrowed freely from his work in the current account, although my own approach varies in certain respects from his work.
38 Clark & Hatfield, 1989.
39 See Buss, 1999.
40 E.g., Sprecher et al., 1994.
41 See Buss, 1999.
42 Buss et al., 2001; Fletcher et al., 2001.
43 Eagly & Wood, 1999. Notably, however, women did not place less emphasis on men's physical attractiveness (nor did men place less emphasis on women's physical attractiveness) as women's empowerment increased.
44 Fletcher et al., 2001. On a seven-point scale the mean scores for the importance of status and resources were 4.79 for women and 3.83 for men.
45 Wilson, 1978, pp. 124–5.
46 Buss & Schmitt, 1993, pp. 207–8.
47 See, e.g., Angier, 1999; Miller, 2000; and Hazan & Diamond, 2000.
48 Based on the information in Baker & Bellis, 1995, the following calculations were made for the probability that one act of (random) copulation would produce the birth of a baby, assuming good levels of health and fertility for both male and female:

1 Probability of fertilization in a normal cycle: approximately .25
2 Probability of fertilization across cycles: $.25 \times .50 = .125$
3 Probability of fertilized egg reaching uterus: $.125 \times .9 = .112$
4 Probability of fertilized egg implanting: $.112 \times .58 = .065$
5 Probability of surviving to twelfth day: $.065 \times .42 = .027$
6 Probability of surviving full term: $.027 \times .80 = .022.$
7 Probability of surviving childbirth: $.022 \times .95 = .021.$

Thus, from a single act of copulation by two healthy young adults the probability a child will result is about 2%. Using a different set of figures, with some additional factors not specified here, by Einon, 1998, produces a figure closer to a 1% probability. The lower figure, however, makes my case even more compelling.

49 Chamberlain, 1991.
50 Van Look et al., 1999; Tommaselli et al., 2000.
51 See, e.g., Miller, 1998; Gangestad & Simpson, 2000. In contrast, David Buss's Sexual Strategies Theory pays considerable attention to how mating criteria influence the development of long-term relationships, and also discusses why specific relationships might switch from short-term to long-term styles. However, this theory is mainly focussed on gender differences, and treats short-term and long-term relationship strategies (desires and goals) as residing in discrete and fundamentally distinct categories (see, e.g., Buss, 1999; Buss & Schmitt, 1993).
52 Buss, 1994.
53 See Simpson et al., 2001.
54 Fletcher et al., 1999; Fletcher et al., 2000b.
55 Fletcher et al., 2000b.
56 Campbell et al., 2001.
57 Fletcher et al., 2000b.
58 Fletcher et al., 2000b.
59 See, e.g., Hazan & Diamond, 2000; Lykken & Tellegen, 1993.
60 Lykken & Tellegen, 1993.
61 Fletcher et al., 2000b.

Chapter 9

1 See, e.g., Crooks & Baur, 1999; Hyde & DeLamater, 1997.
2 Hyde & DeLamater, 1997.
3 Angier, 1999, p. 72.
4 See, e.g., Bogaert & Hershberger, 1999.
5 See Angier, 1999.
6 Michael et al., 1994. All references to the Chicago 1994 sex survey in the text will have this citation.
7 For a review see Baumeister et al., in press.
8 See, e.g., Frank et al., 1978.
9 Symons, 1979; Gould, 1992, ch. 8.
10 See Slob & van der Werff ten Bosch, 1991.
11 Baker & Bellis, 1995.
12 See Gangestad & Simpson, 2000, for a review.

13 Others have argued, more abstrusely, that the sexual systems have been explicitly designed, via evolution, to make women more reliant on the skill and patience of their (male) partners, than vice versa, to achieve sexual pleasure. This is yet another twist on the "women are choosier than men" dictum, which emanates from the observation that women invest more than men in long-term sexual liaisons.

14 Baker & Bellis, 1995.

15 Moore et al., 1999.

16 Birkhead, 2000, p. 29.

17 See Birkhead, 2000.

18 See Birkhead, 2000.

19 See Birkhead, 2000, for all the data reported in this paragraph.

20 Jones, 2000, pp. 86–7.

21 For a recent review of the scientific literature on the hormonal correlates of sexual desire, see Regan, 1999. For a more general and very readable book about testosterone per se, see Dabbs & Dabbs, 2000.

22 See Dabbs & Dabbs, 2000; Meston & Frohlich, 2000.

23 Morris et al., 1987.

24 Shifren et al., 2000.

25 See Regan, 1999.

26 See Meston & Frohlich, 2000.

27 Baumeister et al., in press, p. 21. For all empirical claims in this section on gender differences in sex drive, the reader is directed to the review of Baumeister et al., except where specific studies are cited.

28 Blumstein & Schwartz, 1983.

29 Segraves & Segraves, 1991.

30 Buss, 1989.

31 Buss & Schmitt, 1993.

32 Miller & Fishkin, 1997.

33 See Baumeister et al., in press.

34 Sanders & Reinisch, 1999.

35 Brown & Sinclair, 1999.

36 Angier, 1999.

37 See, e.g., evidence from Gagnon, 1977, concerning the frequency of masturbation, and Hunt, 1974, concerning the perceived pleasure gained from sexual intercourse.

38 I have drawn on historical material here from Michael et al., 1994.

39 Kellogg, 1888.

40 Graham, 1834, p. 58.

41 Arafat & Cotton, 1974.

42 Murphy, 1992.

43 Regan & Berscheid, 1996.

44 Diamond & Savin-Williams, 2000.
45 See Baumeister, 2000.
46 See Baumeister, 2000.
47 See Baumeister, 2000.
48 Davenport, 1977.
49 Davenport, 1977.
50 Davenport, 1977.
51 Gagnon & Simon, 1968.
52 Herdt, 1981; for a useful critique see Elliston, 1995.
53 Gayford, 1997.
54 Buunk et al., 1996; Buss et al., 1999.
55 DeSteno & Salovey, 1996.
56 Daly et al., 1981.
57 Beckerman et al., 1998.
58 Hill & Hurtado, 1996, pp. 229–30.
59 Crocker & Crocker, 1994, pp. 156–7.
60 Crocker & Crocker, 1994, p. 157.
61 Crocker & Crocker, 1994, p. 186.
62 I have appropriated this latter phrase from a quote by Winston Churchill, which he used in a speech broadcast to Britain in 1939 at the beginning of the World War II. He used the phrase to refer to the unpredictable behavior of Russia.
63 Catholic catechism, section 2357.
64 Muscarella, 2000.
65 See Peplau, 2001.
66 Peplau, 2001; Peplau & Garnets, 2000.
67 For a review see LeVay, in press.
68 For a review of studies dealing with the association between childhood cross-gender behavior and sexual orientation see Bailey & Zucker, 1995.
69 LeVay, in press.
70 Bailey & Zucker, 1995.
71 Peplau, 2001.
72 See Lippa & Arad, 1997; Peplau, 2001.
73 Lippa, 2000.
74 Bailey et al., 1994.
75 For reviews see Bailey, 1995; and Peplau et al., 1999. For a general, and up-to-date review of the scientific work dealing with homo-sexuality see an article by LeVay, in press – available at http://www.hometown.aol.com/slevy/
76 See LeVay, in press.
77 See Bailey, 1995; Meyer-Bahlburg, 2001; Peplau, 2001; for reviews.
78 LeVay, 1991.

79 One possibility put forward is that sexual orientation might be related to the number of androgen (including testosterone) receptors in regions of the hypothalamus, rather than size per se. Indeed, women do have a lower density of androgen receptors in certain brain regions than do men. However, a recent study by Kruijver et al., 2001, found no evidence that sexual orientation for men or women was related to the density of androgen receptors in the hypothalamus. Instead, there was clear evidence that higher receptor density was related to higher levels of androgens circulating in the bloodstream in adulthood.

80 Bailey et al., 2000.

81 Hamer et al., 1993.

82 Rice et al., 1999.

83 See Bogaert, 1998; Whitam et al., 1998; Blanchard et al., 2000.

84 Blanchard & Bogaert, 1996.

85 See E. M. Miller, 2000, for an extensive argument to this effect.

Chapter 10

1 See Straus, 1997.

2 See, e.g., Straus & Gelles, 1990; and Magdol et al., 1997. The relationship between socioeconomic status and intimate homicide is especially marked (Polk, 1994).

3 Straus & Gelles, 1990.

4 A revised form of this scale has been developed by Straus et al. 1996. However, I will present the earlier version here, which has been used more frequently by researchers and has also borne the brunt of the criticisms.

5 See Archer, 2000.

6 For a general review see Straus, 1997.

7 Straus & Gelles, 1988.

8 See, e.g., Hanly & O'Neill, 1997; Magdol et al., 1997.

9 See references in notes 4 and 5 above.

10 Carrado et al., 1996; Pan et al., 1994.

11 Stets & Straus, 1990; Sugarman & Hotaling, 1989.

12 Magdol et al., 1997.

13 Magdol et al., 1997.

14 Magdol et al., 1997; Pan et al., 1994.

15 O'Leary et al., 1994; Pan et al., 1994.

16 Magdol et al., 1997.

17 See Archer, 2000, for a recent meta-analysis that supports this generalization.

18 Burke & Follingstad, 1999.
19 Steinmetz & Lucca, 1988.
20 These typically are about .80.
21 O'Leary et al. 1994 reported correlations of .79 for men and .70 for women over a 12-month period in married couples, which reveals exceptional stability over this period of time.
22 Straus et al., 1997.
23 Heyman & Schlee, 1997.
24 Dobash et al., 1992.
25 See, e.g., Szinovacz & Egley, 1995.
26 See, e.g., Babcock et al., 1993; Cantos et al., 1994; Lawrence & Bradbury, in press.
27 Magdol et al., 1997.
28 Babcock et al., 1993; Leonard & Roberts, 1998.
29 Lawrence & Bradbury, in press.
30 See, e.g., Dobash & Dobash, 1984; and Walker, 1984.
31 Magdol et al., 1997.
32 See Straus, 1997.
33 Cascardi & Vivian, 1995.
34 Vivian and Langhinrichsen-Rohling, 1996.
35 Leibrich et al., 1995.
36 New Zealand Ministry of Justice Report, 1996.
37 Johnson, 1995.
38 Holtzworth-Munroe & Stuart, 1994.
39 Magdol et al., 1997.
40 Pan et al., 1994.
41 Pan et al., 1994.
42 Gottman et al., 1995.
43 Babcock et al., 1993.
44 Straus, 1997.
45 Jacobson et al., 1994.
46 US Department of Justice Report, 1998.
47 Scutt, 1983, p. 104.
48 Daly & Wilson, 1988.
49 Data supplied by the research division of the New Zealand Police, showed that in the six years from 1993 to 1998 59 men killed their female partners or ex-partners and 9 women killed their male partners or ex-partners.
50 US Department of Justice Report, 1998.
51 Block & Christakos, 1995; Wilson & Daly, 1992.
52 US Department of Justice Report, 1998.
53 Block & Christakos, 1995; Wilson & Daly, 1992; US Department of Justice Report, 1998.

54 Block & Christakos, 1995.

55 I have put my own spin on the discussion, but have borrowed heavily from the following publications by Wilson and Daly: Daly & Wilson, 1988; Wilson & Daly, 1992; 1993; 1996; Daly et al., 1981.

56 Wilson & Daly, 1993, p. 276.

57 Wilson & Daly, 1993.

58 Polk, 1994.

59 Research on stalking has only just begun, but shows that the majority of stalking occurs after relationship dissolution. The similarities with the data on intimate violence are remarkable. Police reports, criminal convictions, and other research, all support the generalization that women are much more at risk of being injured or attacked by men. However, the initial well-designed surveys, using university student samples, show that women are just as likely to stalk their partners after relationships break up as are men, Davis et al., 2000.

60 Daly & Wilson, 1988; Polk, 1994. Similar findings have also been reported in India (Martin et al., 1999).

61 Levinson, 1989.

62 Fernandez, 1997.

63 Masumura, 1979.

64 See Block & Christakos, 1995.

65 See Holmberg & Veroff, 1996.

66 See Wilson & Daly, 1992.

67 See www.census.gov.nz

68 Daly & Wilson, 1996.

69 See, e.g., Kurz, 1997.

70 A recent example is the response by Jacquelyn White et al., 2000, to John Archer's immaculate and extensive review of the literature in intimate violence. White et al. argued that Archer should have downplayed the findings because they would undermine efforts to eradicate violence against women.

71 Heelas, 1989. Heelas asserts in the same vein that "We must resist asserting that Ilongot youths are aggressive simply because they lop off heads; that Samoan fathers are aggressive simply because they beat their children; or, for that matter, that the British were aggressive when they lined up to exterminate the indigenous people of Tasmania"; Heelas, 1989, p. 240.

72 See Chagnon, 1992.

Chapter 11

1   See, e.g., Fisher, 1992; and G. F. Miller, 2000.
2   See Kelly, 1995.
3   See Shostak, 1983; Lee, 1978; and Kelly, 1995.
4   See, e.g., Simpson & Kenrick, 1997.
5   Palombit, 1994.
6   Palombit, 1994, p. 89.
7   See Hrdy, 1999, for a discussion of this question.
8   Williams, 1996.
9   Schmaltz, 1993.
10 Springer, 1995.

References

Acitelli, L. K., Douvan, E., & Veroff, J. (1993). Perceptions of conflict in the first year of marriage: How important are similarity and understanding? *Journal of Social and Personal Relationships*, 10, 5–19.

Acitelli, L. K., Kenny, D. A., & Weiner, D. (in press). The importance of the similarity and understanding of partners' marital ideals to relationship satisfaction. *Personal Relationships*.

Acitelli, L. K., & Young, A. M. (1996). Gender and thought in relationships. In G. J. O. Fletcher & J. Fitness (eds.), *Knowledge structures in close relationships* (pp. 147–68). Mahwah, NJ: Lawrence Erlbaum.

Ainsworth, M. D. S., Blehar, M. C., Waters, E., & Wall, S. (1978). *Patterns of attachment: A psychological study of the strange situation*. Hillsdale, NJ: Lawrence Erlbaum.

Ambady, N., Hallahan, M., & Rosenthal, R. (1995). On judging and being judged accurately in zero-acquaintance situations. *Journal of Personality and Social Psychology*, 69, 518–29.

Andersson, M. (1994). *Sexual selection*. Princeton, NJ: Princeton University Press.

Angier, N. (1999). *Woman: An intimate geography*. Boston: Houghton Mifflin.

Arafat, I. S., & Cotton, W. L. (1974). Masturbation practices of males and females. *Journal of Sex Research*, 10, 293–307.

Archer, J. (2000). Sex differences in aggression between heterosexual partners: A meta-analytic review. *Psychological Bulletin*, 126, 651–80.

Aron, A., Aron, E. N., & Norman, C. (2001). Self-expansion model of motivation and cognition in close relationships and beyond. In G. J. O. Fletcher & M. S. Clark (eds.), *Blackwell Handbook of Social Psychology: Interpersonal processes* (pp. 478–501). Oxford: Blackwell.

Aron, A., & Westbay, L. (1996). Dimensions of the prototype of love. *Journal of Personality and Social Psychology*, 70, 535–51.

Babcock, J. C., Waltz, J., Jacobson, N. S., & Gottman, J. M. (1993). Power and violence: The relationship between communication patterns, power discrepancies, and domestic violence. *Journal of Consulting and Clinical Psychology*, 61, 40–50.

Bailey, J. M. (1995). Biological perspectives on sexual orientation. In A. R. D'Augelli & C. J. Patterson (eds.), *Lesbian, gay, and bisexual identities over the lifespan* (pp. 104–35). New York: Oxford University Press.

Bailey, J. M., Dunne, M. P., & Martin, N. G. (2000). Genetic and environmental influences on sexual orientation and its correlates in an Australian twin sample. *Journal of Personality and Social Psychology*, 78, 524–36.

Bailey, J. M., Gaulin, S., Agyei, Y., & Gladue, B. A. (1994). Effects of gender and sexual orientation on evolutionarily relevant aspects of human mating psychology. *Journal of Personality and Social Psychology*, 66, 1081–93.

Bailey, J. M. & Zucker, K. J. (1995). Childhood sex-typed behavior and sexual orientation: A conceptual analysis and quantitative review. *Developmental Psychology*, 31, 43–55.

Baker, R. R., & Bellis, M. A. (1995). *Human sperm competition: Copulation, masturbation and infidelity*. London: Chapman & Hall.

Baldwin, M. W. (1994). Primed relational schemas as a source of self-evaluative reactions. *Journal of Social and Clinical Psychology*, 13, 380–403.

Baldwin, M. W., Carrell, S. E., & Lopez, D. F. (1990). Priming relationship schemas: My advisor and the Pope are watching me from the back of my mind. *Journal of Experimental Social Psychology*, 26, 435–54.

Baldwin, M. W., & Fehr, B. (1995). On the instability of attachment style ratings. *Personal Relationships*, 2, 247–61.

Baldwin, M. W., Keelan, J. P. R., Fehr, B., Enns, V., & Koh-Rangarajoo, E. (1996). Social-cognitive conceptualization of attachment working models: Availability and accessibility effects. *Journal of Personality and Social Psychology*, 71, 94–109.

Baumeister, R. F. (2000). Gender differences in erotic plasticity: The female sex drive as socially flexible and responsive. *Psychological Bulletin*, 126, 347–74.

Baumeister, R. F., & Bratslavsky, E. (1999). Passion, intimacy, and time: Passionate love as a function of change in intimacy. *Personality and Social Psychology Review*, 3, 49–67.

Baumeister, R. F., Catanese, K. R., & Vohs, K. D. (in press). Is there a gender difference in strength of sex drive? Theoretical views, conceptual distinctions, and a review of relevant evidence. *Personality and Social Psychology Review*.

Baumeister, R. F., & Leary, M. R. (1995). The need to belong: Desire for interpersonal attachments as a fundamental human motivation. *Psychological Bulletin*, 117, 497–529.

Baumeister, R. F., Smart, L., & Boden, J. M. (1996). Relation of threatened egotism to violence and aggression: The dark side of high self-esteem. *Psy-*

chological Review, 103, 5–33.

Beckerman, S., Lizarralde, R., Ballew, C., Schroeder, S., Fingelton, C., Garrison, A., & Smith, H. (1998). The Barí Partible Paternity Project: Preliminary results. *Current Anthropology*, 39, 164–7.

Belsky, J., Steinberg, L., & Draper, P. (1991). Childhood experience, interpersonal development, and reproductive strategy: An evolutionary theory of socialization. *Child Development*, 62, 647–70.

Berry, D. S. (2000). Attractiveness, attraction, and sexual selection: Evolutionary perspectives on the form and function of physical attractiveness. *Advances in Experimental Social Psychology*, 32, 273–342.

Berscheid, E. (1985). Interpersonal attraction. In G. Lindzey & E. Aronson (eds.), *The handbook of social psychology* (3rd edn., vol. 2, pp. 413–84). New York: Random House.

Berscheid, E., & Peplau, L. A. (1983). The emerging science of close relationships. In H. H. Kelley, E. Berscheid, A. Christensen, J. H. Harvey, T. L. Huston, G. Levinger, E. McClintock, L. A. Peplau, & D. R. Peterson (eds.), *Close relationships* (pp. 1–19). San Francisco: Freeman.

Berscheid, E., & Walster, E. H. (1978). *Interpersonal attraction* (2nd edn.). Reading, MA: Addison-Wesley.

Birkhead, T. (2000). *Promiscuity: An evolutionary history of sperm competition.* Cambridge, MA: Harvard University Press.

Blackmore, S. (1999). *The meme machine.* Oxford: Oxford University Press.

Blanchard, R., Barbaree, H. E., Bogaert, A. F., Dickey, R., Klassen, P., Kuban, M. E., & Zucker, K. J. (2000). Fraternal birth order and sexual orientation in pedophiles. *Archives of Sexual Behavior*, 29, 463–78.

Blanchard, R., & Bogaert, A. F. (1996). Homosexuality in men and a number of older brothers. *American Journal of Psychiatry*, 153, 27–31.

Block, C. R., & Christakos, A. (1995). Intimate partner homicide in Chicago over 29 years. *Crime and Delinquency*, 41, 496–526.

Blumstein, P., & Schwartz, P. (1983). *American couples.* New York: Simon & Schuster.

Bogaert, A. F. (1998). Birth order and sibling sex ratio in homosexual and heterosexual non-white men. *Archives of Sexual Behavior*, 27, 467–73.

Bogaert, A. F. & Hershberger, S. (1999). The relation between sexual orientation and penile size. *Archives of Sexual Behavior*, 28, 213–21.

Bowlby, J. (1969). *Attachment and loss:* Vol. 1. *Attachment.* New York: Basic.

Bowlby, J. (1973). *Attachment and loss:* Vol. 2. *Separation: Anger and anxiety.* New York: Basic.

Bowlby, J. (1979). *The making and breaking of affectional bonds.* London: Tavistock.

Bowlby, J. (1980). *Attachment and loss:* Vol. 3. *Loss.* New York: Basic.

Bradbury, T. N., Campbell, S. M., & Fincham, F. D. (1995). Longitudinal and behavioral analysis of masculinity and femininity in marriage. *Journal of Personality and Social Psychology*, 68, 328–41.

Brennan, K. A., & Shaver, P. R. (1995). Dimensions of adult attachment, affect regulation, and romantic relationship functioning. *Personality and Social Psychology Bulletin*, 21, 267–83.

Brown, D. E. (1991). *Human universals*. New York: McGraw-Hill.

Brown, N. R., & Sinclair, R. C. (1999). Estimating number of lifetime sexual partners: Men and women do it differently. *Journal of Sex Research*, 36, 292–7.

Bunge, M. (1991). A critical examination of the new sociology of science: Part 1. *Philosophy of the Social Sciences*, 21, 524–60.

Bunge, M. (1992). A critical examination of the new sociology of science: Part 2. *Philosophy of the Social Sciences*, 22, 46–76.

Burchfield, J. D. (1975). *Lord Kelvin and the age of the earth*. London: MacMillan.

Burke, L. K, & Follingstad, D. R. (1999). Violence in lesbian and gay relationships: Theory, prevalence, and correlational factors. *Clinical Psychology Review*, 19, 487–512.

Buss, D. M. (1989a). Conflict between the sexes: Strategic interference and the evocation of anger and upset. *Journal of Personality and Social Psychology*, 56, 735–47.

Buss, D. M. (1989b). Sex differences in human mate preferences: Evolutionary hypotheses testing in 37 cultures. *Behavioral and Brain Sciences*, 12, 1–49.

Buss, D. M. (1994). *The evolution of desire: Strategies of human mating*. HarperCollins: Basic.

Buss, D. M. (1999). *Evolutionary Psychology: The new science of the mind*. Boston: Allyn and Bacon.

Buss, D. M., & Barnes, M. (1986). Preferences in human mate selection. *Journal of Personality and Social Psychology*, 50, 559–70.

Buss, D. M., & Schmitt, D. P. (1993). Sexual strategies theory: A contextual evolutionary analysis of human mating. *Psychological Review*, 100, 204–32.

Buss, D. M., Shackelford, T. K., Kirkpatrick, L. A., Choe, J. C., Lim, H. K., Hasegawa, M., Hasegawa, T., & Bennett, K. (1999). Jealousy and the nature of beliefs about infidelity: Tests of competing hypotheses about sex differences in the United States, Korea, and Japan. *Personal Relationships*, 6, 125–50.

Buss, D. M., Shackelford, T. K., Kirkpatrick, L. A., & Larsen, R. J. (2001). *A half century of American mate preferences: The cultural evolution of values*. Unpublished manuscript. Department of Psychology, University of Austin at Texas.

Buunk, B. P., Angleitner, A., Oubaid, V., & Buss, D. M. (1996). Sex differences in jealousy in evolutionary and cultural perspective: Tests from the Netherlands, Germany, and the United States. *Psychological Science*, 7, 359–63.

Campbell, L., Simpson, J. A., Kashy, D. A., & Fletcher, G. J. O. (2001). Ideal standards, the self, and flexibility of ideals in close relationships. *Personality and Social Psychology Bulletin*, 27, 447–62.

Cantos, A. L., Neidig, P. H., & O'Leary, K. D. (1994). Injuries of women and men in a treatment program for domestic violence. *Journal of Family Violence*, 9, 113–24.

Caplan, L. (1984, July 2). Annals of Law: The insanity defense. *New Yorker*, pp. 45–78.

Carrado, M., George, M. J., Loxam, E., Jones, L., & Templar, D. (1996). Aggression in British heterosexual relationships: A descriptive analysis. *Aggressive Behavior*, 22, 401–15.

Carrère, S., Buehlman, K. T., Gottman, J. M., Coan, J. A., & Ruckstuhl, L. (2000). Predicting marital stability and divorce in newly-wed couples. *Journal of Family Psychology*, 14, 42–58.

Cascardi, M., & Vivian, D. (1995). Context for specific episodes of marital violence: Gender and severity of violence differences. *Journal of Family Violence*, 10, 265–93.

Cassidy, J., & Shaver, P. R. (1999). *Handbook of attachment: Theory, research, and clinical applications*. New York: Guilford.

Chagnon, N. A. (1992). *Yanamamö: The last days of Eden*. San Diego: Harcourt Brace Jovanovich.

Chaiken, S., & Trope, Y. (eds.) (1999). *Dual process theories in social psychology*. New York: Guilford.

Chamberlain, W. (1991). A view from above. New York: Villard.

Christensen, A., & Heavey, C. L. (1990). Gender and social structure in the demand/withdraw pattern of marriage conflict. *Journal of Personality and Social Psychology*, 59, 73–81.

Church, A. T., & Lonner, W. J. (1998). The cross-cultural perspective in the study of personality: Rationale and current research. *Journal of Cross-Cultural Psychology*, 29, 32–62.

Clark, M. S., Pataki, S. P., & Carver, V. H. (1996). Some thoughts and findings on self-presentation of emotions in relationships. In G. J. O. Fletcher & J. Fitness (eds.), *Knowledge structures in close relationships* (pp. 247–74). Mahwah, NJ: Lawrence Erlbaum.

Clark, R. D., & Hatfield, E. (1989). Gender differences in receptivity to sexual offers. *Journal of Psychology and Human Sexuality*, 2, 39–55.

Collins, N. L., & Allard, L. M. (2001). Cognitive representations of attachment: The content and function of working models. In G. J. O. Fletcher & M. S. Clark (eds.), *Blackwell handbook of social psychology: Interpersonal processes* (pp. 60–85). London: Blackwell.

References

Collins, W. A., Maccoby, E. E., Steinberg, L., Hetherington, E. M., Bornstein, M. H. (2000). Contemporary research on parenting: The case for nature and nurture. *American Psychologist,* 55, 218–32.

Colvin, C. R., Block, J., & Funder, D.C. (1995). Overly positive self-evaluations and personality: Negative implications for mental health. *Journal of Personality and Social Psychology,* 68, 1152–62.

Corballis, M. C., & Lea, S. E. G. (eds.) (1999). *The descent of mind: Psychological perspectives on hominid evolution.* New York: Oxford University Press.

Crocker, W. H., & Crocker, J. (1994). *The Canela: Bonding through kinship, ritual, and sex.* Fort Worth, TX: Harcourt Brace.

Cronin, H. (1991). *The ant and the peacock: Altruism and sexual selection from Darwin to today.* Cambridge, UK: Cambridge University Press.

Crooks, R. & Baur, K. (1999). *Our sexuality.* Pacific Grove, CA: Brooks/Cole.

Cross, S. E., & Madson, L. (1997). Models of the self: Self-construals and gender. *Psychological Bulletin,* 122, 5–37.

Cunningham, M. R. (1986). Measuring the physical in physical attractiveness: Quasi-experiments on the sociobiology of female facial beauty. *Journal of Personality and Social Psychology,* 50, 925–35.

Cunningham, M. R., Barbee, A. P., & Pike, C. L. (1990). What do women want? Facialmetric assessment of multiple motives in the perception of male facial physical attractiveness. *Journal of Personality and Social Psychology,* 59, 61–72.

Cunningham, M. R., Druen, P. B., & Barbee, A. P. (1997). Angels, mentors, and friends: Trade-offs among evolutionary, social, and individual variables in physical appearance. In J. A. Simpson & D. T. Kenrick (eds.), *Evolutionary social psychology* (pp. 109–40). Mahwah, NJ: Lawrence Erlbaum.

Cunningham, M. R., Roberts, A. R., Barbee, A. P., Druen, P. B., & Wu, C.-H. (1995). "Their ideas of beauty are, on the whole, the same as ours": Consistency and variability in the cross-cultural perception of female physical attractiveness. *Journal of Personality and Social Psychology,* 68, 261–79.

Dabbs, J. M., & Dabbs, M. G. (2000). *Heroes, rogues, and lovers: Testosterone and behavior.* New York: McGraw-Hill.

Daly, M., & Wilson, M. I. (1988). *Homicide.* New York: Aldine de Gruyter.

Daly, M., & Wilson, M. I. (1996). Violence against stepchildren. *Current Directions in Psychological Science,* 5, 77–81.

Daly, M., Wilson, M., & Weghorst, S. J. (1981). Male sexual jealousy. *Ethology and Sociobiology,* 3, 11–27.

Damasio, A. R. (1994). *Descartes' Error: Emotion, reason and the human brain.* New York: G. P. Putnam.

Darwin, C. (1859). *On the origin of the species by means of natural selection, or, preservation of favoured races in the struggle for life.* London: Murray.

References

Darwin, C. (1871). *The descent of man, and selection in relation to sex.* London: Murray,

Darwin, C. (1872). *The expression of the emotions in man and animals.* London: Murray.

Davenport, W. H. (1977). Sex in cross-cultural perspective. In F. A. Beach (ed.), *Human sexuality in four perspectives* (pp. 115–63). Baltimore: The Johns Hopkins University Press.

Davis, K. E., Ace, A., & Andra, M. (2000). Stalking perpetrators and psychological maltreatment of partners: anger-jealousy, attachment insecurity, need for control, and breakup context. *Violence and Victims,* 15, 2000.

Davis, M. H., & Kraus, L. A. (1997). Personality and empathic accuracy. In W. Ickes (ed.), *Empathic accuracy* (pp. 144–68). New York: Guilford.

Dawkins, R. (1986). *The selfish gene.* Oxford: Oxford University Press.

Dawkins, R. (1999/1992). *The extended phenotype: The long reach of the gene.* Oxford: Oxford University Press.

de Munck, V. C. (1998). Lust, love, and arranged marriages in Sri Lanka. In V. C. de Munck (ed.). *Romantic love and sexual behavior: Perspectives from the social sciences* (pp. 295–300). Westport, CT: Praeger.

de Rougemont, D. (1940/1983). *Love in the Western world.* New York: Schocken.

Dennett, D. C. (1995). *Darwin's dangerous idea: Evolution and the meanings of life.* London: Penguin.

Dennett, D. C. (1997, August 14). 'Darwinian Fundamentalism': An Exchange [Letter to the Editors]. *New York Review of Books,* pp. 64–5.

Desmond, A., & Moore, J. (1991). *Darwin: The life of a tormented evolutionist.* New York: W. W. Norton.

DeSteno, D. A., & Salovey, P. (1996). Evolutionary origins of sex differences in jealousy: Questioning the "fitness" of the model. *Psychological Science,* 7, 367–72.

Diamond, L. M., & Savin-Williams, R. C. (2000). Explaining diversity in the development of same-sex sexuality among young women. *Journal of Social Issues,* 56, 297–313.

Dobash, R. E., & Dobash, R. P. (1984). The nature and antecedents of violent events. *British Journal of Criminology,* 24, 269–88.

Dobash, R. P., Dobash, R. E., Wilson, M., & Daly, M. (1992). The myth of sexual symmetry in marital violence. *Social Problems,* 39, 71–91.

Dunbar, R. I. M., & Duncan, N. D. C. (1997). Human conversational behavior. *Human Nature,* 8, 231–46.

Durrant, R., & Ellis, B. J. (in press). Evolutionary psychology: Core assumptions and methodology. In M. Gallagher & R. J. Nelson (eds.), *Comprehensive handbook of psychology.* Vol. 3. *Biological psychology.* New York: Wiley and Sons.

References

Dutton, D., & Aron, A. (1974). Some evidence for heightened sexual attraction under conditions of high anxiety. *Journal of Personality and Social Psychology*, 30, 510–17.

Eagly, A. H., & Wood, W. (1999). The origins of sex differences in human behavior: Evolved dispositions versus social roles. *American Psychologist*, 54, 408–23.

Einon, D. (1998). How many fathers can one man have? *Evolution and Human Behavior*, 19, 413–26.

Ekman, P. (1982). *Emotion in the human face* (2nd edn.). New York: Cambridge University Press.

Eliot, G. (1871–2). *Middlemarch*. London: Penguin. 1965.

Ellis, B. J., & Garber, J. (2000). Psychosocial antecedents of variation in girls' pubertal timing: Maternal depression, stepfather presence, and marital and family stress. *Child Development*, 71, 485–501.

Ellis, B. J., & Kelley, H. H. (1999). The pairing game: A classroom demonstration of the matching phenomenon. *Teaching of Psychology*, 26, 118–21.

Ellis, B. J., McFadyen-Ketchum, S., Dodge, K. A., Pettit, G. S., & Bates, J. E. (1999). Quality of early family relationships and individual differences in the timing of pubertal maturation in girls: A longitudinal test of an evolutionary model. *Journal of Personality and Social Psychology*, 77, 387–401.

Elliston, D. A. (1995). Erotic anthropology: "Ritualized homosexuality" in Melanesia and beyond. *American Ethnologist*, 22, 848–67.

Fehr, B. (1999). Layperson's perception of commitment. *Journal of Personality and Social Psychology*, 76, 90–103.

Fehr, B., & Baldwin, M. (1996). Prototype and script analyses of laypeople's knowledge of anger. In G. J. O. Fletcher & J. Fitness (eds.), *Knowledge structures in close relationships* (pp. 219–45). Mahwah, NJ: Lawrence Erlbaum.

Fernandez, M. (1997). Domestic violence by extended family members in India. *Journal of Interpersonal Violence*, 12, 433–55.

Fincham, F. D. (2001). Attributions in close relationships: From balkanization to integration. In G. J. O. Fletcher & M. S. Clark (eds.), *Blackwell Handbook of Social Psychology: Interpersonal processes* (pp. 3–31). Oxford: Blackwell.

Fincham, F. D., & Bradbury, T. N. (1987). The assessment of marital quality: A reevaluation. *Journal of Marriage and the Family*, 49, 797–809.

Fisher, H. (1992). *Anatomy of Love: A natural history of mating, marriage and why we stray*. New York: Fawcett Columbine.

Fisher, H. E. (1998). Lust, attraction, and attachment in mammalian reproduction. *Human Nature*, 9, 23–52.

Fisher, R. A. (1930). *The genetic theory of natural selection*. Oxford, UK: Clarendon.

Fitness, J. (1996). Emotion knowledge structures in close relationships. In G. J. O. Fletcher & J. Fitness (eds.), *Knowledge structures in close relationships*

References

(pp. 195–217). Mahwah, NJ: Lawrence Erlbaum.

Fitzpatrick, M. (1988). *Between husbands and wives: Communication in marriage*. Newbury Park, CA: Sage.

Fletcher, G. J. O. (1995). *The scientific credibility of folk psychology*. Mahwah, NJ: Lawrence Erlbaum.

Fletcher, G. J. O. (1996). Realism versus relativism in psychology. *American Journal of Psychology*, 109, 409–29.

Fletcher, G. J. O., Danilovics, P., Fernandez, G., Peterson, D., & Reeder, G. D. (1986). Attributional complexity: An individual differences measure. *Journal of Personality and Social Psychology*, 51, 875–84.

Fletcher, G. J. O., & Fincham, F. D. (eds.) (1991a). *Cognition in close relationships*. Hillsdale, NJ: Lawrence Erlbaum.

Fletcher, G. J. O., & Fincham, F. D. (1991b). Attributional processes in close relationships. In G. J. O. Fletcher & F. D. Fincham (eds.), *Cognition in close relationships* (pp. 6–34). Hillsdale, NJ: Lawrence Erlbaum.

Fletcher, G. J. O., & Fitness, J. (eds.) (1996). *Knowledge structures in close relationships*. Mahwah, NJ: Lawrence Erlbaum.

Fletcher, G. J. O., Grigg, F., & Bull, V. (1988). Organization and accuracy of personality impressions: Neophytes versus experts in trait attribution. *New Zealand Journal of Psychology*, 17, 68–77.

Fletcher, G. J. O., & Kininmonth, L. (1991). Interaction and social cognition. In G. J. O. Fletcher & F. D. Fincham (eds.), *Cognition in close relationships* (pp. 234–54). Hillsdale, NJ: Lawrence Erlbaum.

Fletcher, G. J. O., & Kininmonth, L. (1992). Measuring relationship beliefs: An individual differences scale. *Journal of Research in Personality*, 26, 371–97.

Fletcher, G. J. O., Reeder, G. D., & Bull, V. I. (1990). Bias and accuracy in trait attribution: The role of attributional complexity. *Journal of Experimental Social Psychology*, 26, 275–88.

Fletcher, G. J. O., Rosanowski, J., & Fitness, J. (1994). Automatic processing in intimate contexts: The role of close-relationship beliefs. *Journal of Personality and Social Psychology*, 67, 888–97.

Fletcher, G. J. O., Rosanowski J., Rhodes, G., & Lange, C. (1992). Accuracy and speed of causal processing: Experts versus novices in social judgment. *Journal of Experimental Social Psychology*, 28, 320–38.

Fletcher, G. J. O., Simpson, J., & Thomas, G. (2000a). The measurement of relationship quality components: A confirmatory factor analytic study. *Personality and Social Psychology Bulletin*, 26, 340–53.

Fletcher, G. J. O., Simpson, J. A., & Thomas, G. (2000b). Ideals, perceptions, and evaluations in early relationship development. *Journal of Personality and Social Psychology*, 79, 933–40.

Fletcher, G. J. O., Simpson, J. A., Thomas, G., & Giles, L. (1999). Ideals in intimate relationships. *Journal of Personality and Social Psychology*, 76, 72–89.

Fletcher, G. J. O., & Thomas, G. (1996). Close relationship lay theories: Their structure and function. In G. J. O. Fletcher & J. Fitness (eds.), *Knowledge structures in close relationships* (pp. 3–24). Mahwah, NJ: Lawrence Erlbaum.

Fletcher, G. J. O., & Thomas, G. (2000). Behavior and on-line cognition in marital interaction: A longitudinal study. *Personal Relationships*, 7, 111–30.

Fletcher, G. J. O., Thomas, G., & Durrant, R. (1999). Cognitive and behavioral accommodation in relationship interaction. *Journal of Social and Personal Relationships*, 16, 705–30.

Fletcher, G. J. O., Tither, J. M., Durrant, R., & O'Loughlin, C. F. (2001). *Trading off traits in mate selection: Explaining sex differences.* Unpublished manuscript. Department of Psychology, University of Canterbury.

Fletcher, G. J. O., & Ward, C. (1988). Attribution theory and processes: A cross-cultural perspective. In M. Bond (ed.), *The cross-cultural challenge to social psychology* (pp. 231–44). Newburg Park: Sage.

Fodor, J. A. (1983). *The modularity of mind.* Cambridge, MA: MIT Press.

Fowler, B. H. (1994). *Love lyrics of ancient Egypt.* Chapel Hill: University of North Carolina Press.

Frank, E., Anderson, C., & Rubinstein, D. (1978). Frequency of sexual dysfunction in "normal" couples. *New England Journal of Medicine*, 299, 111–15.

Frank-Kamenetskii, M. D. (1997). *Unraveling DNA: The most important molecule of life.* Reading, MA: Addison-Wesley.

Funder, D. C. (1995). On the accuracy of personality judgement: A realistic approach. *Psychological Review*, 102, 652–70.

Funder, D. C., & Dobroth, K. M. (1987). Differences between traits: Properties associated with interjudge agreement. *Journal of Personality and Social Psychology*, 52, 409–18.

Gagné, F. M., & Lydon, J. E. (in press). Mindset and close relationships: When bias leads to (In)accurate predictions. *Journal of Personality and Social Psychology.*

Gagnon, J. H. (1977). *Human sexualities.* Glenview, IL: Scott, Foresman.

Gagnon, J. H., & Simon, W. (1968). The social meaning of prison homosexuality. *Federal Probation*, 32, 28–9.

Gangestad, S. W., & Simpson, J. A. (2000). The evolution of human mating: Trade-offs and strategic pluralism. *Behavioral and Brain Sciences*, 23, 573–644.

Gayford, J. J. (1997). Disorders of sexual preference, or paraphilias: a review of the literature. *Medical Science Law*, 37, 303–15.

Gergen, K. J. (1995). *Realities and relationships: Soundings in social construction.* Cambridge, MA: Harvard University Press

References

Gerrard, M., Gibbons, F.X., Reis-Bergan, M., & Russell, D.W. (2000). Self-esteem, self-serving cognitions, and health risk behavior. *Journal of Personality*, 68, 1177–1201.

Gladue, B. A., & Delaney, H. J. (1990). Gender differences in perception of attractiveness of men and women in bars. *Personality and Social Psychology Bulletin*, 16, 378–91.

Goldman, A. I. (1993). The psychology of folk psychology. *Behavioral and Brain Sciences*, 16, 15–28.

Goode, W. J. (1993). *World changes in divorce patterns.* New Haven: Yale University Press.

Gopnik, A. (1993). How we know our minds: The illusion of first-person knowledge of intentionality. *Behavioral and Brain Sciences*, 16, 1–14.

Gopnik, A., Meltzoff, A. N., & Kuhl, P. K. (1999). *The scientist in the crib: Minds, brains, and how children learn.* New York: William Morrow.

Gottman, J. M. (1990). How marriages change. In G. R. Patterson (ed.), *Depression and aggression in family interaction* (pp. 75-101). Hillsdale, NJ: Erlbaum.

Gottman, J. M. (1994). *What predicts divorce? The relationship between marital processes and marital outcomes.* Hillsdale, NJ: Lawrence Erlbaum.

Gottman, J. M. (1998). Psychology and the study of the marital processes. *Annual Review of Psychology*, 49, 169–97.

Gottman, J. M., & Krokoff, L. J. (1989). Marital interaction and satisfaction: A longitudinal view. *Journal of Consulting and Clinical Psychology*, 57, 47–52.

Gottman, J. M., Coan, J., Carrère, S., & Swanson, C. (1998). Predicting marital happiness and stability from newlywed interactions. *Journal of Marriage and the Family*, 60, 5–22.

Gottman, J. M., Jacobson, N. S, Rushe, R. G., Shortt, J. W., Babcock, J., Lataillade, J. J., & Waltz, J. (1995). The relationship between heart-rate reactivity, emotionally aggressive behavior, and general violence in batterers. *Journal of Family Psychology*, 9, 227–48.

Gould, S. J. (1980). *The panda's thumb.* New York: W. W. Norton.

Gould, S. J. (1992). *Bully for brontosaurus: Reflections in natural history.* New York: W.W. Norton.

Gould, S. J. (1997, June 12 and June 26). Darwinian fundamentalism & evolution: The pleasures of pluralism. *New York Review of Books.* For replies to Gould by his critics, and a response by Gould, see issues published on August 14 and October 9, 1997.

Graham, S. (1834). *A lecture to young men.* Providence: Weeden and Cory. Facsimile repr. edn. (1974). New York: Arno.

Grossmann, K. E., Grossmann, K., Huber, F., & Wartner, U. (1981). German children's behavior towards their mothers at 12 months and their fathers at

18 months in Ainsworth's Strange Situation. *International Journal of Behavioral Development*, 4, 157–81.

Gupta, U., & Singh, P. (1982). Exploratory study of love and liking and type of marriages. *Indian Journal of Applied Psychology*, 19, 92–7.

Gurven, M., Allen-Arave, W., Hill, K., & Hurtado, M. (2000). "It's a Wonderful Life": Signaling generosity among the Ache of Paraguay. *Evolution and Human Behavior*, 21, 263–82.

Haig, B. D., & Durrant, R. (2000). Theory evaluation in evolutionary psychology. *Psychological Inquiry*, 11, 34–8.

Hamer, D. H., Hu, S., Magnuson, V. L., Hu, N. & Pattatucci, A. M. L. (1993). A linkage between DNA markers on the X chromosome and male sexual orientation. *Science*, 261, 321–7.

Hamilton, C. E. (2000). Continuity and discontinuity of attachment from infancy through adolescence. *Child Development*, 71, 690–4.

Hamilton, W. (1964). The genetical evolution of social behavior, Parts 1 and 2. *Journal of Theoretical Biology*, 7, 1–16, 17–52.

Hammond, J. R., & Fletcher, G. J. O. (1991). Attachment styles and relationship satisfaction in the development of close relationships. *New Zealand Journal of Psychology*, 20, 56–62.

Hanly, M. J., & O'Neill, P. (1997). Violence and commitment: A study of dating couples. *Journal of Interpersonal Violence*, 12, 685–703.

Harris, T. G. (1978). Introduction. In E. H. Hatfield & G. W. Walster (eds.), *A new look at love* (pp. v–xi). Reading, MA: Addison-Wesley.

Hatfield, E., & Rapson, R. L. (1993). Love and attachment processes. In M. Lewis & J. M. Haviland (eds.), *Handbook of Emotions* (pp. 595–604). New York: Guilford.

Hatfield, E., & Rapson, R. L. (1987). Passionate love/sexual desire: Can the same paradigm explain both? *Archives of Sexual Behavior*, 16, 259–78.

Haviland, J. B. (1977). *Gossip, reputation and knowledge in Zinacantan*. Chicago: University of Chicago Press.

Hawkes, K. (1991). Showing off: Tests of an hypothesis about men's foraging goals. *Ethology and Sociobiology*, 12, 29–54.

Hazan, C., & Diamond, L. M. (2000). The place of attachment in human mating. *Review of General Psychology*, 4, 186–204.

Hazan, C., & Shaver, P. (1987). Romantic love conceptualized as an attachment process. *Journal of Personality and Social Psychology*, 52, 511–24.

Heelas, P. (1989). Identifying peaceful societies. In S. Howell & R. Willis (eds.), *Societies at peace: Anthropological perspectives* (pp. 225–43). Routledge: New York.

Heider, F. (1958). *The psychology of interpersonal relations*. New York: Wiley.

Heine, S. J., Lehman, D. R., Markus, H. R., & Kitayama S. (1999). Is there a universal need for positive self-regard? *Psychological Review*, 106, 766–94.

References

Herdt, G. H. (1981). *Guardians of the flutes: Idioms of masculinity.* New York: McGraw-Hill.

Hetherington, E. M. (1972). Effects of father absence on personality development in adolescent daughters. *Developmental Psychology, 7,* 313–26.

Heyman, R. E., & Schlee, K. A. (1997). Toward a better estimate of the prevalence of partner abuse: Adjusting rates based on the sensitivity of the Conflict Tactics Scale. *Journal of Family Psychology, 11,* 332–8.

Hill, K., & Hurtado, A. M. (1996). *Ache life history: The ecology and demography of a foraging people.* Hawthorne, New York: Aldine de Gruyter.

Hinde, R. A. (1982). Attachment: Some conceptual and biological issues. In C. Murray Parkes & J. Stevenson-Hinde (eds.), *The place of attachment in human behavior* (pp. 60–76). London: Tavistock Publications.

Hirschfeld, L. A., & Gelman, S. A. (eds.) (1994). *Mapping the mind: Domain specificity in cognition and culture.* New York: Cambridge University Press.

Holmberg, D., & Veroff, J. (1996). Rewriting relationship memories: The effects of courtship and wedding scripts. In G. J. O. Fletcher & J. Fitness (eds.), *Knowledge structures in close relationships* (pp. 345–68). Mahwah, NJ: Lawrence Erlbaum.

Holtzworth-Munroe, A., & Stuart, G. L. (1994). Typologies of male batterers: Three subtypes and the differences among them. *Psychological Bulletin, 116,* 476–97.

Hrdy, S. B. (1999). *Mother Nature: A history of mothers, infants, and natural selection.* New York: Pantheon.

Hunt, M. (1974). *Sexual behavior in the 1970's.* Chicago: Playboy.

Huxley, T. H. (1884). *Biogenesis and abiogenesis; collected essays,* vol. 8. London: Macmillan.

Hyde, J. S., & DeLamater, J. (1997). *Understanding human sexuality* (6th edn.). Boston, MA: McGraw-Hill.

Ickes, W. (1993). Empathic accuracy. *Journal of Personality, 61,* 587–610.

Ickes, W. (ed.) (1997). *Empathic accuracy.* New York: Guilford.

Insel, T. R. (2000). Toward a neurobiology of attachment. *Review of General Psychology, 4,* 176–85.

Jacobson, N. S., & Addis, M. E. (1993). Research on couple therapy: What do we know? Where are we going? *Journal of Consulting and Clinical Psychology, 61,* 85–93.

Jacobson, N. S., & Christensen, A. (1997). *Integrated cognitive behavioral marital therapy.* New York: Guilford.

Jacobson, N. S., Gottman, J. M, Waltz, J., Rushe, R., Babcock, J., & Holtzworth-Munroe, A. (1994). Affect, verbal content, and psychophysiology in the arguments of couples with a violent husband. *Journal of Consulting and Clinical Psychology, 62,* 982–8.

303

Jankowiak, W. R., & Fischer, E. F. (1992). A cross-cultural perspective on romantic love. *Ethnology*, 31, 149–55.

Jockin, V., McGue, M., & Lykken, D. T. (1996). Personality and divorce: A genetic analysis. *Journal of Personality and Social Psychology*, 71, 288–99.

Johnson, M. P. (1995). Patriarchal terrorism and common couple violence: Two forms of violence against women. *Journal of Marriage and the Family*, 57, 283–94.

Jones, S. (2000). *Darwin's ghost: The origin of species updated*. New York: Random House.

Joyce, J. (1936). *Ulysses*. London: Bodley Head.

Kalick, S. M., Zebrowitz, L. A., Langlois, J. H., & Johnson, R. M. (1998). Does human facial attractiveness honestly advertise health? Longitudinal data on an evolutionary question. *Psychological Science*, 9, 8–13.

Karney, B. R., & Bradbury, T. N. (1995). The longitudinal course of marital quality and stability: A review of theory, methods, and research. *Psychological Bulletin*, 118, 3–34.

Kelley, H. H., Berscheid, E., Christensen, A., Harvey, J. H., Huston, T. L., Levinger, G., McClintock, E., Peplau, L. A., & Peterson, D. R. (1983). *Close relationships*. San Francisco: Freeman.

Kellogg, J. H. (1888). *Plain facts for old and young: Embracing the natural history and hygiene of organic life*. Burlington, Iowa: I. F. Segner. Facsimile repr. edn. (1974). New York: Arno.

Kelly, R. L. (1995). *The foraging spectrum: Diversity in hunter-gatherer lifeways*. Washington: Smithsonian Institution.

Kenny, D. A. (1994). *Interpersonal perception: A social relations analysis*. New York: Guilford.

Ketelaar, T., & Ellis, B. J. (2000). Are evolutionary explanations unfalsifiable? Evolutionary psychology and the Lakatosian philosophy of science. *Psychological Inquiry*, 11, 1–21.

Kimble, G. A. (1989). Psychology from the standpoint of the generalist. *American Psychologist*, 44, 491-499.

Kirkpatrick, L. A., & Hazan, C. (1994). Attachment styles and close relationships: A four-year prospective study. *Personal Relationships*, 1, 123–42.

Kruijver, F. P., Fernandez-Guasti, A., Fodor, M., Kraan, E. M., & Swabb, D. F. (2001). Sex differences in androgen receptors of the human mamillary bodies are related to endocrine status rather to sexual orientation or transsexuality. *Journal of Clinical Endocrinology & Metabolism*, 86, 818–27.

Kurz, D. (1997). Physical assaults by male partners: A major social problem. In M. R. Walsh (ed.), *Women, men, & gender* (pp. 222–31). New Haven, CT: Yale University Press.

Langlois, J. H., Kalakanis, L., Rubenstein, A. J., Larson, A., Hallam, M., & Smoot, M. (2000). Maxims or myths of beauty? A meta-analytic and theoretical review. *Psychological Bulletin*, 126, 390–423.

Laudan, L. (1996). *Beyond positivism and relativism: Theory, method and evidence*. Boulder, CO: Westview.

Lawrence, E., & Bradbury, T. N. (in press). Physical aggression and marital dysfunction: A longitudinal analysis. *Journal of Family Psychology*.

Lee, R. B. (1978). Politics, sexual and non-sexual in an egalitarian society. *Social Science Information*, 17, 871–95.

Leibrich, J., Paulin, J., & Ransom, R. (1995). *Hitting home*. New Zealand: Department of Justice, New Zealand.

Leonard, K. E., & Roberts, L. J. (1998). The effects of alcohol on the marital interactions of aggressive and nonaggressive husbands and their wives. *Journal of Abnormal Psychology*, 107, 602–15.

LeVay, S. (1991). A difference in hypothalamic structure between heterosexual and homosexual men. *Science*, 253, 1034–7.

LeVay, S. (in press). Sexual orientation: The science and its social impact. *Reverso*.

Levesque, M. J., & Kenny, D. A. (1993). Accuracy of behavioral predictions at zero acquaintance: A social relations analysis. *Journal of Personality and Social Psychology*, 65, 1178–87.

Levinson, D. (1989). *Family violence in cross-cultural perspective*. Newbury Park, CA: Sage.

Lewin, K. (1951). *Field theory in social science*. New York: Harper & Row.

Lewis, M., Feiring, C., & Rosenthal, S. (2000). Attachment over time. *Child Development*, 71, 707–20.

Lippa, R. A. (2000). Gender-related traits in gay men, lesbian women, and heterosexual men and women: The virtual identity of homosexual–heterosexual diagnosticity and gender diagnosticity. *Journal of Personality*, 68, 899–926.

Lippa, R. A., & Arad, S. (1997). The structure of sexual orientation and its relation to masculinity, femininity, and gender diagnosticity: Different for men and women. *Sex Roles*, 37, 187–208.

Locke, H. J., & Wallace, K. M. (1959). Short marital-adjustment and prediction tests: Their reliability and validity. *Marriage and Family Living*, 21, 251–5.

Lykken, D. T., & Tellegen, A. (1993). Is human mating adventitious or the result of lawful choice? A twin study of mate selection. *Journal of Personality and Social Psychology*, 65, 56–68.

MacDonald, T. K., & Ross, M. (1999). Assessing the accuracy of predictions about dating relationships: How and why do lovers' predictions differ from those made by observers? *Personality and Social Psychology Bulletin*, 25, 1417–29.

MacLean, P. D. (1990). *The triune brain in evolution*. New York: Plenum.

Madey, S. F., Simo, M., Dillworth, D., Kemper, D., Toczynski, A., & Perella,

A. (1996). They do get more attractive at closing time, but only when you are not in a relationship. *Basic and Applied Social Psychology*, 18, 387–93.

Magdol, L., Moffitt, T. E., Caspi, P. A., Newman, D. L., Fagan, J., & Silva, P. A. (1997). Gender differences in partner violence in a birth cohort of 21-year-olds: Bridging the gap between clinical and epidemiological approaches. *Journal of Consulting and Clinical Psychology*, 65, 68–78.

Martin, S. L., Tsui, A. O., Maitra, K., & Marinshaw, R. (1999). Domestic violence in northern India. *American Journal of Epidemiology*, 150, 417–26.

Masumura, W. T. (1979). Wife abuse and other forms of aggression. *Victimology: An International Journal*, 4, 46–59.

McGue, M., & Lykken, D. T. (1992). Genetic influence on risk of divorce. *Psychological Science*, 3, 368–73.

Meston, C. M., & Frohlich, P. F. (2000). The neurobiology of sexual function. *Archives of General Psychiatry*, 57, 1012–30.

Meyer-Bahlburg, H. F. L. (2001). Gender and sexuality in classic congenital adrenal hyperplasia. *Endocrinology and Metabolism clinics of North America*, 30, 155–71.

Michael, R. T., Gagnon, J. H., Laumann, E. O., & Kolata, G. (1994). *Sex in America: A definitive survey*. New York: Warner.

Mikulincer, M., Gillath, O., & Shaver, P. R. (2001). *Activation of the attachment system in adulthood: Threat-related primes increase the accessibility of mental representations of attachment figures*. Unpublished manuscript, Department of Psychology, Bar-Ilan University.

Miller, E. M. (2000). Homosexuality, birth order, and evolution: Toward an equilibrium reproductive economics of homosexuality. *Archives of Sexual Behavior*, 29, 1–34.

Miller, G. F. (1998). How mate choice shaped human nature: A review of sexual selection and human evolution. In C. Crawford & D. L. Krebs (eds.), *Handbook of evolutionary psychology: Ideas, issues and applications* (pp. 87–129). Mahwah, NJ: Lawrence Erlbaum.

Miller, G. F. (2000). *The mating mind: How sexual choice shaped the evolution of human nature*. New York: Doubleday.

Miller, L. C., & Fishkin, S. A. (1997). On the dynamics of human bonding and reproductive success: Seeking windows on the adapted-for human-environmental interface. In J. Simpson & D. Kenrick (eds.), *Evolutionary social psychology* (pp. 197–235). Mahwah, NJ: Erlbaum.

Moore, H. D. M., Martin, M., & Birkhead, T. R. (1999). No evidence for killer sperm or other selective interactions between human spermatozoa in ejaculates of different males in vitro. *Proceedings of the Royal Society of London*, Series B, 266, 2343–50.

Morgan, H. J., & Shaver, P. R. (1999). Attachment processes and commitment to romantic relationships. In J. M. Adams & W. H. Jones (eds.), *Handbook of interpersonal commitment and relationship stability* (pp. 109–24). New York: Kluwer Academic/Plenum.

Morris, N. M., Udry, J. R., Khan-Dawood, F., & Dawood, M. Y. (1987). Marital sex frequency and midcycle female testosterone. *Archives of Sexual Behavior*, 16, 27–37.

Murphy, S. (1992). *A delicate dance: Sexuality, celibacy, and relationships among Catholic clergy and religious*. New York: Crossroad.

Murray, S. L. (2001). Seeking a sense of conviction: Motivated cognition in close relationships. In G. J. O. Fletcher & M. Clark (eds.), *Blackwell Handbook of Social Psychology: Interpersonal Processes* (pp. 107–26). London: Blackwell.

Murray, S. L., & Holmes, J. G. (1993). Seeing virtues in faults: Negativity and the transformation of interpersonal narratives in close relationships. *Journal of Personality and Social Psychology*, 65, 707–22.

Murray, S. L., & Holmes, J. G. (1996). The construction of relationship realities. In G. J. O. Fletcher & J. Fitness (eds.), *Knowledge structures in close relationships* (pp. 91–120). Mahwah, NJ: Lawrence Erlbaum.

Murray, S. L., Holmes, J. G., Bellavia, G., Griffin, D. W., & Dolderman, D. (2001). *Kindred spirits? The benefits of egocentrism in close relationships*. Unpublished manuscript, State University of New York at Buffalo.

Muscarella, F. (2000). The evolution of homoerotic behavior in humans. *Journal of Homosexuality*, 40, 51–77.

Navran, L. (1967). Communication and adjustment in marriage. *Family Process*, 6, 173–84.

New Zealand Ministry of Justice Report (1996). *A summary of crime victims and women's safety surveys* (http://www.justice.govt.nz).

Noller, P., & Ruzzene, M. (1991). Communication in marriage: The influence of affect and cognition. In G. J. O. Fletcher and F. D. Fincham (eds.), *Cognition in Close Relationships*. (pp. 175–202). Hillsdale, NJ: Lawrence Erlbaum.

Noller, P., Feeney, J. A., Bonnell, D., & Callan, V. J. (1994). A longitudinal study of conflict in early marriage. *Journal of Social and Personal Relationships*, 11, 233–52.

O'Leary, K. D., Malone, J., & Tyree, A. (1994). Physical aggression in early marriage: Prerelationship and relationship effects. *Journal of Consulting and Clinical Psychology*, 62, 594–602.

Oatley, K., & Johnson-Laird, P. N. (1987). Toward a cognitive theory of emotions. *Cognition and Emotion*, 1, 29–50.

Okun, B. F. (1997). *Effective Helping: Interviewing and counselling techniques* (5th edn.). London: Brooks Cole.

Ozer, D. J. (1985). Correlation and the coefficient of determination. *Psychological Bulletin*, 97, 307–15.

Page, M. (2000). Connectionist modelling in psychology: A localist manifesto. *Behavioral and Brain Sciences*, 23, 443–512.

Palombit, R. (1994). Dynamic pair bonds in hylobatids: Implications regarding monogamous social systems. *Behavior*, 128, 65–101.

Pan, H. S., Neidig, P. H., & O'Leary, K. D. (1994). Predicting mild and severe husband-to-wife physical aggression. *Journal of Consulting and Clinical Psychology*, 62, 975–81.

Pasch, L. A., & Bradbury, T. N. (1998). Social support, conflict, and the development of marital distress. *Journal of Consulting and Clinical Psychology*, 66, 219–30.

Paulhus, D. L. (1998). Interpersonal and intrapsychic adaptiveness of trait self-enhancement: A mixed blessing. *Journal of personality and social psychology*, 74, 1197–1208.

Pennebaker, J. W., Dyer, M. A., Caulkins, R. S., Litowitz, D. L., Ackreman, P. L., Anderson, D. B., & McGraw, K. M. (1979). Don't the girls get prettier at closing time: A country and western application to psychology. *Personality and Social Psychology Bulletin*, 5, 122–5.

Penton-Voak, I. S., Perrett, D. I., Castles, D., Koyabashi, T., Burt, D. M., Murray, L. K., & Minamisawa, R. (1999). Female preference for male faces changes cyclically. *Nature*, 399, 741–2.

Peplau, L. A. (2001). Rethinking women's sexual orientation: An interdisciplinary, relationship-focused approach. *Personal Relationships*, 8, 1–19.

Peplau, L. A., & Garnets, L. D. (2000). A new paradigm for understanding women's sexuality and sexual orientation. *Journal of Social Issues*, 56, 329–50.

Peplau, L. A., Spalding, L. R., Conley, T. D., & Veniegas, R. C. (1999). The development of sexual orientation in women. *Annual Review of Sex Research*, 10, 70–99.

Petrie, M. (1994). Improved growth and survival of offspring of peacocks with more elaborate trains. *Nature*, 371, 598–9.

Petrie, M., & Halliday, T. (1994). Experimental and natural changes in the peacock's (Pavo cristatus) train can affect mating success. *Behavioral Ecology and Sociobiology*, 35, 213–17.

Pinker, S. (1994). *The language instinct.* New York: HarperCollins.

Pinker, S. (1997). *How the mind works.* New York: W. W. Norton.

Planalp, S., & Rivers, M. (1996). Changes in knowledge of personal relationships. In G. J. O. Fletcher & J. Fitness (eds.), *Knowledge structures in close relationships* (pp. 299–324). Mahwah, NJ: Lawrence Erlbaum.

Polk, K. (1994). *When men kill.* Cambridge University Press.

Regan, P. C. (1999). Hormonal correlates and causes of sexual desire: A review. *Canadian Journal of Human Sexuality*, 8, 1–16.

Regan, P. C., & Berscheid, E. (1996). Beliefs about the state, goals, and objects of sexual desire. *Journal of Sex and Marital Therapy*, 22, 110–20.

Rhodes, G., Hickford, C. & Jeffery, L. (2000). Sex-typicality and attractiveness: Are supermale and superfemale faces super-attractive? *British Journal of Psychology*, 91, 125–40.

Rhodes, G., Proffitt, F., Grady, J. M., & Sumich, A. (1998). Facial symmetry and the perception of beauty. *Psychonomic Bulletin and Review*, 5, 659–69.

Rhodes, G., Sumich, A., & Byatt, G. (1999). Are average facial configuratations attractive only because of their symmetry? *Psychological Science*, 10, 52-58.

Rice, G., Anderson, C., Risch, N., & Ebers, G. (1999). Male homosexuality: Absence of linkage to microsatellite markers at Xq28. *Science*, 284, 665–7.

Ridley, M. (1999). *Genome: The autobiography of a species in 23 chapters*. New York: HarperCollins.

Robins, R. W., Caspi, A., & Moffitt, T. E. (2000). Two personalities, one relationship: Both partners' personality traits shape the quality of their relationship. *Journal of Personality and Social Psychology*, 79, 251–9.

Rockman, H. (1994). Matchmaker matchmaker make me a match: the art and conventions of Jewish arranged marriages. *Sexual and Marital Therapy*, 9, 277–84.

Rogge, R. D., & Bradbury, T. N. (1999). Recent advances in the prediction of marital outcomes. In R. Berger & M. T. Hannah (eds.), *Preventative approaches in couples therapy* (pp. 331–60). New York: Mazel.

Roseman, I. J. (1994). Emotions and emotion families in the emotion system. In N. H. Frijda (ed.), *Proceedings of the 8th meeting of the International Society for Research on Emotions* (pp. 171–5). Cambridge, UK: Cambridge University Press.

Rosenthal, R., & Rubin, D. B. (1982). A simple, general purpose display of magnitude of experimental effect. *Journal of Educational Psychology*, 74, 166–9.

Rubin, Z. (1973). *Liking and loving: An invitation to social psychology*. New York: Holt, Rinehart & Winston.

Rusbult, C. E., Arriaga, X. B., & Agnew, C. R. (2000). Interdependence in close relationships. In G. J. O. Fletcher & M. S. Clark (eds.), *Blackwell Handbook of Social Psychology: Interpersonal Processes* (pp. 359–87). London: Blackwell.

Russell, M. J., Mendelson, T., & Peeke, H. V. (1983). Mothers' identification of their infant's odors. *Ethology and Sociobiology*, 4, 29–31.

Sanders, S. A., & Reinisch, J. M. (1990). Biological and social influences on the endocrinology of puberty: Some additional considerations. In J. Bancroft & J. M. Reinisch (eds.), *A*

Sanders, S. A., & Reinisch, J. M. (1999). Would you say you "had sex" if . . .? *Journal of the American Medical Association*, 281, 275–7.

Sayre, K. M. (1995). *Plato's literary garden: How to read a Platonic dialogue.* Notre Dame: University of Notre Dame Press.

Schachter, S., & Singer, J. E. (1962). Cognitive, social and physiological determinants of emotional state. *Psychological Review,* 69, 379–99.

Schmaltz, J. (1993). Poll finds a an even split on homosexuality's cause. *New York Times,* March 5, 1993.

Scutt, J. (1983). *Even in the best of homes.* Melbourne: Penguin.

Segraves, K., & Segraves, R. T. (1991). Hypoactive sexual desire disorder: Prevalence and comorbidity in 906 subjects. *Journal of Sex and Marital Therapy,* 17, 55–8.

Shaver, P. R., Collins, N., & Clark, C. L. (1996). Attachment styles and internal working models of self and relationship partners. In G. J. O. Fletcher & J. Fitness (eds.), *Knowledge structures in close relationships: A social psychological approach* (pp. 25–62). Mahwah, NJ: Lawrence Erlbaum Associates.

Shaver, P. R., Hazan, C., & Bradshaw, D. (1988). Love as attachment: The integration of three behavioral systems. In R. J. Sternberg & M. L. Barnes (eds.), *The psychology of love* (pp. 68–99). New Haven, CT: Yale University Press.

Shaver, P. R., Morgan, H. J., & Wu, S. (1996). Is love a "basic" emotion? *Personal Relationships,* 3, 81–96.

Shepher, J. (1971). Mate selection among second generation kibbutz adolescents and adults: Incest avoidance and negative imprinting. *Archives of Sexual Behavior,* 1, 293–307.

Shifren, J. L., Braunstein, G. D., Simon, J. A., Casson, P. R., Buster, J. E., Redmond, G. P., Burki, R. E., Ginsburg, E. S., Rosen, R. C., Leiblum, S. R., Caramelli, K. E., & Mazer, N. A. (2000). Transdermal testosterone treatment in women with impaired sexual function after oophorectomy. *New England Journal of Medicine,* 343, 682–8.

Shostak, M. (1981). *Nisa: The life and words of a !Kung woman.* London: Allen Lane.

Siegel, H. (1987). *Relativism refuted: A critique of contemporary methodological relativism.* Boston: Reidel.

Simpson, J. A. (1999). Attachment theory in modern evolutionary perspective. In J. Cassidy & P. R. Shaver (eds.), *Handbook of attachment: Theory, research, and clinical applications* (pp. 115–40). New York: Guilford.

Simpson, J. A., Fletcher, G. J. O., & Campbell, L. (2001). The structure and function of ideal standards in close relationships. In G. J. O. Fletcher & M. S. Clark (eds.), *Blackwell Handbook of Social Psychology: Interpersonal Processes* (pp. 86–106). Oxford: Blackwell.

Simpson, J. A., Gangestad, S. W., Christensen, P. N., & Leck, K. (1999). Fluctuating asymmetry, sociosexuality, and intrasexual competitive tactics. *Journal of Personality and Social Psychology,* 76, 159–72.

Simpson, J. A., Ickes, W., & Blackstone, T. (1995). When the head protects the heart: Empathic accuracy in dating relationships. *Journal of Personality and Social Psychology*, 69, 629–41.

Simpson, J. A., & Kenrick, D. T. (eds.) (1997). *Evolutionary social psychology*. Mahwah, NJ: Lawrence Erlbaum.

Simpson, J. A., Rholes, W. S., & Nelligan, J. S. (1992). Support seeking and support giving within couples in an anxiety-provoking situation: The role of attachment styles. *Journal of Personality and Social Psychology*, 62, 434–46.

Singh, D. (1993). Adaptive significance of female physical attractiveness: Role of waist-to-hip ratio. *Journal of Personality and Social Psychology*, 65, 293–307.

Singh, D. (1994). Is thin really beautiful and good? Relationship between waist-to-hip ratio (WHR) and female attractiveness. *Personality and Individual Differences*, 16, 123–32.

Singh, D., & Luis, S. (1995). Ethnic and gender consensus for the effect of waist-to-hip ratio on judgment of women's attractiveness. *Human Nature*, 6, 51–65.

Slater, A., Von der Schulenburg, C., Brown, E., Badenoch, M., Butterworth, G., Parsons, S., & Samuels, C. (1998). Newborn infants prefer attractive faces. *Infant Behavior and Development*, 21, 345–54.

Slob, A. K., & van der Werff ten Bosch, J. J. (1991). Orgasm in nonhuman species. In P. Kohari & R. Patel (eds.). *Proceedings of the First International Conference on Orgasm* (pp. 135-149). Bombay: VRP.

Smith, E. A., & Bird, R. L. B. (2000). Turtle hunting and tombstone opening: Public generosity as costly signaling. *Evolution and Human Behavior*, 21, 245–61.

Smith, E. R. (1998). Mental representation and memory. In D. T. Gilbert, S. T. Fiske, & G. Lindzey (eds.), *The handbook of social psychology* (4th edn., vol. 1, pp. 391–445). New York: McGraw-Hill.

Spanier, G. B. (1976). Measuring dyadic adjustment: New scales for assessing the quality of marriage and similar dyads. *Journal of Marriage and the Family*, 38, 15–28.

Sprecher, S., Delamater, J., Neuman, N., Neuman, M., Kahn, P., Orbuch, D., & McKinney, K. (1984). Asking questions in bars: The girls (and boys) may not get prettier at closing time and other interesting results. *Personality and Social Psychology Bulletin*, 10, 482–8.

Sprecher, S., Sullivan, Q., & Hatfield, E. (1994). Mate selection preferences: Gender differences examined in a national sample. *Journal of Personality and Social Psychology*, 66, 1074–80.

Springer, J. (1995). *Jerry Springer show*: "I'm furious that you're gay". Multimedia Entertainment.

Stanley, S. M., Bradbury, T. N., & Markman, H. J. (2000). Structural flaws in the bridge from basic research on marriage to interventions for couples. *Journal of Marriage and the Family*, 62, 256–64.

Stanovich, K. E., & West, R. F. (in press). Individual differences in reasoning: Implications for the rationality debate? *Behavior and Brain Sciences.*

Statistics New Zealand Report (1999). *Demographic Trends-Marriage and Divorce* (http://www.stats.govt.nz).

Steinmetz, S. K., & Lucca, J. S. (1988). Husband battering. In V. B. Van Hasselt, R. L. Morrison, A. S. Bellack, & M. S. Hersen (eds.), *Handbook of family violence* (pp. 233–46). New York: Plenum.

Sterelny, K. (2001). *Dawkins vs. Gould: Survival of the fittest.* Cambridge: Icon

Sternberg, R. J., & Beall, A. E. (1991). How can we know what love is? An epistemological analysis. In G. J. O. Fletcher & F. D. Fincham (eds.), *Cognition in close relationships* (pp. 257–78). Hillsdale, NJ: Lawrence Erlbaum.

Stets, J. E., & Straus, M. A. (1990). Gender differences in reporting marital violence and its medical and psychological consequences. In M. A. Straus & R. J. Gelles (eds.), *Physical violence in American families: Risk factors and adaptations to violence in 8,145 families* (pp. 151–65). New Brunswick, NJ: Transaction.

Stoolmiller, M. (1999). Implications of the restricted range of family environments for estimates of heritability and nonshared environment behavior in behavior-genetic adoption studies. *Psychological Bulletin*, 125, 392–409.

Straus, M. A. (1997). Physical assaults by women partners: A major social problem. In M. R. Walsh (ed.), *Women, men, & gender* (pp. 210–21). New Haven, CT: Yale University Press.

Straus, M. A., & Gelles, R. J. (1988). Violence in American families: How much is there and why does it occur? In E. W. Nunnally, C. S. Chilman, & F. M. Cox (eds.), *Troubled relationships* (pp. 141-162). Newbury Park, CA:Sage.

Straus, M. A., & Gelles, R. J. (eds.) (1990). *Physical violence in American families: Risk factors and adaptations to violence in 8,145 families.* New Brunswick, NJ: Transaction.

Straus, M. A., Hamby, S. L., Boney-McCoy, S., & Sugarman, D. B. (1996). The Revised Conflict Tactics Scales (CTS2). *Journal of Family Issues*, 17, 283–316.

Straus, M. A., Kantor, G. K., & Moore, D. W. (1997). Change in cultural norms approving marital violence from 1968 to 1994. In G. K. Kantor & J. L. Jasinski (eds.), *Out of darkness: Contemporary perspectives on family violence (pp. 3-16). Thousand Oaks, CA: Sage.*

Stringer, C., & McKie, R. (1996). *African exodus: The origins of modern humanity.* New York: Henry Holt.

Sugarman, D. B., & Hotaling, G. T. (1989). Dating violence: Prevalence, context and risk markers. In M. A. Pirog-Good & J. E. Stets (eds.), *Violence in dating relationships* (pp. 3–32). New York: Praeger.

Symons, D. (1979). *The evolution of human sexuality.* Oxford: Oxford University Press.

Szinovacz, M. E., & Egley, L. C. (1995). Comparing one-partner and couple data on sensitive marital behaviors: the case of marital violence. *Journal of Marriage and the Family*, 57, 995–1010.

Taylor, S. E., & Brown, J. D. (1988). Illusion and well-being: A social psychological perspective on mental health. *Psychological Bulletin*, 103, 193–210.

Taylor, S. E., & Gollwitzer, P. M. (1995). Effects of mindset on positive illusions. *Journal of Personality and Social Psychology*, 69, 213–26.

Thomas, G. (1998). *Empathic accuracy in close relationships: The role of the perceiver, the target, and the perceiver–target relationship.* Abstracts of the 27th Annual Meeting of the Society of Australasian Social Psychologists, Christchurch, New Zealand, April 16–19.

Thomas, G., Fletcher, G. J. O., & Lange, C. (1997). On-line empathic accuracy in marital interaction. *Journal of Personality and Social Psychology*, 76, 72–89.

Tommaselli, G. A., Guida, M., Palomba, S., Barbato, M. & Nappi, C. (2000). Using complete breastfeeding and lactational amenorrhoea as birth spacing methods. *Contraception*, 61, 253–7.

Tooby, J., & Cosmides, L. (1992). The psychological foundations of culture. In J. H. Barkow, L. Cosmides, & J. Tooby (eds.), *The adapted mind* (pp. 19–136). New York: Oxford University Press.

Trivers, R. L. (1972). Parental investment and sexual selection. In B. Campbell (ed.), *Sexual selection and the descent of man 1871–1971* (pp. 136–79). Chicago: Aldine.

Trivers, R. L. (1974). Parent–offspring conflict. *American Zoologist 14*, 249–64.

Turkheimer, E. (2000). Three laws of behavior genetics and what they mean. *Current Directions in Psychological Science*, 9, 160–3.

US Department of Justice Report (1998). *Violence by Intimates* (http://www.ojp.usdoj.gov/bjs/).

Van Look, P. F. A., von Hertzen, H., Glasier, A., Howie, P. W., Kennedy, K. I., Thalabard, J. C., Labbok, M., Bhatnagar, S., Burger, H. G., Delgado, H. L., Dada, O. O. A., Gross, B. A., Hofvander, Y., Lavin, P. A., Guang-hua, T., Ayeni, O., Pinol, A. P. Y., Chevrot, A. J. M., Vucurevic, M., & Nagi, V. S. (1999). The World Health Organization multinational study of breast-feeding and lactational amenorrhoea: # 3. Pregnancy during breast-feeding. *Fertility and Sterility*, 72, 431–40.

Vivian, D., & Langhinrichsen-Rohling, J. (1996). Are bi-directionally violent couples mutually victimized? In L. K. Hamberger & C. Renzetti (eds.), *Domestic Partner Abuse* (pp. 23–52). New York: Springer.

References

Walker, L. E. (1984). *The Battered Woman Syndrome*. New York: Springer.

Waters, E., Merrick, S., Treboux, D., Crowell, J., & Albersheim, L. (2000). Attachment security in infancy and early adulthood: A twenty-year longitudinal study. *Child Development*, 71, 684–9.

Wegner, D. M., & Bargh, J. A. (1998). Control and automaticity in social life. In D. T. Gilbert , S. T. Fiske, & G. Lindzey (eds.), *The handbook of social psychology* (4th edn., vol. 1, pp. 446–96). New York: McGraw-Hill.

Weinfield, N. S., Sroufe, L. A., & Egeland, B. (2000). Attachment from infancy to early adulthood in a high-risk sample: Continuity, discontinuity, and their correlates. *Child Development*, 71, 695–702.

Whitam, F. L., Daskalos, C., Sobolewski, C. G., & Padilla, P. (1998). The emergence of lesbian sexuality and identity cross-culturally: Brazil, Peru, the Philippines, and the United States. *Archives of Sexual Behavior*, 27, 31–56.

White, J. M. (1985). Perceived similarity and understanding in married couples. *Journal of Social and Personal Relationships*, 2, 45–57.

White, J. W., Smith, P. H., Koss, M. P., & Figueredo, A. J. (2000). Intimate partner aggression – What have we learned? Comment on Archer (2000). *Psychological Bulletin*, 126, 690–6.

Wile, D. B. (1995). *After the fight: A night in the life of a couple*. New York: Guilford.

Williams, G. (1996). *Adaptation and natural selection*. Princeton, NJ: Princeton University Press.

Wilson, E. O. (1978). *On human nature*. Cambridge: Harvard University Press.

Wilson, E. O. (1998). *Consilience: The unity of knowledge*. London: Little, Brown.

Wilson, M., & Daly, M. (1992). Who kills whom in spouse killings? On the exceptional sex ratio of spousal homicides in the United States. *Criminology*, 30, 189–215.

Wilson, M., & Daly, M. (1993). An evolutionary psychological perspective on male sexual proprietariness and violence against wives. *Violence and Victims*, 18, 271–94.

Wilson, M., & Daly, M. (1996). Male sexual proprietariness and violence against wives. *Current Directions in Psychological Science*, 5, 2–7.

Wolf, A. P. (1995). *Sexual attraction and childhood association: A Chinese brief for Edward Westermarck*. Stanford, CA: Stanford University Press.

Young, H., & Uenukukopako, T. (1995). *Hinemoa & Tutenekai: A Te Arawa legend*. New Zealand: Huia.

Zaadstra, B. M., Seidell, J. C., van Noord, P. A. H., te Velde, E. R., Habbema, J. D. F., Vrieswijk, B., & Karbaat, J. (1993). Fat and female fecundity: Prospective study of effect of body fat distribution on conception rates. *British Medical Journal*, 306, 484–7.

References

Zebrowitz, L. A., & Rhodes, G. (in press). Nature let a hundred flowers bloom: The multiple ways and wherefores of attractiveness. In G. Rhodes & L. A. Zebrowitz (eds.), *Facial attractiveness: Evolutionary, cognitive, cultural, and motivational perspectives.* Westport, CT: Ablex.

Index

and good communication model,
128–34
and good management model,
128–34
and lay relationship theories,
130–1, 137, 141
and marital therapy, 138–41
predicting, 134–45
see also anger
Rhodes, Gillian, 175
Rosanowski, Janette, 44
Rosenthal, Robert, 31
Rubin, Donald, 31
Rubin, Zick, 5
Rusbult, Caryl, 129
Rutherford, Ernest, 13–14

Salovey, Peter, 219
Sambia, 217
Schachter, Stanley, 81–2
Schlee, Karin, 235
Science,
and correlations, 30–4
and criteria for theory evaluation,
11–14, 24, 65–6, 269
and experiments, 30–4
and folk psychology, 14–16, 25,
46–9, 197–8, 211, 261, 269
and history of science of
relationships, 5, 17–18
and intimate relationships, 3, 18
and is/ought distinction, 17
and love, 268
and measurement, 234, 236–7
model of, 11–12
and natural sciences, 16
and positivism, 8, 10–11
and postmodernism, 8–11, 69,
106, 147
and predicting relationship
phenomena, 268
and relativism, 9–11, 172

and testability of evolutionary
theory, 65–6, 268–9
theory-knitting approach to, 6
and third variables, 32–3
and truth, 17
Scutt, Jocelynne, 241–2
self-help books, *see* pop-psychology
Selleck, Tom, 175
Senator Proxmire, 18
Sex,
and 1994 Chicago sex survey,
200–1
and chimpanzees, 266
and culture, 217
extramarital, 99–101
and hormones, 205–7
and the human clitoris, 199
and the human penis, 198–9, 202
and Kinsey's sex surveys, 200
and menstrual cycle, 266
and moral and legal concerns,
269–71
and orgasms, 199–202
and passion, 214–15
sex drive defined, 207
and sex surveys, 200
and sexual capacity, 207
and testosterone, 205–7
see also evolutionary psychology;
gender differences in sex drive;
love
sexual dimorphism, 54
sexual orientation,
and accuracy of stereotypes, 225
and congenital adrenal hyperplasia
(CAH), 226
and cross-cultural evidence, 223
and homophobia, 270
and number of homosexuals, 223
in Plato's symposium, 1
and similarity of homosexuals to
heterosexuals, 224–5